KU-237-189

BRIGHT LIGHT, WHITE WATER

*The story of Irish lighthouses
and their people*

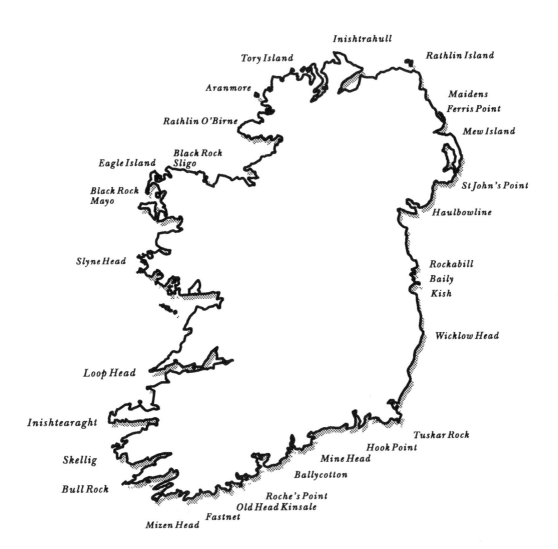

Inishtrahull

Tory Island

Rathlin Island

Aranmore

Maidens
Ferris Point

Rathlin O'Birne

Mew Island

Black Rock
Sligo

Eagle Island

St John's Point

Black Rock
Mayo

Haulbowline

Slyne Head

Rockabill

Baily

Kish

Wicklow Head

Loop Head

Inishtearaght

Tuskar Rock

Hook Point

Mine Head

Skellig

Ballycotton

Bull Rock

Roche's Point

Old Head Kinsale

Mizen Head

Fastnet

WITHDRAWN FROM STOCK

3 0012 00248960 6

BRIGHT LIGHT, WHITE WATER

*The story of Irish lighthouses
and their people*

BILL LONG

LIMERICK COUNTY LIBRARY

387.155

53770

WITHDRAWN FROM STOCK

NEW
ISLAND
BOOKS

(With the generous assistance of
E.B.S. Building Society)

BRIGHT LIGHT, WHITE WATER
Is first published in 1993 by
NEW ISLAND BOOKS
2 Brookside
Dundrum Road
Dublin 14
Ireland.

New Island Books gratefully acknowledges the generous
financial assistance of **E.B.S. Building Society** in
reproducing the colour photographs in this book.

All text © Bill Long, 1993.

All colour photographs © their respective photographers.
See page 217 for list of photographers.
Black and white photographs from the records of Irish Life.
Callwell drawings from Robert Callwell's original manuscript, 1869.

ISBN 1 874597 40 5

The author has asserted his moral rights.

A catalogue copy of this book is available from The British Library.

Colour cover photographs by Richard Cummins. Cover design by Jon Berkeley.
Inside design by Graphic Resources. Printed in Ireland by Colour Books Ltd.,
Baldoyle.

CONTENTS

Dedicated to all those who kept the light
Remembering Lyonesse

"When I came back from Lyonesse
With magic in my eyes,
All marked with mute surmise
My radiance rare and fathomless,
When I came back from Lyonesse
With magic in my eyes."

Thomas Hardy.

FOREWORD

Bill Long's story of Irish Lighthouses and their People is timely for the saddest of reasons. His faithful account almost coincides with the completion of the Commissioners of Irish Lights automation programme. The micro chip seems to me to be too small to have a soul; it replaces a noble human tradition which, over the years, has produced an unusual and special group of people who have lived and served at remote headlands and on isolated rock stations. For generations, the Lighthouse Keepers have been the custodians of that flame of light, which provides the glow that leads the mariner safely on his voyage. They have seen the sea in all its moods; they have wondered at its mystery and at its power, as curtains of spray lash the window panes high up on the Fastnet dome; they have observed the majesty of the universe in clear skies, without the intrusion of light pollution, which obscures the heaven's beauties from the city dweller. The Lighthouse Keepers have lived close to nature and their knowledge and understanding of life is all the better for it.

The service must continue in those radically changed circumstances. Our Service's motto is, 'In salutem Omnium'. The Lights do not belong to us; they belong to the seafarers who earn their living on the deep. Our duty is to serve; to be as faithful as the sunrise and to provide that shaft of light which reassures mariners that they are not alone.

John Gore-Grimes
Chairman,
Commissioners of Irish Lights.

"There it loomed up stark and straight, glaring white and black, and one could see the waves breaking in white splinters, like smashed glass against the rocks. One could see the lines and creases in the rocks. One could see the windows clearly; a dab of white on one of them and little tufts of green on the rock. A man had come out and looked at them through a glass and gone in again. So, it was like that, James thought, the Lighthouse one had seen across the bay all these years; it was a stark tower on a bare rock. It satisfied him. It confirmed some obscure feeling about his own character."

Virginia Woolf. 'To The Lighthouse'

Introduction

I was born, and grew up, in an old thatched farmhouse on the Waterford coast. It stood between two great sea-lights; Hook Head, seven miles to the East, with a landmass intervening, and Mine Head to the South-West, across six miles of open water. Capricious water, that whispered or roared as wind and tide dictated.

From early childhood I remember the two great beams raking the night sky. On cloudy nights the lights were two long, yellow fingers stabbing the darkness with relentless regularity; on clear nights they polished the stars with their ceaseless sweeping. And, when mist crept in off the sea and hung, like tattered lace, along the edges of the thatched eaves outside my bedroom window, I could hear the fog signals. The rifle crack of Hook Head, and the deep, reverberating boom of the Coningbeg Lightship, like the bellow of a wounded bull. So, from my country cradle, lighthouse beam and boom, were my lamp and my lullaby.

I was seven years old when I first visited a lighthouse. My grandfather knew a keeper on the Hook and we were invited to spend a day there. We crossed, by fishing boat, from Dunmore East. Standing in the deep well of the boat, rolling in the huge Atlantic swell sweeping up the estuary, the black and white striped lighthouse was the most solid building I had ever seen. As we wallowed in the trough of the big seas, it towered above us on its bare promontory, dominating the landscape and the seascape. Seaward, to the South-East, two coasters ploughed their way Westward, their decks awash, toy boats, dwarfed, swallowed up in the great moving maw of blue and white water. And, behind the white perimeter wall of the lighthouse compound, the keepers' dwellings looked like toy houses in the shadow of the great tower.

In those days, the late 1930's, the keepers' families lived at the lighthouse, and I spent most of the day playing with some of the children. In the afternoon, my grandfather's friend took us to the tower, and with him, I climbed the spiralling stone steps, right up to the great lantern itself. My grandfather couldn't make that climb, for he had a permanently disabled hip; a legacy of the Civil War. The keeper explained, as we climbed, how the 'new' light-house tower had been built round the old tower, which had been a monastery. He showed me the monks' cells, tiny cramped places, set into the old walls, and the lovely vaulted ceiling of what had once been their chapel in the centre of the tower. And, at every level on the tortuous climb to the top, there were long, narrow windows, framing views of sea, and sky, and green, undulating Summer country.

When we reached the lantern at the top of the tower my head was spinning. Spinning from the climbing, and spinning also from the tales the keeper was telling me. Of how this was the oldest lighthouse in the British Isles, dating back to the 5th century, when Saint Dubhan, a Welsh monk and hermit had established the first primitive beacon here. This was a crude iron 'chauffer', or stove, set on top of a mound of stones, in which a coal, or wood fire was kept burning during the hours of darkness, as a navig-ational aid to ships entering the estuary, bound for the Port of Waterford. Poor Dubhan, the keeper said, had got so tired of removing the bodies of drowned sailors from the rocks, after their ships had foundered, that he decided to do something practical by way of establishing that first warning light.

From that first, long ago visit to Hook Head, I have been in love with lighthouses. In love with the lonely places where they are set. In love with the spartan, though comfortable, conditions. In love with the cleanliness of the great towers, with their polished lanterns and their shining brass-work. In love, above all, with the great lights, raking the sea and sky, endlessly, night after night, warning ships of the perils of ragged rock and white water. And full of admiration for the men, and sometimes women, who have ensured that the lights never fail to be lit and kept burning.

There are, for me, two places where I will always go, regularly, on 'pilgrimage' — the lighthouse and the Cistercian monastery. For me they have much in common; the loneliness of the location, the spartan living conditions, the great, unbroken silences, the quiet camaraderie and the ambience so conducive to bringing me face-to-face with myself, where there is no possibility of escaping that necessary confrontation.

I feel a close affinity with James in Virginia Woolf's novel, *To The Lighthouse,* when, looking out at the lighthouse, he feels that—"It satisfied him. It confirmed some obscure feeling about his own character." Ever since that first visit to Hook Head, the lighthouse has been inextricably linked to the monastery for me. And, many years later, when I began my research for this book, I was delighted, but not really surprised, to find that, from the 11th to the 15th century, monks and hermits were among the most assiduous keepers of beacons in Europe. In those post Dark Ages times, when Europe was, quite literally, beginning to 'light up', the first primitive, tentative beacons, on lonely cape and off-shore island, were built by philanthropic laymen and tended by monks, priests and hermits, whose 'living' was conditional on their 'keeping the lights'.

During the researching and writing of this book I lived for long spells in the Baily lighthouse at Howth. I needed some isolation from the the social scene, while, at the same time, remaining close enough to Maynooth and Dublin to honour lecturing and broadcasting committments. And the Baily, tucked under the cliff at the extreme North-East end of Dublin Bay, proved to be the ideal place; accessible, yet remote. For me, there was a particular point on the descent, just below the lightkeepers' dwellings, where the road corkscrews steeply to the lighthouse itself, which was a demarcation line. Beyond that one entered a sort of time tunnel; the gleaming walls of the white-washed out-buildings; the tower itself; the sea seeming to wrap one round; the distant mountains across the Bay, their foothills peppered with toy houses; the coastline stretching to Wicklow Head; the Kish lighthouse three miles off-shore, remote, austere; the city, distant, bandaged in smog, yet only forty-five minutes away by public transport. All this conspired to make one feel "away from it all".

The point of rock on which Baily is built, in addition to being the pivotal point for all shipping wheeling North or North-East out of the Port of Dublin, is also, I am sure, the epicentre of all the contrary wind currents in Christendom. At night, shutters up, wind wailing and whistling against the three-foot thick walls of the granite tower, sea soughing and sucking along the base of the cliff, one might well be on some remote rock station. And, when fog insidiously crept in from the Kish sandbank, the great diaphonic horn in the 'engine room' beside the tower, relentlessly ground out its warning; its *basso profundo* echoing along the cliff-face, obliterating all other sound.

I worked through many nights on Baily, researching, writing various drafts, time forgotten; sustained by the work in progress, and the thought that, above me in the lonely tower, there was always a keeper on duty. And that, whenever I felt tired, or needed to check a fact, or elicit an honest opinion, I could climb and join him where he sat in front of his short wave radio. There we would listen to the disembodied voices through the static crackle; track the little moving islands of light that were ships moving in and out of harbour, tracers on the natural radar screen of the pitch black sea; watch the dancing horse-shoe of lights around the Bay, and drink tea and talk.

The unfailing courtesy, kindliness, humour, and patience with my often elementary questions, of the lighkeepers on Baily, will never be forgotten. John Noel Crowley, Peter Duggan, Eddie Copeland, Al Hamilton, Paraic Keane, Pat Kennedy and Leo Jones.

Automation is far advanced now. By 1997 all our lighthouses will be automated and de-manned. The lonely beacons, on rocky promontories and off-shore rocks and islands, will be lonelier still after the departure of the last keepers. Leaving a lighthouse after its automation, some years ago, an old keeper, going 'ashore' for the last time, looked back and down from our rapidly rising helicopter at the slim, white spiral of the tower, dwindling into distance, and said to me: "Isn't it like a big white pencil stuck in the rock." And that set me thinking. Thinking that lighthouse keepers, working, as they do, a month on and a month off, spend half their working lives living inside pencils stuck on rocks.

An Historical Sketch:
World Sea-lights and Sea-marks

When the first primitive man hollowed out the first log to make the first primitive canoe, or bound logs together to make the first primitive raft, he ventured off-shore in search of food and trade. In so doing he discovered that, sometimes, wind, weather and tide, made return to shore impossible before nightfall. Returning with daylight he had the crude towers and totems, set up by his friends on beach and headland, to guide him back. But, with the onset of night, a stygian darkness bandaged land and sea, making navigation impossible. And so the concept of the 'sea-light' was born. Fires were lit along the shore, and kept burning through the night to guide the voyager home.

From such primitive beginnings evolved the lighthouse system of today; a highly sophisticated branch of engineering, involving many sciences — architecture, radio, electronics, optics, oceanography and acoustics. An international system, using a common language of visual and aural signals, to keep the sea-ways safe for ships and protect the lives of those who sail in them.

Less than accurate charts and sea surveys, untrustworthy 'sailing instructions' and totally inadequate navigational instruments, left those early mariners largely dependent on what they could actually see. It was all very well steering by the stars, when one could see the stars. But, when cloud and fog obliterated them, the pioneer navigator was sailing blind, and without any intimation of hazard, was suddenly in white water, inexorably driving onto rock. The lighthouse then, even in its most primitive form, was undoubtedly the greatest blessing ever for mariners.

The first lighthouses, of which we have any record, were constructed by the coastal tribesmen of Lower Egypt — the Sybians and Cushites. The buildings were towers which doubled as monasteries; the first light-keepers being monks and priests, who, in additon to their liturgical offices, also taught various aspects of seamanship, pilotage, hydrography and astronomy. With the exception of the teaching function, this was very close to the monastery-lighthouse, operated by Saint Dubhan at Hook Head, several centuries later.

The first regularly-operated lighthouse was that situated on a headland in the Troad, at Sigaeum. This was functional around 650 B.C. and was an invaluable navigational aid to ships bound for Troy, Hellespont and the ports of the Bosphorus and the Black Sea. The Colossus of Rhodes could also be termed one of the earliest lighthouses. The figure of Apollo was over one hundred feet high, made of bronze, and stood with legs astride the entrance to Rhodes Harbour, holding aloft a torch, lighted at night. It was built around 300 B.C., but, for such a monumental structure, had a relatively short life, being destroyed by an earthquake about eighty years later.

Undoubtedly, the greatest lighthouse of all time must be the incomparable Pharos of Alexandria; its name derived from the island on which it was built, in 261 B.C., by King Ptolemy II. One of the seven wonders of the ancient world, it is unique in history, both for its size and length of service — an astonishing 1500 years. It was 450 feet high, built on a 100 feet square base, and its open fire was visible from a distance of 29 miles. A 13th century account of a visit to the Pharos is given by an Arabian geographer: *"This lighthouse has not its equal in the world for excellence of construction and for strength, for not only is it constructed of a fine quality stone, called 'kedan', but the various blocks are so strongly cemented together with melted lead, that the whole is imperishable, although the waves of the sea continually break against its Northern face."* The great lighthouse survived the onslaughts of weather, sea and time until, in the 13th century, it was destroyed by an earthquake.

This method of 'cementing' blocks of stone together with melted lead was used by the architect of the second Eddystone lighthouse, Rudyerd, over 2,000 years later. In 1709 he built, against seemingly impossible odds, the great tower on the grim, red rocks, fourteen miles off Plymouth.

So great a wonder, so fine an achievement, was King Ptolemy's lighthouse, that the word 'pharos' became generic in lighthouse terminology. Pharology is the word still used to describe the science of lighthouse engineering.

The Romans were great builders of lighthouses round the coasts of Europe. Usually these towers were dual-purpose; to light the coast and to protect themselves against the raids of Saxon and Danish pirates. Remains of Roman light-towers may still be found at various points on the English coast; part of a Roman tower still stands at Dover castle, and was once used, in the 13th century, as a bell-tower for the church of St. Mary.

At the end of the 5th century, with the decline of the Roman Empire, many of the fortified lighthouses they had built were sacked or vandalised by pirates and invaders and, one by one, the beacons were extinguished, as the forbidding shadow of the Dark Ages loomed. And, after the centuries of darkness, when trading between nations became possible again, and ships began to venture out onto the seaways, the lights were lit along the coasts of Europe.

Now, the first keepers of these re-kindled, post Dark Ages lights, were monks and priests and hermits; especially along the French and English coasts. Dating from that time, there are the remains of a stone lantern, set in a corner of the great tower of St Michael's Mount. In this lantern was displayed a light, mainly to help local fishermen, but also of immense help to passing ships. Near Ilfracombe was Lantern Hill, which was originally the chapel of Saint Nicholas. Here, the monks maintained, through the night, a beacon fire to guide passing ships. And, in several places, wealthy patrons and donors, financed 'livings' for monks and hermits, on conditon they established and tended lighted beacons. This philanthropic system worked very well until the Dissolution of the Monasteries. Men who had devoted their lives to the altruistic serving of others, by establishing and maintaining these coastal lights were, arbitrarily, removed, with disastrous results for shipping.

The line between genuine philanthropy and speculation is a thin one; the philanthropist, by his enthusiasm showing the viability of a scheme, is inevitably, albeit unwittingly, spawning the calulating speculator. In the matter of the development of some kind of lighthouse system the Dissolution of the Monasteries certainly accelerated this process. Indeed, in an ironic way, there is evidence that the process was already at work before the monks, priests and hermits were removed. Near the start of the fifteenth century a hermit lived in a stone tower on a bluff above the river Humber. He had once been a wealthy merchant and landowner, but had renounced his wealth and property in favour of a more frugal, eremitic life. Still, his old instinct for recognising an opportunity to make a profit remained with him. He first established a beacon on top of his hermit's tower and then, having proved its value to ships using the harbour, petitioned King Richard II to grant him leave to levy tolls on all such traffic. He was granted a license and, to his credit, all income was spent on the building of a lighthouse proper and the maintainance of the light. Long after the original hermit had died the lighthouse continued to function, until tower and hermitage were both eroded by the sea and disappeared.

In 1536, King Henry VIII, under pressure from merchants and harbour authorities because of the decline in trade, realised that this was an unfortuante, and unwanted side-effect of his persecution of the monks, priests and hermits. He was well-advised to grant a charter to a group called the Guild of the Blessed Trinity of Newcastle, to design, build and maintain suitable lighthouse towers on that Northern part of the coast. He gave them license to impose tolls and levies on passing ships; the income going to defray the expense of running the lighthouses. This Guild functioned, very successfully, for two hundred years.

At that time, possibly because of the negligible cost of maintaining them, sea-marks, of one kind or other, were considered to be quite important. Important enough to be the subject of an Act of Parliament, passed by Henry's successor, Elizabeth, in 1565. "Steeples, woods, ancient ruins or any other marks standing upon the main shores adjoining the sea" became subject to a preservation order; "removal, alteration, or defacement" was punished by a "fine of one hundred pounds, or the alternative of outlawry".

During the next two hundred years this specious system of operating a lighthouse service of sorts, operated in both Ireland and England. The private patentees, the franchise holders, ever greedy for more and more profit, kept their outgoings to a minimum. The enormous cost of fuel in these old coal, wood and peat burning beacons and the additional cost of hoisting it, with primitive machinery, to the tops of towers, meant that many of the actual 'lights' were inefficient. Wages were paltry; at the beginning of the 17th century, thirty-seven pounds per annum for a man, much less for a woman. And, in those days, women were often given the job of keeper, for that reason, often with disaster resulting, as in the case of the Caistor light, where an old woman was employed as keeper, being paid a pittance. She lived at a remove of several miles from the beacon, and when the light was most needed, in foul weather, failed to make the journey, so that the tower remained in darkness. This situation remained for many years, ending only when a ship, with all hands, was lost, and the patentee's license withdrawn.

On certain parts of the English coast there was opposition to the establishment of lighthouses from the 'wreckers'. These were often whole families who, traditionally, for several generations, had made a good living from looting wrecks along the coast; in many instances luring storm-tossed ships onto the rocks with false beacons strategically placed to take them off-course. In addition to looting the cargo, the 'wreckers' killed all survivors, as in the superstition-ridden tradition of their nefarious vocation, survivors of shipwreck brought ill luck to a neighbourhood. In the early part of the 19th century the political jobbery, bribery and general corruption involved in this system of granting patents, franchises and licences to unscrupulous speculators, was halted, once and for all by the Government, with Trinity House being given control of all English and Irish lights.

Subsequently the control of development and maintainance of lighthouses round the Irish coast, devolved from Trinity House to The Customs Office and the Ballast Board to The Commissioners of Irish Lights. Undoubtedly, the 19th century was to be the golden age of lighthouse development in the British Isles, particularly in Ireland.

Part One

The East Coast: Carlingford to Hook

Carlingford Lights - Dundalk - Drogheda Lights - Balbriggan - Rockabill - Howth Pier - Baily - Poolbeg - Dun Laoghaire Lights - Kish - Muglins - Wicklow Head - Tuskar Rock - Coningbeg - Barrels - Hook Head.

"For the great plateful of water was before her; the hoary lighthouse, distant and austere, in the midst and on the right, as far as the eye could see, fading and falling, in soft low pleats, the green sand dunes, with the wild, flowing grasses on them, which always seemed to be running away into some moon country, uninhabited of men."

Virginia Woolf: "To The Lighthouse".

Commissioners on tour - pre-helicopter

Carlingford Lights

Carlingford Lough has three working lighthouses; Haulbowline, a main sea light, which also serves to guide vessels from seaward through the narrow entrance channel into the Lough itself; and Vidal Bank and Green Island, two Leading Lights. There was a fourth, Greenore, which after a century and a half of service, was discontinued on 1st August, 1986. Haulbowline was built after a request from the Merchants of Newry, in 1817, to the Ballast Board of Dublin, to replace the old 1803 Light at Cranfield Point. The Board agreed that Cranfield was in a poor position for marking the dangerous rocks at the entrance to Carlingford Lough; it was also inadequate in guiding vessels at the West end of the Lough.

Haulbowline's cut-stone tower was designed by George Halpin Snr., and built, under his direction by workmen of the Ballast Board. It was originally painted white, but restored to its original stone-work in 1946. The fixed, white light was first exhibited on 1st September, 1824, with a half-tide light exhibited half-way up the seaward side of the tower. In daylight, a large ball was hoisted on a mast above the lantern, to indicate the tide. A bell was struck, by a machine, every 30 seconds in foggy weather. As with most stations there was constant changing and experimenting with the fog signal and with the main light. The bell gave way to an explosive signal, which, in turn, gave way to an electric horn. The light changed, over the years, from fixed to occulting, and subsequently to flashing. Haulbowline was converted to electric and demanned on St. Patrick's Day, 1965. From 1824 until 1922 the Keepers and their families lived at Cranfield Point, in the dwellings attached to the old lighthouse, moving eventually to new dwellings at Greencastle. The old Cranfield tower fell to bad coastal erosion in the 1860's, tumbling onto the foreshore.

In 1868, the Carlingford Lough Commissioners began a scheme to deepen the channel through the Bar and up into the Lough. They wrote to Irish Lights informing them of this and requesting two Leading Lights for the channel. The lights are screw-pile structures, with adequate housing for the light on top. They are 500 yards apart and the front Light, Vidal Bank, is 28 feet high; the rear Light, Green Island, 45 feet high. Fixed white lights were established in both on 28th February, 1873. They were both converted from oil to acetylene in 1922, and their character altered from fixed to occulting. The same Attendant has responsibility for looking after these two Leading Lights, together with Haulbowline and the local Irish Lights buoys.

Greenore was a harbour light, built on Greenore Point, in Carlingford Lough, by George Halpin Snr, in 1830. The light first established on 20th December of that year, was 30 feet above high water and visible for nine miles in clear weather. The cut stone tower was always painted white. At that time Greenore itself was a thriving place. From the early 1860's the L.N.W.R. (London North-Western Railway Company) had been investing steadily in the development of the Dundalk-Greenore Railway and the Port of Greenore. They had created a small town at Greenore, with a quay wall, railway station, hotel and cattle lairs. Its two streets were named Euston Street and Anglesey Street; there was a co-op store and a library. And the cottages had an unmistakable "L.N.W.R. - Crewe" look about them. At one stage of this hectic development, there was a valid complaint from the Dundalk & Newry Steam Packet Company, that the height of the hotel and railway station was impeding the view of the Greenore Light for ships going seaward from Newry and Warrenpoint. The possibility of moving the lighthouse was considered, but then abandoned in favour of a light on the pierhead. This pier light formed a front Leading Light with Greenore Point, but was not in the jurisdiction of Irish lights. In 1955 it was considered to be "unreliable" and struck- off the Admiralty List of Lights in the 1981 edition.

After the General Strike, in May, 1926, the passenger service on the steamers ceased. After the Second World War the cattle trade declined, as did the Dundalk, Newry and Greenore Railway. This led to the eventual closing-down of both Railway and Steamship services on 31st December, 1951. The last sailing out of Greenore was that of the old *Slieve League*, to Holyhead, on the 29th.

Dundalk

The light in Dundalk Bay is a pile light. One of Alexander Mitchell's structures, similar to the Spit Bank in Cork Harbour; the system that failed on the Kish, Arklow and Blackwater Banks, but was eminently successful in other places — Maplin Sands in the Thames, Wyer near Fleetwood, and Morecambe Bay. Mitchell was a blind Belfast Engineer, who had patented a wrought and cast-iron screw pile. These piles were screwed into the sandy bottom and supported a wooden 'deck', on which was built limited accommodation for the keeper, and a lantern. In 1846, the Dundalk Harbour Commissioners wrote to the Ballast Board

Our Lady's Finger and Maiden Tower.
(R. Callwell).

requesting that two lights be placed at strategic positions in Dundalk Bay. There was an ever increasing volume of shipping using the Harbour, largely due to the town being the centre of the Great Northern Railway of Ireland. As it was such a busy cross-roads for both imports and exports, action was taken relatively quickly. George Halpin inspected the channel and wrote his report, and without much delay the Board replied to the Harbour Commissioners that it was "favourably inclined to erect two small lighthouses at Dundalk." Trinity House endorsed this, but stated that they must be maintained out of local revenue, from Port dues, and not a burden on the Mercantile Marine Fund.

Early in 1847 a 300 ton vessel went aground in the channel, and this incident helped speed up the building of the lights. For this type of screw-pile light there had to be considerable time spent in sinking trial piles. This took over a year and it was not until the end of 1848 that work proper began on the lighthouse. Just one light, not two as originally sanctioned. The whole structure was built by the end of June, 1849. However, shortly after its completion, Inspector Halpin noticed distinct signs of scouring and shifting sand in the vicinity of the piles. This concerned him and he decided to allow some time to elapse before ordering the lantern to be fitted. At the end of 1852 he again surveyed the channel and the new lighthouse. He found that, though the lighthouse had been built on the South side of the channel, it was now standing in mid-channel. This area was notorious for the shifting sands and scouring had taken place, so altering the position of the structure. However, it was decided that the light would be just as effective, and safe, in mid-channel, so work proceeded with the installation of the lantern. This work was impeded by further shifting of the sands and when the light was eventually exhibited, on the night of 18th June, 1855, the lighthouse was on the North side of the channel. Two semi-detatched cottages were built for the Keepers at Soldier's Point, on the South side of the estuary. A third dwelling, detatched, was erected there in 1886.

Soon after the light was first exhibited, a fog signal bell was installed. This worked well, but was discontinued in 1967, when it was replaced by a horn fog signal, with a character of 3 blasts of 1.5 seconds each, every 60 seconds. For the mariner this was fine, a good, strong signal; but, for the unfortunate residents of nearby Annaloughan, it was a near nightmare. The residents lodged many complaints, in the early 1970's; some of them stating that the signal often boomed out, even when there was no fog. They lamented the passing of the pleasant tone of the old bell and queried the Commissioners of Irish Lights right to inflict such a nuisance on them. On investigation it was found that roosting cormorants in front of the fog detector were triggering off the signal horn at the oddest times. The detector was repositioned and bird repellant used, reasonably successfully, in attempting to placate the irate residents.

Drogheda Lights

The mouth of the River Boyne, the entrance to the channel that leads up to the busy Port of Drogheda, is a place of sandhills and sandbanks, where the noble river straggles out in little deltas to the sea. This has always been a difficult approach for inward bound ships. As far back as the middle of the 16th century the Maiden Tower and Lady's Finger, built in the sandhills, were leading daymarks to help vessels approach the mouth of the river. But, as trade flourished in the port, it became obvious that unlighted beacons were not enough. In 1838, the Drogheda Harbour Commissioners wrote to the Ballast Board, applying for a light to be erected at the entrance to the River Boyne. George Halpin surveyed the area and recommended that two lights were needed, on the sandhills in the vicinity of the 16th century towers; a third light, he added, in his report, would be advantageous. As two, and a possible three lights were involved, Trinity House reserved the right to make their own inspection. This was done and sanction given for the erection of three lighthouses, in June 1839.

Two of these were to be "placed at discriminate elevations on the Southern side of the entrance, about East and West of each other, to lead vessels over the bar, and up to the third lighthouse." Because of the sandy nature of the place, and the scouring and shifting of the sands, it was decided that the three structures should be of temporary, timber construction, supported on parallel beams, to allow re-alignment, should the channel change. The East and West Lights were 27 feet and 40 feet above high water and 100 yards apart. In clear weather they could be seen at a distance of 6 to 7 miles. The North Light was 23 feet above high water; all three having fixed lights. They were, all three, exhibited for the first time on 1st March, 1842.

Considering the lights were built as "temporary" originally, they proved weatherworthy and reasonably durable. Over the years several alterations were made to all three stations, usually when timbers had rotted. A large proportion of ironwork was introduced into the framing. In 1949, the Department of Industry and Commerce in Dublin received a letter from a London Shipping Company, requesting improvement in the actual lighting at the entrance to the Boyne. This request was passed to Irish Lights, whose subsequent investigation led to the eventual conversion to electric. This meant that from 24th November, 1953, the three Drogheda Lights became unwatched. At one stage, when the lights were still watched, there were two female Assistant Keepers employed. In 1960-1961 the Drogheda Harbour Commissioners informed Irish Lights that they were considering seeking modification of the lights, in connection with dredging operations for a new channel. Despite many meetings and various inspections these modifications never materialised, but toward the end of 1978, the East and West Lights ceased to be leading lights and became Lights in Line. These two still remain the responsibility of Irish Lights; the North Light has been given over to the Drogheda Harbour Commissioners.

Balbriggan

The lighthouse at the end of the pier at Balbriggan, was built, in 1769, as a sea light for vessels navigating off the East coast, and to mark the entrance to Balbriggan Harbour. For the first forty years of its life it was unique in having, as "keeper of the light", a clergyman. From 1769 to 1811, the Reverend George Hamilton was paid two-hundred pounds per annum by the Revenue Commissioners to take care of the light; in those days candles being the means of illumination.

After responsibility had passed to the Ballast Board a Keeper was appointed, but not before the Reverend Hamilton had recommended that the tower should be raised, to prevent damage to the lantern glass from the heavy seas that regularly pounded the harbour. The glass had been broken on several occasions, during his term as "Keeper". However, it was March 1820 before work commenced on the "new" tower and lantern; five oil lamps, each with a reflector, replacing the candles. Ground for the new Keeper's dwelling was leased from the Reverend Hamilton. When Rockabill Light was exhibited, on 1st July, 1860, Balbriggan ceased to be a sea light, becoming a minor Harbour Light. The light was eventually made unwatched and converted to electric in 1960. The lighthouse tower was debauched, to a degree, by the removal of the old lantern and the dome, and is not nearly as aesthetically pleasing as it was in its old form. In 1989 responsibility for the Balbriggan light passed from Irish Lights to Dublin Port & Docks Board.

Rockabill

The Rockabill lighthouse stands on the larger of the two Rockabill Rocks directly off Skerries, to the North of Lambay Island, where the dreaded Taylor Rocks lie one and a half cables off Scotch Point. It is an imposing tower, tall and slim, one of the most elegant on the whole coast. Recently, visiting Jack Roche at his home in Skerries, we sat in his back garden and looked across a few miles of calm blue sea to the Rockabill. Jack, now retired, served on Rockabill for several years, and smiled as he remembered the frustration of being able to see into his own back garden from the lighthouse tower. It was, he said, less frustrating to be away on the West coast, on Eagle Island, than to be so near home.

In the first half of the 19th century there had been several wrecks on this coast in the area of the Taylor Rocks and Lambay Island. In response to various requests perches and beacons had been erected, but to very little avail. They were invariably damaged, or washed away by the enormous seas. There was no light on the coast from The Baily, at Howth, to the mouth of the Boyne, apart from the pier head light at Balbriggan. This, though listed as a sea light, was less than effective in foggy weather in warning of the dangers of Lambay and Taylor Rocks. On the 21th January, 1854, the Australian registered emigrant ship *Tayleur*, on her maiden voyage, went aground on rocks at Lambay Island; a total wreck, with 290 passengers and crew drowned. This tragedy pointed up the need for a light in this area. Rockabill seemed to be the most suitable location. The lighthouse was built by Burgess Bros. of Limerick, and the light first exhibited on 1st July, 1860.

The *Tayleur*, ahead of her time in design and construction, built largely of steel, left the Mersey at noon on Thursday, 19th January, 1854, in fair weather. Shortly after leaving port the weather came on to blow and the gale increased in force through Thursday night and right through Friday. Close-reefing of the topsails became necessary, but with insufficient crew, some of them foreigners unable to understand fully the orders, the ship drifted steadily to leeward in a narrow sea. During Friday night a fatal defect made itself manifest; all the compasses on board were disturbed by the iron hull and differed from each other. Under these conditions and in thick haze, the captain lost all knowledge of his position. Then at 4 a.m. on Saturday morning the light on The Skerries, off the tip of Anglesea, was sighted. The *Tayleur* continued to sail on and sometime later the wind freshened and the haze cleared. Land was dead ahead and it was now too late to alter course. Two anchors were dropped, but the chain-cables snapped and the ship drifted onto the rocks at Lambay Island. Of 528 persons on board, 290 drowned. The ship sank quickly. Dead bodies littered the rocks along the island's shore; 80 corpses were buried on the island. The remainder were, together with the spars and luggage from the wreck, swept out to sea by the current.

In recent years, sub-aqua divers have been very active around the wreck of the *Tayleur*, and have recovered some magnificent Willow Pattern pottery, in a remarkable state of preservation; salt and pepper pots, a jug, and plates. The Rockabill became fully automated in 1989, when the last keepers were withdrawn from the Rock. Rockabill is a well-known bird sanctuary, with a big population of terns. At last census, in 1993, the following was the count: Roseate Tern - 427 pairs, Common Tern - 280 pairs, Arctic Tern - 17 pairs, Kittiwake - 80 pairs, Black Guillemot - 20 pairs.

Howth Harbour, East Pier

Like Dunmore East, Howth Harbour and its lighthouse came to be built as a result of a decision by the British Post Office, in the early part of the 19th century, to make both fishing villages Packet Stations. There had been a small quay at Howth since the 17th century, just large enough to meet the needs of local fishermen and to off-load "coal, fuel and other necessaries and conveniences" for transporting by horse and cart up to the lighthouse at Baily, on Howth Head. This primitive quay would, obviously, be in-adequate for the mail packet, so John Rennie, who afterwards designed Dun Laoghaire Harbour, was commissioned to design a Harbour and Lighthouse for Howth.

The first stone of the new harbour was laid in 1807, the granite being quarried locally, at Kilrock, above Balscadden Bay. The new harbour did not function satisfactorily as a Packet Station for very long. Sand and mud began to fill the harbour very rapidly and it became increasingly difficult to maintain sufficient depth for the Holyhead packets. Eventually, it was decided to build a harbour at Dun Laoghaire, where depth would not be a problem, and site the Packet Station there. John Rennie was again commissioned to design the harbour, and construction began in 1817.

The Commissioners of Howth Harbour, even though they might lose the Packet Station, were not to be denied their lighthouse. The new harbour, though too shallow for packet ships,in the long term, could be developed for fishing vessels. To their credit, the Harbour Commissioners were perspicacious enough to see that the place could develop into one of the country's major fishing ports. They, consequently, decided to push the Corporation for the establishment of the long proposed light on the pier-head at Howth. Their persistence paid-off and the new lighthouse was completed in the early part of 1818. The elegant little cut-stone tower was very similar to the tower, also designed by John Rennie about the same time, for Salt Island in Holyhead Harbour.

However, when George Halpin inspected the new tower he was surprised to find that it was "neither ready for a lightkeeper, nor suitably constructed for lighting the harbour." He demanded that "the apartment be made as comfortable as possible for the keeper and that the sheet iron be replaced by plate glass, so that the light can be seen from inside the harbour, and on entering or leaving it." His demands were complied with, to the letter, and the new light was exhibited on 1st July, 1818. It comprised twelve Argand lamps, with red lamp glasses, and silvered copper catoptric reflectors.

The living quarters in the tower were very cramped for the keeper and, in 1821, it was decided to build a separate residence, adjoining the lighthouse. Originally a single storey dwelling was built; a second storey was added some years later.

In 1836, the Lords Commissioners of H.M. Treasury questioned the necessity to retain a light at Howth Harbour. George Halpin quickly responded that, although the harbour was no longer a Packet Station, it was a very useful harbour of refuge and, consequently, a light must be maintained. In the early 1980's Howth Harbour was modernised, and the old 1818 light was replaced by a new tower and light at the end of the East Pier Extension. This was established on 19th May, 1982, with a character of two one-second flashes, white and red, every 7.5 seconds, and is automatic, remote controlled.

The Baily

It seems entirely fitting that the Baily lighthouse, at the Eastern tip of Howth Head, should be the last of all our Irish lighthouses to be automated. It is scheduled to be fully automatic and ready for de-manning in 1996. For, this is, next to Hook Head, the oldest light in Ireland. In one form or other the Baily light has guided ships in and out of the port of Dublin for over 300 years, as well as being a familiar, and often welcome, landmark for ships plying North, or South, along the East coast.

Lighthouse Relief

Over the years, thousands of flights, in and out, of Dublin Airport, have passed directly over Baily. And the air-traveller's eye is invariably drawn to the neatness of the splash of startlingly white buildings, on the black rock under the cliff. Sea-travellers know it too, for all ships in and out of Dublin Port or Dun Laoghaire, must pass it. From Dun Laoghaire to Merrion gates, DART commuters have an uninterrupted view of Baily; by day, remote and austere, or close and friendly, depending on the light; by night a warm, friendly wink, every 20 seconds across the waters of the bay. And when the great, grey sea-fogs bandage the whole bay area, there is not a place, in all the urban and suburban sprawl, where Baily's bellowing fog-horn does not reverberate.

From the early part of the 9th century there was a light, albeit primitive, on Baily. Not on the site of the present lighthouse, but on a part of Howth Summit, known as 'The Green Bayly'. From the scant information we have, this was no more than a fire lit on a rock, or mound of stones, but sufficient to warn mariners of the dangers of towering cliff and white water. In all probability, not very well organised, and certainly not 'commercial'; rather, the work of some altruistic souls, possibly local fishermen, or their families, who, through personal experience, had come to appreciate how helpful some guiding beacon could be.

Not until the second half of the 17th century was there any attempt to build a lighthouse on the Head. In 1665, Sir Robert Reading was given the 'franchise'— Letters Patent — to build six lighthouses on the Irish coast; two at Kinsale, one at Hook Head, one at Isle of Magee, near Carrickfergus, and two at Howth. Of the two at Howth, one was "to mark the land", the other "to come over the bar." The lighthouse intended to light ships across the bar was never built; some sort of crude perch and buoy was put in its place. But, the other was established in 1668; a cottage-type lighthouse, with a coal-burning beacon. This beacon was lit atop a square, squat tower built against the cottage's Eastern gable. As it consumed a great quantity of coal, Sir Robert had a special quay constructed at Howth village to service the lighthouse. The necessary coal and other requisites were transported up the steep hill by horse-drawn carts.

The next lighthouse on Howth was built by Thomas Rogers, in 1790, on the same site as the old cottage-lighthouse. By the standards of that time it was of very advanced design; a lantern with a light source of 6 Argand oil lamps, each with a silvered copper parabolic reflector. This reflector directed the light through 6 "bulls eye" panes of glass which worked as lenses. He had also invented catadioptric lights, and was, obviously, a man very much in the forefront of lighthouse development, design and construction. He came to Ireland at the express invitation of the Lord Lieutenant, The Marquis of Buckingham, to construct the new lighthouse at Howth. The Irish Government was impressed by his work and invited him to join the Revenue Commissioners as "Lighthouse Contractor and Inspector." His contract gave him autonomy in all matters relating to lighthouses, as the body controlling them at the time, The Revenue Commissioners, was not really interested in things maritime.

Over the next twelve years Rogers built new lighthouses at Cranfield at the entrance to Carlingford Lough, at Cape Clear, at Loop Head and at Clare Island. Eventually, perhaps from lack of any control, Rogers grew careless in his administration of the lighthouses under his management. In an effort to maximise his personal profit from them, he hired too few helpers and paid them badly; an average of £15 per annum to a lightkeeper. Naturally, they began to seek other ways of making some money "on the side" and Rogers, in an effort to keep them happy turned a blind eye. He allowed them to use their dwellings for various puropses; the practice of herbal medicine, shoemaking, carpentry, prostitution, illegal distilling, basket weaving. The Government in London began to receive many complaints as to the inefficient manner in which the Irish lighthouse service was run, and this started a series of investigations and reports which eventually led to a special Act of Parliament being passed in 1810. This replaced the Revenue Commissioners as the controlling body for Irish light-houses. The Ballast Board of Dublin, who had managed the Port of Dublin and the Poolbeg light for over thirty years, was given responsibility instead.

The first act of the new Board was to appoint George Halpin Snr., the Engineer to the Board, as Inspector of Lighthouses. For the moment Thomas Rogers remained in his position of Lighthouse Contractor, presumably not aware of the investigation. Halpin found the lights to be in a semi-derelict condition, for want of maintenance; lens were broken, the towers themselves were far from watertight, equipment was rusting. The lanterns were so exposed that "the rain beat through them." Rogers had his con-tract terminated, and George Halpin Snr., given full charge of lighthouses by the Ballast Board, began a period of unprecedented development in the infant Lighthouse Service.

It is significant that, in 1810, when the Ballast Board took over, Thomas Rogers's contract price "for annual maintainance of nine lights" was £5,899. After 12 years of George Halpin's 'management', the same nine lighthouses cost only £3,363. And Rogers had deployed only one keeper at each lighthouse, where, 12 years on, each light had several keepers.

As was to be the case with other lights, the lighthouse built by Rogers on Howth was found to be positioned at much too high an elevation. Fog, mist and low cloud frequently obscured the lantern, and it was the subject of regular complaint from ships' owners and merchants of the Port of Dublin. So, on 5th December 1811, the Ballast Board recommended that a new lighthouse be built, further down the hill, at a spot known then as Little Baily. This was a rock, standing in the sea, below the level of the cliff, but joined to it; a place where King Crimthan, two thousand years before, had built his fortress. A place, sometimes, even now, called Duncriffan Point.

George Halpin Snr., designed and supervised the building of the new Baily tower, and the fixed white catopric light, with twenty four Argand oil lamps and reflectors, was established on 17th March, 1814. Originally the cut granite tower was painted white, and remained so until 1910, when the then Engineer-in-Chief, C.W. Scott, had it restored to its natural granite.

In the early days of the new lighthouse there was the saga of "the Bells of Baily." This began with an accident. On 3rd August, 1846, the City of Dublin Steam Packet Company's paddle steamer *Prince* was making for Dublin Port, in thick fog. Near the 'Nose of Howth', about 1 mile North of the Baily, she struck the cliffs and was badly holed, but with no loss of life. The Ballast Board, or anyone else for that matter, could not be sure that, if fog bells had been in operation at the Baily, the accident would have been prevented. Still, in such matters, they reckoned it was better to give the benefit of the doubt, and have fog bells installed.

Then, seven years later, in a blinding snow-storm, on the night of 15th February, 1853, another City of Dublin Steam Packet vessel, Queen Victoria, in passage from Liverpool to Dublin, ran onto the Casana Rock, between the 'Nose' and the Baily. This rock is not far from the mainland, so eight of the passengers scrambled ashore and reached the lighthouse. After they had left, the Captain managed to reverse the vessel off the rock. Not realising how badly holed she was he made to round Baily, but taking water rapidly she drifted and struck the rocks directly below the lighthouse, sinking with her bows touching the shore. Meantime, the P.S *Roscommon,* another City of Dublin Steam Packet Company vessel had come to the assistance of the *Queen Victoria,* saving 47 lives; unfortunately, 58 lives were lost, including the Captain. No bell had been sounded in the snow-storm. For, the bells promised seven years before had not yet been installed.

At a public trial the jury found the Captain and Mate "guilty of culpable negligence in failing to reduce speed, during a snow-storm which had obscured all lights." The Ballast Board conducted their own inquiry. It concluded that "the light was in perfect order"; but further found that the Assistant Keeper, who should have been on watch when the *Queen Victoria* struck, had gone to his bed early. He was dismissed from his post immediately. Regarding the fog bells that should have been erected after the first accident in 1846, Inspector George Halpin said that, due to the urgency of a number of new works being undertaken around the coast, the erection of the bells at Baily had been postponed. Within two months the Ballast Board informed the Board of Trade that a fog-bell was in course of manufacture. The bell served well until a reed-horn signal, activated by compressed air, was installed in November, 1867. The horn was replaced by a siren in 1879, and the siren by a diaphone in 1926. The bell, however, was not removed until 1890, when it was returned to the Kingstown stores.

Poolbeg

The South Wall of the Port of Dublin is one of the longest sea-walls in Europe. It extends from Ringsend nearly four miles out into the Bay and, at its seaward tip stands the Poolbeg lighthouse. The original Poolbeg tower was built in 1768, but, even before that there had been a light, in one form or other, at the end of this sea-wall. The 'wall' itself was commenced in 1717 and was, originally, built of a frame-work of wooden piles, reinforced with baskets made of salley willows cut at Booterstown, across the Bay.

This wall extended as far as a place which became known as the Pigeon House; approximately the point at which the two gigantic ESB chimneys stand today. Now, the Pigeon House derived its name from the massive wooden shed built by the Port Authority to facilitate the work on that original sea-wall. The shed served as a store-room for the tools being used, and as a shelter for the workmen. The caretaker, a man called Pidgeon, had reasonably comfortable living quarters adjacent to it, where he lived with his wife. During the Summer months small pleasure boats took people on trips to see the work in progress and the Pidgeons were perspicacious enough to see the need for certain 'services'. They fitted out part of their living-quarters as a hostelry and supplied meals and refreshments to the trippers. That original wooden shed has, of course, long since gone; a fort was built over its ruins in 1815. But, the name 'The Pigeon House' remains.

This 'wall' of wooden piles and kishes was not very long-lasting, and by 1735 it had been replaced by a double granite wall, with the cavity filled with rocks and gravel. To mark the end of this wall, a floating light, the first in Ireland, was moored there that same year. This was managed by James Palmer and became known as Palmer's Lightship, or the Dublin Lightship. About 1753 the wall was extended to a deep pool at the East end of the South Bull, called Poolbeg, again using the wooden piles and salley kishes. The Lightship was moved to mark the new extremity of the wall and thereafter became known as "the lightship at the kishes". Maintainance on this 'wall' was so expensive that, in 1761 work commenced on the building of a new stone sea-wall, similar to that linking Ringsend and the Pigeon House. It was decided, about the same time, to build a proper lighthouse tower at Poolbeg. The granite for the replacement wall was quarried in Dalkey and shipped across the bay from Sandycove and Bullock Harbours.

The first light was exhibited in the new tower in 1768 and the old Lightship continued to function until 1782. The lighthouse attained its present form between 1819 and 1820, when it was completely re-designed and re-built, under the direction of Inspector George Halpin Snr. In 1846 there was much legal wrangling over the status of the light; whether it should be classed a harbour or a coast light. The question was raised by the City of Dublin Steam Packet Company. They were querying the light dues of the Poolbeg, and were eventually refunded the dues they had paid on the head of it being a coastal light; the Attorney General deciding it should be classified as a harbour light. Incredibly, it was not until 1856 that dues were completely withdrawn.

It was again in the legal wars when it was passed from the jurisdiction of Commissioners of Irish Lights to that of the Dublin Port and Docks Board; a wrangle about storm-damage repairs and maintainance. This again involved the Attorney General, but was eventually settled through the intervention of the Board of Trade, who offered £1,500 for immediate repairs, on condition that the Port and Docks would accept full responsibility thereafter.

Over the years the colour of the tower has changed from white to black and then to its present colour, red. Inevitably the Poolbeg was automated and the last keeper was withdrawn from the tower on 1st January, 1969.

Dun Laoghaire Lights

The first harbour light was established in Dun Laoghaire, then Anglicized Dunleary, as early as 1813. Dunleary only became known as Kingstown after the visit of King George IV in 1821. It remained Kingstown until 1920, when it reverted to being Dun Laoghaire, the name of the original fishing village. The actual harbour was then quite small, occupying the space between a short pier and the steep cliffs East of where the Purty Kitchen now stands. It was a sheltered and safe anchorage and served the cross-channel steam packet and local fishing boats. At that time the Dunleary terminus of the Dublin and Kingstown Railway Company was located at what is now the landward end of the West Pier. This line became operational in 1834, and by 1837 had been extended to the site of the present railway station. This extension necessitated building a causeway across the old harbour, cutting-off a large portion of it between the new railway line and the cliff. This cut-off was eventually filled in and became the site, initially for the Kingstown Gas Works, and subsequently for the Albright & Wilson Chemical Plant. The site is now derelict and awaiting re-development.

Old Dunleary's little harbour had, before the building of the extended railway line across it, been the refuge for ships waiting to get into the Port of Dublin. The Port was quite congested at that time due to silting-up and, with a growing sea-traffic, Dunleary's capacity to accommodate the over-flow was totally inadequate. So, in 1817, work commenced on the mammoth task of building the new harbour; the West Pier and the East Pier. Designed by John Rennie, using thousands of tons of granite from Dalkey quarries, this project took over twenty-five years to complete. As the two arms grew in length, a temporary light on a wooden frame was established on each, and moved out with the progress of the piers. When the construction was completed the present lighthouses were built; the East Pier light being established on 1st October, 1847, the West Pier on 29th September, 1852. Keepers' dwellings were also constructed on each Pier.

These lights functioned very well until 1892, when the City of Dublin Steam Packet Company lodged a complaint regarding "the poor lighting at Kingstown East and West". By the end of 1896 both lights had been modified, with greatly increased power. When King Edward VII and Queen Alexandra vivited the Port, in July, 1907, the whole harbour was en fête. The two lighthouses and the keepers' dwellings were outlined with fairy lights, and vessels in the Port were dressed overall, including the Lighthouse Service tenders.

As cross-Channel traffic grew, the various shipping companies, plying in and out of Kingstown, demanded more navigational aids from the Lighthouse Service. In 1909, the London North-Western

Railway requested that a fog horn be sounded from Kingstown West for their vessels. As they were willing to contribute an equitable sum toward the cost of this additional service it was sanctioned; a certain keeper being designated to sound the horn, for which he was paid an extra £5 per annum.

Dun Laoghaire West became an unwatched station on 1st April, 1930, and the fixed red light was changed to three red flashes every 10 seconds; this being shortened, in July 1933, to 7.5 seconds. The East Pier became a three-keeper station in 1949, with the Principal Keeper moving to live in the old West Pier dwelling and the two Assistants living, with their families, in the dwellings at the base of the East Pier tower. In March 1955, the station became relieving and the families moved out.

Watch Room — Pre-automation

Kish Bank

The ultra-modern tower on the Kish sandbank, three miles off-shore, at the entrance to Dublin Bay, is unique among Irish lighthouses. Built on the telescopic principle, it was intended to be the first of several such lights along our East Coast. However, just a few years after its commissioning, in November 1965, that thinking had changed, and already the automation of all our lighthouses was being planned. In the new scheme of things such elaborate and expensive structures would not be needed to house the remote-controlled lights of the future.

So, in the context of Irish lighthouses, the Kish remains a 'one-off' feat of modern engineering; its luxurious, well-appointed living quarters and work-stations deserted and silent since its automation in May 1992. The irony of those now unused facilities brings a wry, sometimes cynical smile to the faces of retired keepers who, prior to 1965, suffered the extreme discomfort of the cramped, damp and cold quarters of the last of the old Kish lightships. Life aboard a lightship, in addition to the spartan quarters and the incessant rolling, could also be hazardous. There was the constant danger of drifting and, without propulsive power in high seas, capsizing. Right up to 1965 there were regular applications before the Commissioners of Irish Lights for grant aid to replace sets of false teeth, lost over the side, by lamplighters and fog-signalmen, in rough weather. And, there was the hazard of collision. The old Kish lightvessel was run-down four times; on one occasion being sunk by the Dun Laoghaire-Holyhead mailboat.

One of those retired keepers, though he never worked on the Kish, is D.J. O'Sullivan, an octogenarian, now living in Donegal. D.J.'s father was a lighthouse keeper also and lost his life in a tragic accident on Bull Rock when D.J. was just a boy. In time D.J., and his brother Eugene, became lighthouse keepers.

The life of a lighthouse keeper gave D.J. O'Sullivan ample time to pursue his two great interests — writing and the study of flora and fauna. He has published poetry and short stories and, for over twenty years wrote the much loved 'Land and Water' column in the 'Irish Press'. He is accepted as one of the most erudite natural-ists in Europe and has lectured widely, both here and in the USA. One of his poems, much anthologied, is called 'Kish', and it describes, very graphically, the constrictions imposed on the keeper of the light in the new lighthouse.

"A lone tower, the lighthouse
Rises out of the sandy ocean bed,
And the man who walks the balcony
In prescribed circuit, round and round,
Counts the railing's uprights, cross-pieces,
To pass his hours of watch away.
With never room to make a change,
But pace and stop, retrace and pace
Along a single narrow track.
Not side to side, or to and fro,
Confined within the murette's range,
A type of roofless iron cage.
While, here and there, with beady eyes,
The grey gulls watch him move around;
In disdain spread their wings, or swim
Free as the tidal currents run.
The choice is theirs; he has no choice,
Impounded by the catwalk's rim."

Even without the title the Kish is instantly recognisable in this poem. It is the only "wave-washed" tower on the Irish coast which imposes such strict restraints on the keeper's mobility. Built on sand, it rises sheer out of the sea. Even Fastnet has its strip of rock with a heli-pad, where a man may walk, weather permitting. But, on the Kish sandbank there is no rock. There is a heli-pad, but that is atop the tower and is much too exposed a place to take a stroll. So, the keeper on Kish has to take his exercise on the endless circle of the catwalk, called the murette, that portion of the lantern house between the balcony and the glass.

The first light-ship in the British Isles, at the Nore, was established around 1735, six years before the first Irish light-ship, the 'Dublin L.V.', was placed on station. This vessel marked the seaward end of the South Wall, which ran from O'Connell Bridge to what later became known as the Poolbeg lighthouse. A distance of four and a half miles, this is considered to be the longest sea-wall in Europe. It was constructed by making large baskets of salley willows, cut at Booterstown, filling these with stones, and sinking them to make a solid sea-wall. As the Irish for basket is 'kish', the light-ship moored at the end of this wall became known as "the light-ship at the kishes" — abbreviated, through common usage to 'The Kish'. That first light served well enough for over forty years, being withdrawn in 1782, when lighthouses proper had been established at either side of the Liffey entrance. Some sources say that the Kish Bank took its name from this original light-ship; others maintain that the Bank was known as the Kish long before that time.

The first light-ship was established on the Kish Bank in 1811, when an old Dutch galliot was converted and moored there. The Bank being so far out to sea, the light was of inestimable value to all shipping in East Coast waters. Not only did it benefit ships entering and leaving the Port of Dublin, it was also of great use to ships plying North and South along the coast.

That first, primitive beacon on the sands consisted of three lights arranged in a triangle; for a fog signal the crew took turns in beating a loud gong. In fog there was a special arrangement with the Dun Laoghaire-Holyhead packet. When she was due off Kish, the keepers fired an 18-pounder gun — two shots, at fifteen minute intervals. The packet, when she had slipped safely past the hazardous sandbank, fired a single shot in acknowledgement. And, on only four occasions was there collision. A surprisingly low incidence considering the mail-packet rounded the Kish, inward and outward bound, twice a day, every day throughout the year.

The converted galliot served its purpose well for over thirty years. Then, in the early 1840's, the first governing body of Irish Light-houses, the Dublin Ballast Office, began to plan the replacement of the light-ship with a more modern, fixed structure. This would mean, quite literally, building a lighthouse on the sand. The challenge to the engineer-pharologist was enormous, for the sand-bank lay, at low-tide, in 54 feet of water, at high-tide 68 feet, with a constant, treacherous tide-rip of nearly 3 knots. To compound the problem, solid rock-bottom was buried under 300 feet of sand.

Of the embryo ideas and detailed plans presented to the Ballast Board by the best engineering brains of that time, one seemed to have a greater chance of success than all the others. It was a 'screw pile' system of building on sandy foundations, developed by Alexander Mitchell, a blind engineer. He was given the contract to build the first lighthouse on the Kish Bank. Though his patent was used, with great success, in other locations — the Spit bank at Cobh and the pile lights in Dundalk Bay and Carlingford Lough — it was not a success on the Kish Bank. The piles became 'prostrated', in a fierce November gale, in 1842, and the project was abandoned. It had already cost £2,500, a huge sum in those days. Local fishermen, returning from a day's trawling in the area of the Bank, can still be heard to complain of having their nets damaged by the submerged wreckage of "Mitchell's bloody piles."

After this costly set-back it was to be, incredibly, a century and a half before another attempt was made to build a lighthouse on the Kish. The new scheme had its genesis in a visit, by Irish Lights Engineer-in-Chief, Desmond Martin and two Commissioners, to the Sixth Annual Lighthouse Conference in Washington, in 1960. Here, among other exhibits, the plans and models of the 'legged' platforms used for oil-rigs were on show. The Irish party was impressed, and perspicacious enough to see the possibilities of adapting this method of building in the construction of 'wave-washed' lighthouses. On their return the Board of Commissioners of Irish Lights looked favourably on the idea and tenders were invited.

Nine designs were eventually tendered, and the one selected was quite revolutionary, differing greatly from the original concept of the 'legged' structure, similar to the oil-rig platforms. It came from the Danish firm of Christiani & Nielsen, and was based on a method devised by Robert Gellerstad of the Swedish Lighthouse Board. Their proposal was for a telescopic caisson, approximately 100 feet in diameter, inside which, in another caisson, the light-house tower would be constructed. When completed, it would be towed to the Kish Bank; the outer caisson would then be flooded and the tower telescoped up to its full height of 110 feet above low-water.

One of the big advantages of this method was that virtually all the construction work could be done in the relative shelter of Dun Laoghaire Harbour. Simultaneously, the work of preparing the sea-bed on the Bank could be progressed; divers working in ten fathoms of water, preparing a 120 diameter radial screed on the ocean floor. This would form the base for a 6-inch-thick layer of heavy gravel on which the caisson would rest.

Construction started on this unique project in the old Coal Harbour in Dun Laoghaire, in August 1963. By the end of that year the outer caisson was completed. The workers, mostly locals, who had worked round-the-clock shifts to achieve this, celebrated in the local pubs. But, even as they celebrated, disaster struck;

41

the kind of disaster the sadistic sea saves for those who have the temerity to challenge its power by attempting near-impossible things. In a December gale of incredible ferocity, huge seas invaded even the normally sheltered Inner Harbour, and the newly-constructed caisson was sunk and damaged beyond repair. The whole process had to be started all over again.

With great ingenuity the engineers decided to salvage as much as they could from the wreckage; the old caisson was roofed over and used as a pontoon on which the new one could be built. To prevent adherence to the new base slab a one-inch layer of sand was spread on the roof. Work progressed satisfactorily, and when the combined weight of the two caissons was still such that the whole would float in the 18-feet of water in the Inner Harbour, the structure was towed to a berth in the deeper water of the Outer Harbour. Here, work was continued to the point where its weight still permitted it to be floated off the pontoon. At this point the ballast water was pumped out of the new structure; it then seperated from the old. This stage of the work was completed by November 1964.

Such was the public interest in the building of this extraordinary structure that crowds flocked to Dun Laoghaire, from all over the country to see the work in progress. As a safety precaution, and to prevent crowds encroaching on the actual workplace, a wooden 'viewing stand' was constructed for the day trippers. It was a boom time in Dun Laoghaire. After a time of great depression in the late '50's, the building of the Kish brought much-needed employment to the Borough. Many people were working again for the first time in over a decade; and working for above average pay — the shift-work rate being much higher than the straight day-rate. The workers and their families began to enjoy a social life they had not known for years. Hope flowered again and with it a pride in what they were doing — building the 'new' Kish.

Labour relations between workers and contractor were excellent. Morale was high and an enlightened management showed its appreciation by encouraging 'social' activity. For special occasions, such as Christmas, Easter, the completion of a phase in production, the workers had established a collective. The money saved in this was matched, pound-for-pound by the contractors, and many a 'celebration' was held in local hostelries — The Purty Kitchen and The Cumberland being within 'spittin' distance' of the work-site, and Walter's slightly further away at the other end of Dun Laoghaire. One of the workmen, recently retired from Irish Lights, told me that he remembers the largest round ever ordered in Walter's Pub; the 'keeper of the purse' calling for drinks for 72 people out of the collective fund.

During the building of the tower at the Coal Harbour, there were, among the many visitors to the site, two whose lives have been dedicated to the Irish Lighthouse Service. One, J.J. (Jack) Roche, a PK (Principal Keeper), who had spent a lifetime working on the most remote lighthouses round our coast, and was now being honoured by being offered the position as first Principal Keeper on the 'new' Kish. The other, Mel Boyd, an Engineering student at Trinity College, who, at that time, could not even have guessed that he would, some years later, join the Irish Lights organisation and eventually become its Chief Executive.

Jack Roche's initial reaction, on being shown the futuristic, pre-fabricated, telescopic shell of the new tower was: "My God, they expect me to live in this 'thing', with walls 10 inches thick, when, all my working life, I've been in granite towers with walls 8 feet thick." Nevertheless, he took the posting and was to enjoy several happy years on the Kish before his retirement. Mel Boyd re-members being tremendously impressed by the technical achievement and engineering skills.

In a long career in the Irish Lights Service Jack Roche had served on many stations round the coast. His last posting was to Kish, where he served for four years until his retirement in 1969. He told me that his Kish days were the happiest in his whole working life; he loved the new tower, quite literally, making it his own to such a degree, that for his time there, it became affectionately known as 'Roche's Tower'. He has so many memories of his days there.

"I think the most extraordinary thing I saw in my time on the Kish, was a migration of birds," Jack told me. "It was a kind of soft, slightly misty night, and I came on watch at twelve o'clock. When I went out on the balcony I just couldn't get over it. In the rays of the light the birds must have been in countless thousands. I went up onto the helicopter platform and there wasn't a vacant space on that. All the little balcony rails were lined with birds, shoulder to shoulder, everywhere. It reminded me of a migration I saw when I was a young keeper at the Old Head of Kinsale, but there, we had to sweep the dead birds off the balcony after they'd struck the light. On the Kish, thank God, there were no dead birds. Whatever way the lantern was situated they didn't strike it."

Jack is enjoying his retirement but, he told me, "One thing I miss very much is the shipping. When I was on the Kish I made a lot of friends. Ships got to know me, although I never met, or saw, their captains or officers. They'd call me up on the radio telephone at all times, day and night, and we'd swap yarns. The radio telephone meant an awful lot to us, especially on the long night watches. I talked to all kinds of men. I remember once talking to a skipper in the Bay of Biscay. That's a long way away. He was bound for one of the English East coast ports, with a cargo of phosphates. That was my amusement. They kept me informed of new ships coming out of the yards, ships that were sold, ships that had changed their names, what passage they were on, what trades they were on. I miss all that a lot."

In June 1965 the building of the tower was completed, and on the 29th of that month the whole structure was towed, by two tugs, to its site on the Kish Bank, three miles out to sea. The coast, from Dun Laoghaire to Dalkey, was *en fête* for the occasion. Boats from the various Yacht Clubs accompanied the tugs and thousands of people lined the sea front, jostling for a vantage point from which to view the slow progress of the strange convoy. The floating lighthouse was a large structure, weighing seven thousand tons and drawing 30 feet of water. To most of the onlookers it seemed a miracle that the ungainly looking mass could actually float.

On arrival at its prepared site, the new tower was made fast to four prepared moorings, pending being manoeuvered into its correct position on the Bank. Throughout the day there had been a gentle Northerly breeze; unfortunately, this now freshened to force 4, accompanied by the dreaded Kish Bank fog. One of the mooring lines snapped. There was no option but to sink the unit where it stood, which was several hundred feet to the South of its intended siting.

It was to remain in this position until July 15th, clearly visible from Dun Laoghaire, Howth and the South Dublin coast. Stuck out there in the great maw of water, silhouetted against the sky, it presented a tilted, 'drunken' image, like the leaning tower of Pisa; it was the butt of many jokes for the local Jeremiahs, especially among the sailing fraternity. Some of them had, from the start predicted disaster for the project. To their chagrin it was refloated and successfully positioned on the bed prepared for it. A dredger was then deployed to pump sand ino the lower part of the annular space between the outer wall of the caisson and the tower proper. This done, the tower was then raised by flooding the inner cylinder of the caisson with water. The space left by the tower was filled in with sand and stones, and the remaining space, between tower and caisson, was filled with concrete.

Over the next four months there was a constant shuttle of work-boats between Dun Laoghaire and the Kish, as it was furnished and fitted-out with the most modern equipment. This included a radio-beacon, which, 25 years later, was tranferred to the Baily, on the automation of the Kish. The keepers' quarters are luxurious compared to any other lighthouse on our coasts; seperate bedroom for each keeper, well-equipped kitchen, dining room, games room and television lounge.

The new light was established on 9th November 1965, and the lightship towed away. This was before the advent of the helicopter to effect reliefs and emergency 'lifts', in case of accident or illness. John de Courcy Ireland, then Secretary of the Dun Laoghaire Lifeboat, wondered if there would be any problems for the lifeboat coming alongside the new tower, used as it was to the lighthship. He decided their next 'excercise' would be to the new Kish, to look at the structure and estimate what problems they might have should it be necessary to take a man off. "The day we picked for the trip," John said, "was abominable. High wind and a ferocious sea running. Indeed the whole of the interior of Dun Laoghaire harbour seemed to be breaking out, over the sea-wall, into Scotsman's Bay. So bad that, on the way out, two of the lifeboat crew got sick, a most unusual occurrence. Now, we had all seen the tower being built in Dun Laoghaire Harbour, but here we were seeing it in its natural element, with this enormous sea breaking around it, indeed the waves were climbing half-way up the tower. John Jenkins, the lifeboat coxwain, came in as close as he dared, ran his experienced eye over the massive tower, made his mental measurements and assured us that, if and when the need arose, we could manage it."

Although the telescopic system of building lighthouses had been used before, mostly in the Scandanavian countries, this was the first time it had been used in Irish waters; a significant event in marine engineering, and a tribute to all who worked on the project. This huge and complex construction was completed without any loss of life; without a single serious accident; and without any serious engineering hitch. The only set-backs were those caused by the weather.

Throughout the whole operation the most sophisticated engineering methods were used. However, when it came to the most efficient way of measuring the strength of the tide-race, on the ocean floor at the Kish Bank, man's ingenuity was called on to devise a simple method, using very 'domestic' components; a baby's bottle, a cork, some Bird's Jelly, a string and a brick.

The bottle was half-filled with jelly. A hole was drilled in the cork and one end of the string passed through, before sealing the cork in the bottle. The other end of the string was tied round the brick. The bottle was placed in boiling water until the jelly had melted, then the unit was attached to a heaving line and thrown overboard. The brick lay on the sandy bottom with the bottle floating upside down, pulled by the tide-race. Left for fifteen minutes, the jelly had solidified at a certain angle, and by measuring this the strength of the tide-race was accurately gauged. As a final 'refinement', direction as well as strength could be gauged by floating a compass needle in the liquid jelly.

The great pride in the tremendous achievement of building the beacon on the sands was epitomised for me recently in talking to an Irish Lights employee, Charlie O'Shea, who had worked on the construction of the lighthouse. "Sometimes now," he said, "I like to take my grandchildren on day trips to Holyhead. And, when the mailboat is passing the Kish, one of them always says, very proudly, "Grandad, didn't you build that lighthouse?" And I always answer — 'Yes, I did'."

John de Courcy Ireland talked to me, for a Radio programme I was making, on the occasion of the automation of the Kish, in May 1992. He paid tribute to the generations of keepers who had kept the light there, and who had also been vigilant over and above the call of duty. "I can think of at least half-a-dozen occasions, when incidents occurred in the area of the Kish, and had the keepers not been there, watching, lives would definitely have been lost. And this should be our great worry for the future, when there's nobody watching."

The Muglins

From the 9th century to the 18th century, Dublin itself was far from ideal as a port from which to conduct foreign trade. Entry was impeded by a sandbank, and the rivers Liffey, Dodder and Tolka flooded regularly, making it more of a hazard than a safe haven for ships. For several centuries therefore, Dalkey, two miles South-East of Dun Laoghaire, was the Port for Dublin. From its sheltered anchorage Danish settlers traded with several European countries and a cross-Channel trade flourished, with the ports of Chester, Chepstow, Gloucester and Bristol. The Normans found Dalkey equally suitable and built seven castles there. These castles, in addition to being residences and watch-towers, were also fortified warehouses, and were the constant target for bands of marauding mountain men from Wicklow.

Protecting the haven of Dalkey Sound is the large Dalkey Island, with its Napoleonic Martello tower, disused battery and monastic ruins of St. Begnet's church. There is also a protecting chain of smaller islands, or rocks — Lamb Island, Clare Rock and Carrig Rock — all to the North-West of Dalkey Island. About 500 meters to the North-East lie the Muglins, treacherous, jagged rocks, which are not part of the protective chain, but rather a great hazard to shipping. At one time, when piracy flourished on this coast, gibbets were raised on the Muglins, and the bodies of executed pirates left to swing in the sea-wind.

Over the years many ships foundered here, but it was not until 1873 that the suggestion of a light on the Muglins was raised. In that year the Kingstown Harbour Master, Captain William Hutchinson, published a plea, in 'Saunder's Newsletter', for a light on "these siren rocks". He subsequently furnished a list of twelve vessels lost, but, despite this, there was indecision between Trinity House, The Board of Trade and the Commissioners of Irish Lights. When a thirteenth wreck was added to Captain Hutchinson's list in 1876, the question became a live issue again. However, it was not until 1880 that a conical stone beacon, 30 feet high, was erected on the Muglins. This was painted white; a red centre-belt being added in 1883. On the 23rd June, 1906, an occulting red light was established on the Muglins Beacon. Then, on 30th July, 1979, the Muglins was raised from the status of "lighted beacon" to "lighthouse", to avoid confusion with the modified IALA Buoyage System A in Dublin Bay.

Wicklow Head

During the eighteenth and nineteenth centuries there was a genuine effort made to light some of the main hazards on the Irish coast. Lighthouses were built, at enormous cost, and then, often after several years, found to be in the wrong specific location. The design was good, the construction painstakingly done, the lantern as powerful as the limitations of the time allowed; but the engineers had yet to learn that the highest point on cliff, or headland, was not necessarily the best specific location. This mistake was made in several places, among them Howth, Clear Island, Old Head of Kinsale and Wicklow Head.

Wicklow Head's first light, after nearly fifty years in service, was deemed to be on too high an elevation and, consequently, very often obscured in fog. That first light, established on 1st September 1781, was actually part of a unique pair of lighthouses built on Wicklow Head at the same time. One was on Long Hill, and known as the upper, or rear light; the other was on the saddle of the headland above the sea, and known as the lower, or front light. The Revenue Commissioners then had responsibility for light-houses, and the twin towers were designed by their Engineer, John Trail.

Two separate towers were deemed necessary, as ships approach-ing the East coast might confuse a single light with Hook Head, to the South, and Howth, to the North; these being the only other lights on the whole East coast at that time. That Wicklow Head should be lit was imperative; it was landfall for a growing traffic, plying out of English West coast ports, and gave a lead West-North-West between the South end of the India Bank and the North end of the Arklow Bank. It would also be of inestimable value to inshore traffic through the Swash, making for the anchor-age at Wicklow town, behind the Murrow, or trying to find the coastal channel to Dublin.

The twin towers were octagonal in design and built of cut stone. Nothing now remains of the front tower, on the headland saddle nearest the sea, but the old rear tower still stands on Long Hill. It is approximately 95 feet high, in a good state of preservation, and still functional as a long-established sea-mark. There is not even a drawing extant to tell us anything of the front tower, but we can safely assume that it was similar in style to its twin. One report, written in March 1812, describes it as "the second tower, which is a smaller one, in a proportionable degree, has also got a lantern, the light source of which is twenty tallow candles at the focus of a large mirror-reflector."

In 1810 The Corporation for Preserving and Improving the Port of Dublin took over responsibility for the lights from the Revenue Commissioners. One of their first considerations was the replacement of the twin lights on the Head. There were two reasons for this. The upper light was at such an elevation that it was constantly obscured in foggy weather. And, because of poor maintainance by the Revenue Commissioners, the lanterns in both towers were in a very dilapidated state, rotten and rusty, with tarnished reflectors.

At the time there seemed a great urgency to effect these very necessary changes, yet the mills of bureaucracy grind slowly indeed, and it was almost five years before approval for the re-building was granted by Trinity House and the Lord Lieutenant. In the interim, several attempts were made to make the rotting lanterns efficient; all stop-gap and not very successful. Small pieces of looking-glass were cemented into the large catoptric reflectors, with six candles placed in their assumed focus. And so, for over fours years, the lights functioned with this makeshift apparatus.

Then, in 1816, approval was given to George Halpin Snr., the Corporation's Inspector of Works, to go ahead with his design. Work commenced on the two towers that year. They were both built on the same bearing as the 1781 towers; the new upper lighthouse very close to the old front lighthouse on the headland saddle; the new front lighthouse much lower down the cliff, just 121 feet above high water level. The old front tower was demolished, and the light in the old upper tower was discontinued on, or about, the 12th November 1818, when the new lights were exhibited for the first time. They were both fixed lights, each lantern housing fifteen Argand oil lamps and reflectors. A definite improvement on the twenty tallow candles in the old lanterns. The upper tower was 75 feet high, the lower tower 45 feet.

This change from tallow candles to, in their time, state-of-the-art oil lamps, precipitated the first recorded 'trade dispute' in the new Lighthouse Service. George Halpin, in a report to his Board, recommended that the two long-serving keepers at Wicklow Head,

Leonard Manley and George Wilkinson should "have their employment terminated and be made to surrender their light-keepers' dwellings." In his judgement, they were "unqualified to work in the new lighthouses." Presumably, years of faithfully, and efficiently, tending tallow candles, didn't necessarily mean they were fit to trim the wicks and fill the tanks of oil lamps. So, in a way, it could be said they lost out to progress, to the state-of-the-art. Halpin also recommended that "C. Dudgeon, the Wicklow Lighthouses Collector and Inspector, should be informed his services are unnecessary, and be given payment to the end of the present quarter, December 1818." Neither he, nor the Board, could have anticipated the stance taken by the three very agg-rieved men. They appealed on the grounds of "long and faithful service" for a reconsideration of their situation, and, after much demur, the Board eventually awarded Manley and Wilkinson pensions of fifteen pounds a year for life, and Dudgeon a lump sum of fifty pounds, "in respect of his twenty years service."

During their period of management of the lighthouses, 1796 to 1810, the Revenue Commissioners had deployed a Preventive Water Guard at the station. This Guard was dismissed, soon after the Corporation took over. Then, ten years on, in 1821, the Commissioners proposed that they be allowed to re-instate this Water Guard, along with a flag-mast, and take over the two vacant lightkeepers' "cabins". However the Corporation would not count-enance such an arrogant proposal, replying that "the regulations of the Service prevented the Board from complying with the request."

In a storm, on the night of 10th October, 1836, the old rear tower on Long Hill was struck by lightning. In the fire that followed the interior was gutted on all floors, and the lantern destroyed. George Halpin went to inspect the damage, and in his report, recom-mended that "as the tower forms a useful landmark by day it should be re-roofed next Spring." The Board quickly agreed that this should be done. Yet, once again, the mills of bureaucracy ground slowly indeed, and thirty years were to pass before the present brick dome was put on, in 1866.

In the middle of the nineteenth century there was an appreciable increase in the number of ships plying between English ports and the East coast of Ireland. Pressure was put on the Corporation by ship owners, agents, merchants and port authorities, to improve the lighting on the South and South-Eastern approaches to

Dublin; especially the stretch between Tuskar Rock and Kish Bank. A special committee was formed, in 1863, to study this situation and make recommendations. As a consequence, a new lightvessel, the *Wicklow Swash*, was moored off Wicklow Head, and the upper light was discontinued. Simultaneously, improvements were carried out to the lower light. The 1818 lantern was replaced by a cast-iron lantern manufactured by Edmundson & Co., Dublin; the fixed catoptric apparatus being replaced by a first order dioptric lens, made by Chance Brothers, of Birmingham. With a revolving shade this gave an occulting character of ten seconds flash every fifteen seconds. Captain Nesbit, of Trinity House, designd the oil lamp, which was manufactured by W. Wilkins, of London. The *Wicklow Swash* lightvessel had a relatively short life; it was withdrawn from service on 10th October, 1867, when the *Codling* and *North Arklow* light-vessels were established.

About this time, John R. Wigham, of Edmundson & Co., Dublin, who specialised in the manufacture of lighthouse lanterns, patented his invention for illuminating with gas. He was directed by the Corporation to commence experiments at the Baily lighthouse, on Howth Head, in 1865. At first the gas was made from oil, then shale, and finally good quality cannel coal. A small gasworks was set up at Baily. So successful was this that other stations also converted to gas, among them Wicklow Head.

Wicklow light was converted to gas on 4th January, 1868; the supply coming from a gas-works built at the station. Initially the gas was made from oil, but later cannel coal was used very effectively. Altogether there were 108 jets in the light; an inner group of 28, plus four other circles of jets, each with 20 fish-tail jets. This made it possible to employ lights of five different powers. The flame produced by these jets was concentrated into a mica funnel, set at the focal point of the lens.

Gas proved to be quite satisfactory at Wicklow Head and relatively economical. It continued to be used at the lighthouse until 1906. In August of that year it was changed to incandescent paraffin vapour, with a 50mm diameter mantle. At that time the optic was also changed to a third order revolving apparatus, driven by a clockwork rotation machine. This new set-up gave three flashes every ten seconds. This method of lighting was extremely satisfactory and continued to be used for the next seventy years.

In October 1974 the station became relieving, and shortly afterwards work commenced on a major modernising. A new watch-room was built over the keeper's quarters, to house, among other things, the monitoring equipment for the two new Lanby buoys, which, in May 1976, replaced the old Codling and Arklow light-vessels. The station had, meantime, in March 1976, converted from paraffin to electric.

As part of the modernising and up-dating programme, a Radio Beacon was added to the station in 1978. The aerial for this is slung between masts specially erected; one on top of the remains of the old 1818 tower, the other on the headland just above the present lighthouse. The beacon became operational on 5th April, 1978 and has a link with six other Radio Beacons. These are located at: Skerries, off North-West Anglesea, Bardsey Island, off the Lleyn Peninsula, Cardigan Bay, Cregneish, Isle of Man, Point of Ayre, Isle of Man, and South Rock lightfloat, off County Down. Each station transmits its own signal in Morse, once every six minutes. Wicklow Head's signal is—W K—(.＿ ＿ ＿ . ＿).

The upper tower, dating from 1818, and the two light-keepers' cottages attached to it, remain in good condition, having been leased to various tenants from 1891 until 1942. The first lessee was the Admiralty (Coast Guard) in 1891. The Board of Works were there from 1922 for several years. They were followed by a couple of private lessees and, finally, from 1935 to 1942, the Irish Youth Hostel Association. On three sides this tower commands magnificent views of the Wicklow countryside; fertile fields, woodlands and towering mountain peaks. On the fourth side is the sea.

Wicklow Head would seem to be one of the most 'popular' stations on the whole Irish coast. I have spoken to keepers who served there — many of them, like John Noel Crowley with their families. And they are unanimous in their praise of it —"a very happy place to live and work." Indeed, John Noel and his brother Oliver, presently Principal Keeper at Wicklow Head, are the end of a great dynasty of lightkeepers, going back to their father and grand-father. A dynasty that would almost certainly have had another Crowly or two join the Service if automation had not ended ended recruitment.

A lighthouse lantern

Tuskar Rock

Of all the lighthouses on our coasts the Tuskar, seven miles off the South-East tip of Ireland, must be more familiar to more Irish people than any other. It lies directly in the path of all sea-traffic entering, or leaving, the ports of Rosslare Harbour and Wexford. Millions of emigrants, from, quite literally, every county in Ireland, have been through Rosslare, outward and inward bound, passing, at a safe distance, the flat islet on which the massive, granite tower stands most of them unaware of the treacherous rocky shoals that plague this Wexford coast; shoals which have probably caused more wrecks than any other navigational hazard on our seaboard.

In 1810, when the Corporation for Preserving and Improving the Port of Dublin took over the management of lighthouses from the Revenue Commissioners, their Board was very aware of the danger the unmarked and unlit Tuskar Rock presented to shipping. The following year, George Halpin Snr., together with three other Board members, inspected the Rock and prepared a proposal for a lighthouse. His detailed drawing was submitted to the Corporation, who first approved the plans, afterwards informing Trinity House. To their surprise, however, the Elder Brethern, did not look with great favour on Halpin's design for the Tuskar. He had proposed a tower similar in construction to those at South Rock, County Down, built in 1797, and the Poolbeg, in Dublin Bay, built in 1768. The Trinity House Board visualised a tower similar to the South Stack, near Holyhead, designed by D. A. Alexander, the Trinity House Surveyor, and completed just two years before. With their letter of disapproval they enclosed the book of drawings of South Stack.

By the end of that year Trinity House gave their approval to the Tuskar project, presumably after some compromise, as to the design of the new lighthouse, had been reached. There was a belated attempt made by the Waterford Chamber of Commerce to have the new lighthouse constructed on the Saltee Islands, 18 miles West-South-West of the Tuskar Rock; in their opinion, that being a better site. That there was a certain vested interest in this cannot be doubted, the Saltees being considerably closer to the entrance to Waterford Harbour, and the Chamber of Commerce representing the merchants and traders of that City. The Corporation did not entertain such a proposal, stating in their reply that they considered that Hook Head lighthouse served Waterford-bound shipping very efficiently, and no other light was needed in that immediate vicinity. Building commenced in 1812.

Now, the building of lighthouses, largely because of their location, is a hazardous business; particularly those on wave-washed rocks. Exposed to wind, weather and the vagaries of a capricious sea, snatching working-time between tides and gales, workmen really gambled with their lives. Indeed it is surprising that, thanks to God, or Davy Jones, or whatever agency ordains such things, there were so very few fatalities, or even serious accidents. For instance, when one thinks of Fastnet, besieged for days on end by enormous waves breaking right over the tower, one wonders how it ever came to be built, without a single life being lost. Sadly, Tuskar was not so fortunate. It claimed twelve lives; eleven during its construction, and one during World War Two.

On the night of 18th October 1812, a sudden, severe storm hit the Wexford coast. This South-Eastern tip of Ireland is plagued by such storms. This is where ocean and channel meet; where the long, mountainous Atlantic rollers are in head-on collision with the sweeping tides and choppy cross-currents of the St. George's Channel. This is where the colliding waters are whipped to a white frenzy, by Southern gales blowing, unharnessed, all the way out of the Bay of Biscay. A playground of contrary winds and squalls and tide-rips and swirling currents; a graveyard of ships. And, on that October night, the graveyard of ten workmen on the Rock, whose wooden dormitories were swept into the seething waters. Fourteen survived, managing to find a purchase on the sea-swept rock, clinging there, in desperation, for forty-eight hours until they were taken off. A Mr. W. Johnson, employed at the Wexford Custom House, was their "good samaritan", ensuring that they were rescued as soon as possible and given "all necessary care." He was highly commended by the Corporation for his "humane inter-ference" and was empowered to advance the survivors, and the relatives of those lost, such immediate relief as he thought necessary.

The ten men who drowned were: Philip Brady, Samuel Croke, Patrick Byrne, William Bishop, William Devereaux, James Nowlan, Josiah Corish, and Myles Ryan — all married; and John Kehoe and John Salmon — unmarried.

The inequities of the compensatory system of that time are evident in the "awards" made to those whose lives were so dramatically effected by the Tuskar disaster. Each "widow, or destitute mother" was awarded a "pension" of six pounds per annum. Each child up to 16 years, three pounds per annum. A survivor, who had his leg amputated was awarded ten pounds per annum. There was "a fund of forty-pounds" set up, out which "survivors are to be compensated for loss of clothing." Six of the survivors were paid "lump-sums of half-a-guinea for two weeks, or an extra week's wages", as compensation. Two years later, when the tower was nearing completion, a stone-cutter fell from a height of 72 feet and was killed. There is no record of what his family, specifically, received in compensation. We can only assume that the settlement was as inequitable as that granted the others.

Incredibly, all of the survivors returned, after a very short recovery period, to their work on the Rock and, when that work was finished, moved directly on to Inishtrahull off the North coast of

Donegal, to build another lighthouse. Ballads were sung about them at the time, extolling their bravery and gallantry, and while they obviously possessed these qualities, sheer pragmatism must also have been a powerful motivating factor. They had a job to do, however difficult or dangerous; they had families to support; permanent employment was hard to come by. It was largely a matter of expediency . They were locked in a system, and a brush with death could not be allowed to alter their lives too much.

The first light on Tuskar was exhibited on the 4th June, 1815 and its first fog signal was a simple bell, tolled every thirty seconds. The light was a first order catoptric, with three faces — two white and one red; each flash was visible for ten seconds, with a two minute interval between each flash. The optic was supplied by Messrs. G. Robinson of London.

In the 178 years since then, there has been only one night on which that light failed to be lit; a single occasion when the Tuskar remained in darkness. Thankfully, no tragedy resulted from this lapse. And lapse it was; a very 'human' lapse, a very rare lapse; a lapse that really was the exception proving the rule. The rule being that, over the years, lightkeepers had been always above reproach in adhering, very strictly, to the code of the Service. On this occasion two of them, by their dereliction of duty, precipitated a situation that resulted in their careers being ruined. It was also an episode that had all the elements of a Gilbert and Sullivan operetta, or a Whitehall farce.

And it all began with a consignment of contraband brandy. The Wexford coast had long been a favourite landfall for smugglers, running "excisable commodities" from French ports. Using manageable, manoeuverable craft — luggers and cutters — they were able to 'wear' in to the smaller harbours and creeks and off-load their precious cargo. On a fine morning in 1821, the cutter *Shark*, out of Le Havre, made landfall off Tuskar about 3 a.m. The skipper intended running up to Wexford Port, but, seeing coastguard and customs officials in a launch patrolling the entrance to the channel, he 'wore' the *Shark* into the 'cothole' on the Rock and landed, in the half-light, according to his unofficial manifest, "a large cask and several smaller kegs of French brandy, 40 pounds of sperm candles, a tin box of playing cards, and several other excisable commodities." He explained his predicament to the two lighthouse keepers, Michael Wisheart and Charles Hunter, 'buying' their confidence and collusion by promising them "a present", on his return to claim the goods, if they were untouched. He then sailed up to Wexford, was overhauled by the Coastguard and Customs officers, and searched. Nothing was found.

The *Shark* lay-up in Wexford for a few days, during which time her skipper made plans to return to the Tuskar and remove his contraband cargo. He planned to land it on the mainland at Ballytrent, where he had some accomplices, who had a whale-boat lying there, ready to make the run to the Rock. One of his own crew was locked into a wooden bathing box on the beach to keep a lookout for patrolling coastguards. This look-out had a candle in a lantern with which he was to signal his skipper on Tuskar, waiting with the loaded whaleboat to run back to Ballytrent.

Leaving Ballytrent, after dark, the smuggler was surprised to find that there was no light on Tuskar. On reaching the Rock he entered the tower where he found the two lighkeepers; "Hunter dead drunk on his back, and Wisheart in the same state on his side." They had 'tapped the Admiral' — broached the brandy cask — and had, to judge from the level remaining, been imbibing heavily. The smuggler left them to their slumbers and ran what remained of his cargo safely to Ballytrent. By an extraordinary coincidence, that very night, "a wild, wet night", King George IV, aboard the *Royal Yacht,* in convoy with some ships of the Fleet, was en route to Kingstown. When they failed to find the Tuskar light, they were very perplexed, and, guided by The Smalls light on the English side they ran for shelter to Milford Haven.

Such dereliction of duty deserved, and got, severe censure and punishment. An immediate examination was ordered into the affair, and, on 23rd October, 1821, the following resolution was made at a meeting of the Corporation in the Ballast Office, Dublin. *"An examination having taken place into the conduct of Michael Wisheart and Charles Hunter, relative to a Smuggling transaction at Tuskar Lighthouse, it was resolved that: In consequence of the inattention of Michael Wisheart to his charge at the Tuskar Light-house, a quantity of contraband goods were deposited on the Rock, and of which he neglected to acquaint the officers of the Board, to remove him from the situation of First Light-keeper, and that he be placed as second in some other lighthouse. It was also resolved that: Charles Hunter (Assistant Light-keeper at Tuskar), having per-mitted the landing of these goods, that he be removed from the situation of a lightkeeper, and that he may hereafter be employed as a working blacksmith (from which employment he had been taken into the Lighthouse Service)."*

Charles Hunter returned to work, as a blacksmith, in 'Halpin's Pool' in Dublin, and gave many years of loyal service there. Alas, poor Wisheart was sent to the Skellig's Rock, a place so inhospitable and difficult of access, that he was very unlikely to find the wherewithal to 'tap the Admiral' there. For a while his main off-duty occupation seemed to be ensuring that his cow had enough grass from the wind-swept rock. Cutting grass one day, near the cliff's edge, he fell over and was killed. So ended this tragi-comic episode, thankfully, without direct loss of life on that night when the light was not lit. When one thinks of the possible ramifications of that single dereliction of duty, one realises that the *Royal Yacht* might have run aground on the treacherous Wexford shoals.

Houses for the families of the Tuskar keepers were built at Ballyhire, between Greenore and Carnsore Points, in 1817. However, in 1834, these houses were sold and accommodation for the families made ready on the Rock itself. The reason given by the Board was "the disgraceful attitude of the keepers when they were ashore." For some years after that the Board eneavoured to ensure that keepers assigned to Tuskar were men with small families, or no families. The dwellings at the base of the tower were increased in size in the 1850's and 60's, but there was a limit as to what could be done on such a small islet. Eventually, in 1886, permission was given to build four dwellings ashore, at Rosslare. The Tuskar keepers and their families, moved into those new houses in 1890, and they were occupied by Lighthouse families until 1973, when they were bought by the Railway Hotel Company.

Certain recommendations were made in 1879, in a special report on wrecks along the Wexford coast. It was mooted that Tuskar should have a first order optic showing red and white alternately at sixty second intervals. While sanctioning the change in optic, Trinity House observed that, in their opinion, many of the ship-wrecks were due to negligence. True to form, there was a long interim between the sanctioning and the actual commencement of work. Not until the Summer of 1885 did the improvements commence on the Rock. These improvements being largely to the lantern and balcony it was necessary to moor a temporary light-vessel just off the Rock. She remained in place until the 20th November, 1885, when the new light was exhibited. This new light was a tremendous improvement on the old Aragand oil lamps and reflectors. It had a first order biform lens, each lens with a multi-wick oil lamp, all supplied by Edmundsons of Dublin.

These multi-wick burners functioned well for many years, being replaced on the 20th May 1910, by triple 35mm incandescent paraffin vapour burners. And this type of burner remained in use until the light was converted to electricity on 7th July 1938. Tuskar was the third Irish lighthouse to be converted to electricity, the first being Donagahdee in 1934, the second Chaine Tower, Larne, in 1935. The biform lens was replaced by a Chance Brothers' 500mm annular lens, with a 3000 W lamp, giving two white flashes every 7.5 seconds.

Simultaneously, on July 7th, a wireless beacon, as it was then called, was established on Tuskar. During fog conditions only, this transmitted the signal E I K . During World War Two, from September 1939 to May 1944, the beacon was discontinued. In August 1953 the morse character was changed to T R, and Tuskar was linked with five other Radio Beacon stations, transmitting continuously. Another, more sophisticated navigational aid was added to Tuskar Rock on 6th August 1969; a Radar Beacon.

During the war, small, low-lying rocks, or islets, like Tuskar, were particularly vulnerable to the hazard of drifting mines. On 2nd December, 1941, a mine struck the rock and exploded, injuring two Assistant Keepers, W. J. Cahill and P. Scanlan. Both were rushed ashore by the Rosslare lifeboat, but, sadly, Patrick Scanlan died in hospital next day.

October 1969 saw the arrival of the greatest boon since the deep-freeze. The helicopter began to be used for reliefs. It was now possible to lift men off and on the most hazardous rocks, in conditions where boat reliefs would have been impossible. At that time, however, Tuskar was not ready for helicopters. It had no level space large enough for a landing place. In 1972 a concrete heli-pad was built on the Rock and reliefs commenced on 30th January, 1975.

The Barrels and Coninbeg Rocks

The Barrels Rock and the Coningbeg Rock are two names closely linked with Tuskar in the minds of every mariner who has sailed in these waters. Both lie South-West of Tuskar; the Barrells at 10 miles, the Coningbeg at 25 miles. The Coningbeg Rock, or Coney Rock, to seaward of the Southern tip of the great Saltee Island, had been marked by a lightvessel, the *Seagull*, since 1824. She was the third lightvessel to be established off the Irish coast; the first being Palmer's lighthship in the Liffey in 1735; the second, the Kish Bank lightship in 1811.

The Coningbeg Rock is the Rock that nearly had a lighthouse, but had to settle for a lightship instead. George Halpin Snr., in 1818, proposed a tower for Coningbeg; a tower that would, at first, be used just as a fog-signalling station, with bells operated by machine, and could later be converted into a lighthouse. Only after much dithering, and a long silence, did Trinity House finally decide, four years later, to have a lightvessel instead of a lighthouse. But, Inspector Halpin remained convinced that a lighthouse was the best method of lighting the Coningbeg Rock. After an interval of nearly twenty years he again approached his Board on the matter. This time with a plan to erect an adaptation of Alexander Mitchell's screw-pile structure on the Rock. In his proposal he specified that he would not use screw-piles, but would drill holes in the rock for straight piles, grouting them with lead. He received permission to proceed with his plans in July 1842.

Now, it must be explained at this stage of the Coningbeg saga, that there were two Halpins, father and son, both named George, and both employed by the Corporation for Preserving and Improving the Port. George , the elder, had been Inspector of Lighthouses and Works since 1800. George, the younger, had joined the Corporation as Assistant to his father in 1830. As the official registration of births, deaths and marriages did not commence until 1864 in Ireland, it is difficult to ascertain for certain exactly when George Snr. died. There is an entry in the 'Dublin Evening Post' of July 11th, 1854: *"We deeply regret to have to state the death of George Halpin, who for nearly half-a-century, has filled the important office of Engineer to the Ballast Board. The melancholy event took place on Saturday morning. Mr. Halpin was, we believe, in his 80th year."* His burial in Mount Jerome took place on the 12th July, 1854, and he was recorded there as being 75 years old. It is quite impossible at this remove to even attempt to reconcile the ages.

Some months after the death of George Snr., on 1st September, 1854, there is an entry in the Journal of the Ballast Board: *"George Halpin, Assistant Inspector of Lighthouses and Works, having been appointed Inspector of Lighthouses and Works in room of his father Mr George Halpin, at a salary of £665.7.5d per annum. Chargeable to the Lighthouse fund and £184.12.4d chargeable to the Port Fund as hitherto paid to the late Inspector."* As all the records from this time merely refer to George Halpin, or Inspector Halpin, it is impossible to be certain when the younger man began to take over survey and on-site work from his father. It was probably sometime during the prolonged work on the Coningbeg piles. George Halpin Jun. did not enjoy as long a term of office as his father. He was *"pensioned due to ill-health"* in 1862. Neither, ironically, did he enjoy the same reputation as his father, who was hyper-active, as a lighthouse designer and builder, during a truly golden period of lighthouse construction in Ireland. I say, iron- ically, for George Snr. had never trained as an Engineer and was never one in the professional sense; though he had been "brought up as a builder", according to the Municipal Corporation's (Ireland) Report of 1835. While the younger George, his son, had trained and formally qualified as an Engineer.

From the start Halpin, or the Halpins, experienced difficulty on Coningbeg Rock. The particular rock-type was difficult to drill and was exposed only for very short intervals at low-water. And even during those short intervals, open as it was to the huge Atlantic swell, waves still washed over the rock, making drilling an almost impossible operation. And, the failure of Mitchell's screw-pile efforts on the Kish Bank, in November 1842, cannot have helped confidence or morale.

Hampered so much by the weather and the tides, work progressed very slowly. So slowly that, six years later, only seven of the nine requisite holes had been drilled, and hoplessly behind schedule, only one pile had been sunk and grouted with lead by November 1848. As work had to be suspended during the Winter months, this lonely pile stood there taking the brunt of Atlantic gales and huge seas. It withstood all the hammering and buffetting, and by 1850 all nine piles had been sunk and grouted. Hopeful of success at last, but commendably cautious, George Halpin decided to leave these piles for two years, before building the platform, dwelling and lantern on them. They almost passed this test of time and elements, but, in a severe South-Westerly storm during the Winter of 1852-1853, they were twisted beyond repair. The Inspecting Committee on Tour decided, in August 1853, to abandon all idea of placing a permanent structure on the Rock. Just a month later, George Halpin, most probably the younger, proposed the building of two lighthouses, at different levels, on the nearby Saltee Islands. This was shelved by the Board and the whole matter left in abeyance for almost ten years, until the Waterford Harbour Board began agitating for a light on the Coningbeg. The Rock was, once again, inspected during the Spring of 1872. The Inspecting Committee reported *"of the nine pillars erected twenty years ago, the centre one has broken off three feet above the rock, one has disappeared and the remaining seven are much bent."*

By this time, responsibility for the development of the lighthouse service had been transferred to the Commissioners of Irish Lights. The new body, set up by the Act of Victoria in 1867, on the advice of Trinity House, had carried out this latest survey; the Engineer-in-Chief, J.S. Sloane, recommending the building of a granite tower on the Rock. He submitted drawings for the new lighthouse three months later. Again, after years of discussion and prevarication, it was decided, finally, to establish a larger lightvessel on the Coningbeg Rock.

In 1879 complaints were received by the Ballast Office that ships were mistaking the Coningbeg light for the Tuskar light. Trinity House found this difficult to comprehend, as the Coningbeg had two fixed white lights, and the Tuskar a single revolving light, giving two white flashes and one red. At first they dismissed the claims of ships being wrecked and put it down to negligence and bad seamanship. Gradually, however, they accepted the point that, as the Tuskar's red flash was not visible beyond ten miles, there could well have been confusion as to the identity of the lights. It was, reluctantly, decided to establish a lightvessel on the Barrels, and the light was exhibited for the first time in October 1880. The Barrels lightvessel was withdrawn from station during World War Two, being replaced by a lighted whistle-buoy. She was re-established in March 1960, serving for another ten years, and then, replaced again by another whistle-buoy.

Hook Head

It is generally accepted that the Tower of Hook, on Hook Head, in County Wexford, is the oldest established light in the British Isles. It dates from the 5th century, and St. Dubhán, its founder, must be regarded, albeit unofficially, as the patron Saint of the Irish Lighthouse Service. The Saint gave his name, *Rinn Dubhain* to this windswept, flat and treeless promontory, called, before he came, *Hy-Kinsellagh.*

Now, by a strange, though fortuitous, coincidence, the word *Dubhán,* in Irish, means 'hook'; or, more specifically, 'fishing hook'. So the name 'Hook Point' seems singularly appropriate for a place where fishermen had plied their trade from time immemorial, and where the altruistic Welsh monk, Dubhán, established, and personally 'kept', that first, primitive light.

Dubhán, an uncle of St. David of Wales, in search of solitude, chose this place for his tiny cell and oratory, because it was remote; surrounded on three sides by the sea. And he cannot have been long settled here before he became aware of the terrible hazards of this rock bound coast, with its treacherous currents and hidden rock-shoals. There was no shelter here from any wind; from whichever quarter. No respite from the incessant pounding of the sea. Indeed, poor Dubhán must often have wondered, as he went his eremitic round of days and nights, if the seas would not engulf this wild headland he had chosen for his home, and sweep him away.

He survived; but many others, on that inhospitable coast, did not. Ships making for the Port of Waterford in bad weather, were regularly driven onto the rocky headland and wrecked. Dubhán, after a night of storm, would often find the mariners' bodies on the rocks below his cell; some dead, some near-dead. So his tiny settlement became, at the same time, mortuary and hospital.

Dubhán, in an effort to warn mariners of the killer cape on which he lived, had a local blacksmith make him a huge iron basket, or 'chauffer', which he suspended from a mast, near the edge of the cliff. In this chauffer he lit a fire at sunset and personally stoked it through the night. A difficult task this, especially in wet, windy and stormy weather, when it was most needed. Climbing the narrow ladder attached to the mast, and carrying the necessary fuel, must have been very hazardous. The fuel used varied from coal to charcoal, from wood to tar, depending on supply. The one fuel always in supply was the driftwood from wrecked ships, collected by Dubhán from the rock shelves and shingle coves near the beacon.

Others joined Dubhán at his little oratory and gradually a small community was established. On his death-bed he entrusted the care and maintenance of the light to his fellow-monks and they, in faithful succession, continued to 'keep' it until about fifty years before the Anglo-Norman invasion. One tradition tells us that the Tower of Hook was built by Strongbow's wife, Eva; a second tradition, that it was built by Raymond le Gros, who was married to Strongbow's only sister, Basilia. One way or the other, we can be sure it was built as a fortress and watchtower, at this most strategic location, by the newly-arrived Normans, in an effort to consolidate and protect their conquests.

The massive tower was built around 1172, and is, today, after more than 800 years, in such excellent condition that there seems no reason why it should not be functional for another millenium. There is not the slightest evidence of structural senility; no damp-ness, no subsidence. The walls vary in thickness from 9 feet to 13 feet; in the substance of the walls are stone steps leading to the top of the tower. The tower is divided into three storeys, each one of beautiful vaulted construction, with windows in embrasures.

The new tower was vested in the monks of Churchtown, the nearby site of Dubhán's original oratory; they having, sometime prior to the Anglo-Norman invasion, become affiliated to the Priory of Saint Augustine at Ross (now New Ross). They had named their new monastery-tower, Saint Saviour's of Rendenaun. In 1247, John FitzGeoffrey, Justiciar of Ireland, was instructed that, for as long as the lands of Walter, late Earl of Pembroke, were under his control, he should *"cause the custodian and Chaplains of St Saviour of Rendenaun, who there built a tower as a beacon for ships, to have, out of the issue of these lands, a maintenance, in money and otherwise, with all arrears due to them."* In 1307 the custody of the tower was transferred to the Sovereign and the Bailiffs of New Ross, and, sometime between that and the Dissolution of the Monasteries in the 16th century, the monks left the 'keeping' of the light to others.

In the early 17th century there is evidence that the tower was still being used as a lighthouse, but also doubling as a centre for the coining of counterfeit money. It was certainly an ideal location for this, situated as it was on the very end of a bare and treeless promontory, commanding an unobstructed view of a vast hinterland, across which any raiding party would have to travel. A look-out had ample time to alert the counterfeiters, who would then hide away their coining paraphernalia in the sea or on the foreshore. This 'industry' seemed to thrive up to the outbreak of the 1641 Rebellion.

After the Rebellion, the beacon at Hook was abandoned for over a quarter of a century. Then, in 1657, the Down Survey noted "this tower, which formerly hath been a lighthouse to conduct shipps into ye Harbour". In the same year the Commissioners of Public Revenue were petitioned by various factions, representing merchants, ship-owners and mariners, to restore the beacon on Hook Head. The petition read *"There is a Towre called ye Towre of Hook, standing upon ye mouth of ye River of Waterford, on a cape of land running into the sea, which had formerly been maintained for a lighthouse, and used to be white limed for a land marke by day, and to have a great fire kept on the topp thereof for a marke by night. For want of ye maintainance of which, several shipp wracks have lately been on these coasts to the discouragement of Merchants, Seamen and Others."*

This petition was unsuccessful. No action was taken in restoring the tower as a lighthouse until 1665, when Sir Robert Reading was granted a franchise by King Charles II to erect and maintain six lighthouses round the Irish coast. Sometime between then and 1667 the beacon on Hook Head was re-established. Though we cannot be certain, it is very likely that Reading was responsible for the construction of a special 'lantern' to house the beacon fire on top of the tower. This had a very special brick dome to withstand the tremendous heat of the fire, with a flue through the dome to help conduct the smoke clear of the flame; so, giving the mariner a much brighter light. In a Report on the state of Irish Lighthouses, dated 1704, there is a reference to an estimate for *"the repair and alteration of the lanthorn at Hook Lighthouse, lyme for pointing and ruffcasting the outside of the tower, and other mason's work about the lanthorn and battlements, also 140 foott of glass for the lanthorn, iron for the great bricks for the breast of the lanthorn."* In that same year, 1704, Queen Anne passed all responsibility for Irish lighthouses to the Revenue Commissioners.

In the years of Sir Robert Reading's management the tower had been enlarged, though there is no certainty as to who was responsible for that work. The height was increased by approximately 6 meters, and the diameter by 3.5 meters. Whether deliberate, or indeliberate, the tower is not truly circular. A new wall was built outside the old wall and a stone stairway built between the two.

Now, at the time of the Revenue Commissioners taking over the lighthouses, Hook Head presented a major problem for them. It was held, on a twenty-one year lease by the Loftus family, of nearby Loftus Hall, and they engaged the Commisioners in a lengthy battle in relation to the renewal of the lease. The dispute lasted two years, during which time the light, fortunately, was not extinguished. However, having survived so many crises, the tower was allowed to fall into a state of disrepair toward the end of the 18th century. Then, in 1791, the ex-Trinity House Engineer, Thomas Rogers, was given the contract, by the Revenue Board, to maintain and staff Hook lighthouse among others; Howth, Kilwarlin (South Rock), Copeland Island, Aranmore, Loop Head, Old Head of Kinsale, Charles Fort (Kinsale) and Duncannon Fort.

Now, Rogers, who had invented catadioptric lights, while still with Trinity House, refurbished the old tower and installed, what for that time was 'state-of-the-art' lighting equipment; a new 3.65 meter diameter lantern, and 12 Argand oil lamps with reflectors. His reign was short lived, however, as all Irish lighthouses were transferred, by Act of Parliament in 1810, to the Board of the Corporation for Preserving and Improving the Port of Dublin (the Ballast Office). Two years later the apparatus was improved and then, in 1864, a new lantern and fixed dioptric lens replaced the old lantern and catoptric apparatus. At the time of fitting this, cinders from Sir Richard Reading's old coal burning grate were found on top of the tower, underneath Rogers' 1791 lantern.

In 1871, six years after it was first used at Baily, coal-gas replaced oil at the Hook, and a small gas-works was built beside the lighthouse to produce the gas. This functioned very satisfactorily until it was replaced by vapourised paraffin in 1911 and, subsequently, by electricity in 1972.

The first fog-signal, a bell, was introduced in 1838. This bell was originally rung by hand; usually by the keeper on duty, but sometimes by a bell-ringer, employed on a casual basis during periods of fog and poor visibility. And, on this coastline, where fogs could sometimes last for five or six days on end, ringing the bell by hand was an exhausting task. So, about 1850, a very basic, but nevertheless effective, piece of machinery was installed, to activate the bell at the required intervals. Then, in 1872, the bell was replaced by a gun, which gave way to an explosive charge in 1905. The explosive charge was effective but, in the early 1970's became quite a security hazard. Keeping the requisite stock of explosives at a lighthouse made it an instant target for certain subversive elements anxious to acquire any component usable in their bomb-making. It was not unusual, at that time, for light-houses to be raided, keepers held at gun point, and explosives stolen. So, in the interests of personal safety, the explosive charge was discontinued and replaced by a Supertyfon Emitter, operated by compressed air. Racon was established in 1974.

In 1977 families were withdrawn from the dwellings at Hook Head and the lighthouse then became 'relieving', like the off-shore stations. In my visits to various lighthouses, and talks with keepers, I have met many who, prior to 1977, lived with their familes at the Hook. Most had children born and grow up there during their time attached to the station, and all spoke affect-ionately of it as a great place in which to live and rear a family. And I often think of those children I played with at Hook Head, when I visited it as a boy of seven, over fifty years ago. I cannot remember their names at this remove, for I only met them once. But I do remember that they were happy and friendly and kindly. To me, then, they were children from another world; an enchanted world of white houses on a green strip of headland, above dark rocks and an ever-moving, ever-sounding, blue-grey sea; with, always, the comforting bulk of the great tower guarding them. And I envied them in their kingdom by the sea, and often wondered what became of them. Perhaps some of them became lighthouse keepers, for, it is a vocation passed on, in many families, from one generation to another, in dynastic fashion.

Poolbeg. Callwell.

Part Two

The South Coast:
Dunmore East to Fastnet Rock

Dunmore East - Duncannon - Ballinacourty - Mine Head - Youghal - Ballycotton - Roche's Point - Spitbank - Charles Fort - Old Head of Kinsale - Galley Head - Fastnet Rock.

"These poor fellows who must be bored to death sitting all day long with nothing to do but polish the lamp, and trim the wick, and rake about on their scrap of garden. For, how would you like to be shut up for a whole month at a time, and possibly more in stormy weather, upon a rock the size of a tennis lawn, she would ask. And to have no letters, or newspapers, and to see nobody; if you were married not to see your wife, not to know how your children were - if they were, if they had fallen down and broken their legs and arms; to see the same dreary waves breaking week after week, and then a dreadful storm coming, and the windows covered with spray, and birds dashing against the lamp, and the whole place rocking, and not to be able to put your nose out of doors for fear of being swept into the sea."

Virginia Woolf: "To The Lighthouse".

Youghal Lighthouse on site of old convent.

Dunmore East and Duncannon North

These are two harbour lights serving shipping leaving and entering Waterford Harbour. The Dunmore East light is situated on the pier-head directly across the estuary from the tower of Hook, on the Waterford shore. The Duncannon North light is three miles further up the estuary, on the opposite, Wexford shore. The Dunmore light was first exhbited in the fall of 1825; the Duncannon light 13 years later, in 1838.

Dunmore East today is a picturesque, up-market seaside town and a very busy fishing port; a place where several very different 'cultures' live amicably together. The fishermen and their families who have been here from time immemorial; the wealthy Waterford merchants and professional people who began to settle here from the mid-19th century; and the *nouveau riche* who have infiltrated the town in the past thirty years.

In 1814, when Dunmore East was a tiny fishing hamlet, it was chosen by the British Post Office to be the Irish terminal for a new Mail Packet route from Milford Haven. The Post Office retained the services of an eminent Scottish Engineer, Alexander Nimmo, to design and build a harbour and lighthouse to accommodate the new Mail Packet Service. In building the new harbour Nimmo made excellent use of the local red sandstone, and his lighthouse took the form of a fluted Doric column, with the lantern on top of the capital. This, together with the cast-iron lattice balcony makes Dunmore East special among Irish lighthouses. The passenger and mail service operated between Milford and Dunmore for over ten years, before Waterford Port became the Irish terminal; this obviated the 10 mile road journey from Dunmore East.

Oil lamps and reflectors were used until 1922; the light was then converted to acetylene. In that year also an attendant replaced the lightkeeper and the station became 'unwatched'. In January 1964 the power was converted yet again; this time to electric.

Duncannon North is a harbour light forming with Duncannon Fort leading lights to guide ships over the bar of Duncannon. The tower at Duncannon was originally built at Roche's Point, at the entrance to Cork Harbour, in 1817. After nearly twenty years service there, it was deemed to be too small to accommodate a lantern big enough to maintain a good light. It was dismantled in 1838 and re-built at Duncannon. Originally oil-burning, it was changed to acetylene in 1937, and finally converted to electric in May 1971.

Tramore Beacons

There is no lighthouse at the entrance to Tramore Bay, but the headlands on each side are marked by quite unique beacons, or seamarks, sometimes referred to as caution towers. Two towers mark the headland to the East, Brownstown Head; and three towers mark the headland to the West, Great Newtown Head. With a different number of towers on each headland, the mariner would not confuse one with the other; and would, obviously, not be likely to confuse either with the single tower on Hook Head, six miles due East, at the entrance to Waterford Harbour. The beacons were designed by George Halpin Snr., and completed in 1824. Halpin had originally intended to have the twelve-feet-high figure of a sailor, arm extended to warn ships, atop a tower on each headland, but, by some extraordinary carelessness, one of the figures was lost, and so Brownstown remains, to this day, without a 'Metalman'. Over the years, however, Tramore's 'Metalman' has become a local institution and a great tourist attraction. Tradition, and superstition, would have us believe that any eligible maiden who hops, on one foot, three times round the base of the 'Metalman's' tower, will find a good husband within the year. As the hopping distance is about eighty yards and the ground, worn from so many feet, very uneven, not many complete the course.

Agitation for some seamarks, beacons or lights in Tramore Bay, began as early as 1811. Mr. R. Pope, the Waterford Agent of the London Assurance Company, wrote to the Corporation for Preserving and Improving the Port of Dublin, to complain about "two recent shipwrecks in the Bay." The sloop, *Commerce*, out of Plymouth, with a cargo of bacon, bound for Waterford, was lost in the Bay. And the schooner, *Grinder*, out of London, bound for Lisbon, with a cargo of wool, had blown off course and gone aground on the sands. "Her cargo has been saved, but I am very apprehensive about the future of the vessel herself." Mr. Pope blamed a Government signal tower on Brownstown Head for these wrecks. "This unlighted tower, can, quite easily in bad weather, be mistaken for the tower at Hook Head, thus leading unsuspecting mariners into Tramore Bay, instead of Waterford Harbour. I request that this evil tower be removed forthwith. At time of writing the tower has not been used for over a twelvemonth."

However, despite much letter writing at top level, and much talking and lobbying, nothing was done. Until another wreck occurred in 1816, when a troop-ship, returning from the Peninsular War, was wrecked in the Bay with a loss of 360 lives. This caused a public outcry, and relatively quick action, for the Corporation that is. The Tramore beacons only took another eight years to build.

Throughout the years Tramore Beacons have changed colour. Up to 1930, both Brownstown towers and Newtown towers were whitewashed. From 1930 to 1957 Brownstown towers were tarred and Newtown towers whitewashed. Then, in 1957, the brickwork badly needed pointing and after this work had been completed it was decided neither to paint nor tar them. The sailor is painted, as the need arises every three or four years.

Ballinacourty Point

In the early part of the 19th century Dungarvan, on the Waterford coast, was a flourishing port, with a growing traffic to and from several English and European ports. And the entrance to the harbour was totally unlit. Indeed, there was no light on all this coast from Hook Head to Roche's Point, in 1845, when the merchants and shipowners, requested a harbour light to help guide ships into Dungarvan Bay and up to safe anchorage. There were sea-marks on both Brownstown and Newtown Heads, but these were of little or no help to ships making for Dungarvan. This long stretch of unlit coast was causing great concern to the Cork Harbour Commissioners about this time, and at their behest, lights were established on Mine Head, a few miles South of Helvick Head, and on Ballycotton Island on the same day, 1st June, 1851. Originally it was planned to establish the new harbour light at Youghal on that same day, but George Halpin decided to wait until February 1st of the following year to exhibit that.

The Ballast Board looked favourably on the request for a harbour light in Dungarvan and acted relatively quickly. Ballinacourty Point, on the Northern shore of Dungarvan Bay was selected as being the most suitable location for a lighthouse. A tower, designed by George Halpin was built there, using local limestone rock, and the light was exhibited for the first time on 1st July, 1858. Viewed from the sea, or from Helvick Head across the Bay, Ballinacourty tower stands out dramatically on its low lying headland, with the bulk of the Comeragh Mountains rising behind it.

Mine Head

A few miles South of Helvick Head, the Southern extremity of Dungarvan Bay, stands the major sea light on Mine Head. The George Halpin designed tower is strategically located on the high, sheer, inaccessible cliffs between Dungarvan and Ardmore. It has the highest elevation of any lighthouse in Ireland, 285 feet; 3 feet more than Blackrock, Mayo. Built of old red sandstone, it was first exhibited, together with Ballycotton light, on 1st June, 1851.

After years of pressure from shipowners and merchants in the Youghal and Cork areas, the Ballast Board had, in 1847, begun to build a tower on Capel Island, off Youghal. This decision was taken despite George Halpin's opinion that the second major sea-light on this coast, in addition to Ballycotton, should be on Mine Head. Work had already commenced on the Capel Island light when the pressure group changed its mind and demanded that the light be on Mine Head. The Admiralty and Trinity House were consulted and it was decided to suspend work on Capel Island and build a tower on Mine Head. It was generally agreed, at the time, that going with the U-turn was the right decision, and the light on Mine Head continues to serve shipping on this difficult stretch of coast with great efficiency.

Youghal And Capel Island

Driving through the town of Youghal towards Cork, where the road runs uphill just above the sea, there is a moment when you think the lighthouse ahead is actually standing in the middle of the road. This momentary optical illusion is quickly dispelled as you mount the hill and get a different perspective. The neat, gleaming white tower is, you realise, built, not in the middle of the street, but on the side of the street, overlooking the entrance to the bay. From the lighthouse, you can see, half-a-mile offshore, Capel Island, and the squat tower at its Western end; the sea-mark that nearly became a lighthouse in the mid-19th century.

In the early part of that century much attention was directed to the South coast between the entrance to the port of Waterford and the entrance to the port of Cork. There was neither sea-light nor seamark between Hook Head and the Old Head of Kinsale; the Roche's Point light being regarded merely as a harbour light. And the seventy-odd miles of coastline between the two sea lights was strewn with navigational hazards; a real threat to the growing sea-traffic to ports like Youghal and Dungarvan, and to Cork itself.

Youghal, in particular, in the 1820's was becoming a really important and busy port. For that period in history there was an unprecedented movement of ships in and out of Youghal. Statistics for the year 1831 show, very graphically, how both imports and exports had grown. In that year nine ships brought 2,000 tons of timber from North America and 440 colliers brought 28,000 tons of coal and 26,000 tons of anthracite, or culm, as it was then called, into the port of Youghal. And there was a total, that same year, of 3,000 tons of goods exported through the port; a combination of oats, wheat, barley, flour, calves, pigs, sheep, bacon and butter. There was also a growing sea-going fishing fleet of 250 vessels.

Now, that kind of traffic on an unlit coast was a sure recipe for disaster. Over a five year period 30 vessels had gone aground on this stretch of coastline. Then, in 1828, a merchant of Youghal, Thomas Harvey, began to agitate for the erection of a lighthouse, and was backed by his fellow-merchants in Cork, together with shipowners and master mariners. The Corporation for Improving the Port of Dublin was bombarded with letters, many of them with over 100 signatures, all demanding that urgent attention be paid to the lighting of this hazardous coast. A coast so dangerous that, 650 years before, in 1190, Maurice Fitzgerald had built a 'Light Tower', on the site where the present tower stands. He had endowed the Convent of St Anne for the purpose of maintaining this light, and for over 350 years the nuns had been the conscientious keepers of the flame here; maintaining lighted torches on the tower at night, to guide ships in and out of harbour. In 1542 the community of nuns was dissolved and the light discontinued. Darkness reigned until the present light was established in 1852, just over 300 years later.

Now, in 1828, the Corporation Board and its Engineer, George Halpin Snr., were surprised that the requests were for the establishing of a light, not on the site of the old nunnery light, but on Capel Island at the Western extremity of Youghal Bay. They duly informed Thomas Harvey that they did not consider Capel Island a suitable location for a lighthouse; it being "not in the best situation for passing vessels, and not much better for local shipping unless there was a second light placed at the entrance to Youghal Harbour." Unwittingly they had started a wrangle as to where the light should be placed, which was to continue for over twenty years; one of the longest arguments about location in the whole history of Irish lighthouses.

George Halpin, in his wisdom, was totally convinced that the major sea-lights, on this coast, should be built at Mine Head and at Ballycotton, with a harbour light at Youghal, on the exact site of the old nunnery tower. He maintained that it was not without significance that only the local Youghal and Cork interests were clamouring for a light on Capel Island; the main channel trade not being involved. However, after years of pressure the Dublin Ballast Board deemed it expedient to sanction the building of a lighthouse on the island and Halpin was instructed to prepare plans. Work commenced on the site in April 1847, progressing quickly, and by January of the following year the new tower had reached a height of six feet above the cut-stone base.

However, just before work had commenced on the new lighthouse, an incident occurred which would eventually have serious ramifications. On 16th January, 1847, the steam ship *Sirius*, in a dense fog, ran aground on the Smith's Rock, West of Ballycotton. Her Captain managed to have her refloated on a high-tide and attempted to run her into Ballycotton Harbour, but near the coast she became a total wreck. The *Sirius* had enjoyed a distinguished working life. She was the first ship to make the Atlantic crossing from Passage West to New York, completely under steam, in April 1838, beating Brunel's *Great Western* by half-a-day. Captain Denham R.N. was appointed by the Board of Trade, under a Steam Navigation Act, to investigate the loss of the *Sirius*. In his subsequent report he recommended to the Ballast Board that two lighthouses should be erected, on a transit to clear Smith's Rock; one on Ballycotton Island, the other on either Helvick or Ballymacart Head, now Mine Head. Meantime, work was progressing on the Capel Island light and the concerned parties in Cork and Youghal, who had long been agitating for the light were informed, by letter, of this.

Then, on 24th February, 1848, the Dublin Ballast Board received a memo from the Admiralty — "Herewith enclosed copy of a letter received from the Cork Harbour Commissioners, merchants, traders and ship owners of Cork City and County." This letter was a complete reversal of all they had sought in the past. They now wanted lights on Mine Head and Ballycotton, and not on Capel Island. The letter stated that "if there was a loss sustained in removing stones from the incomplete tower on Capel Island to Mine Head it should not be considered a question of such magnitude as the protection of shipping, life, and property." The Ballast Board protested strongly to the Admiralty about the Cork and Youghal Merchants' U-turn, pointing out that what they were now, belatedly demanding, had been Inspector Halpin's first preference. This was to no avail and two weeks later the Admiralty suggested that Trinity House should acquiesce to the suspension of work on Capel Island, and sanction the building of lighthouses at Mine Head and Ballycotton, with a smaller light inside the bar at the entrance to Youghal Harbour.

So, the present lighthouse came to be built on the site of the old Convent "Light Tower' and the half-finished Capel Island tower was finished off as a beacon, or sea-mark; the most expensive on the coast at a cost of £2,137.14.2d. It still serves as a navigational beacon and is rented by a group of ornithologists who monitor the migrations of birds in that area.

Work on the new tower in Youghal commenced in the Summer of 1848 and the masonry part of it was completed by July 1849. During the following Winter the lantern was added, but there was a hold-up on the copper-work of the dome, as the Corporation's coppersmiths were deployed at Ballycotton which, together with Mine Head, was being built at the same time. Originally it was planned to put all three lightouses into operation on the same day, but Inspector Halpin did not agree with this, insisting that Youghal be lit after the other two. Ballycotton and Mine Head were exhibited on 1st June, 1851; Youghal was exhibited on 1st, February 1852.

The tower is built of granite, has three floors and is 43 feet high to the top of the dome ventilator. It stands 78 feet above high water. That first light was a fixed dioptric showing white, and was visible for ten miles. After several changes over the years it was converted to electric in 1964, now showing white and red and with increased power.

From 1860, three unsuccessful attempts were made, by various Railway Companies to acquire some of the lighthouse ground, in order to extend lines into the centre of Youghal town, or through the town. On one occasion the Ballast Board's Civil Engineer reported that there would be serious damage to the lighthouse itself if the railway line was allowed to pass through the garden. The garden he described as being small but of great fertility. This, however, is very different to what the Attendant J. Higginbotham, told Michael Costeloe of Irish Lights, when he visited the lighthouse in 1963. Higginbotham said that anything he'd ever planted in the same garden was burnt out of the ground by the salt from the sea-spray, and cabbage heads were twisted off their stalks, by the wind, like cork-screws.

In 1906, the schooner *Annett* was wrecked near Youghal and the jury, following the inquest on the ill-fated ship, recommended a newer and much brighter light. The Commissioners informed the Board of Trade that they considered the light to be "quite sufficient." There had been a Tidal Light exhibited since December, 1870; this from a window in the tower, two hours before high water and one hour after. A local man, E. Youdall, was paid a wage of ten shillings a week to tend this light. In 1916, the Inspector, Captain Dean, reported that "Signalman Youdall has become too feeble to attend regularly to his work, and the job should be handed over to the Principal Keeper and his family, with an increase in salary of £10 per annum."

Ballycotton

In the early to mid-19th century, when long stretches of the Irish coast were being lit for the first time, it was not always an easy task for the Ballast Board, Trinity House and the Board of Trade to concur as to the best specific location for a particular light. The requests for these new lights invariably came from Harbour Authorities, merchants, shipowners and the masters of ships using unlit ports along the coast. Very often vested interests, and politics, were involved with those who pressed and agitated for lights to be erected at certain locations, and the three deciding bodies had the impossible task of trying to accommodate everybody's request and still be seen to do the right thing.

The tragedy of the *Sirius* caused a re-think among the many factions who had pressed for the erection of a lighthouse on Capel Island; there was a split. The Cork Steamship Company, together with some merchants and shipowners, wrote, urging the Board to complete the building of the Capel Island lighthouse. Others, headed by the Cork Harbour Board, did a U-turn, and requested the Board to suspend work on Capel Island, and build a lighthouse on Ballycotton Island instead. The Ballast Board, in a quandary at such ambivalence, appealed to the Admiralty for some directive. That body, in its wisdom, advised them that they must "determine a course which seems best calculated for the benefit of the public." They were also of the opinion that, "pending the final decision, work should be suspended on the Capel Island tower." As that building had only reached a height of 6 feet, it was proposed that perhaps it could be removed and re-erected on Ballycotton Island. This was quickly dismissed as being uneconomic and a new tower sanctioned for Ballycotton. It was considered best to establish two lights on a transit to clear the notorious Smith's Rock; one at Ballycotton and the other either on Helvick Head or Mine Head.

The Ballycotton tower was built on Ballycotton Island, which stands at the entrance to the Harbour, close inshore. George Halpin designed the tower and the keepers' dwellings and the contract for the construction was awarded to the Cork firm of W. & P. Brash, in November, 1848. The tower and dwellings were built with old red sandstone quarried on the island. An interesting fact was revealed during the 'inquisition' to establish an equitable price for the island. The owners included the Archbishop of Dublin and the Bishop of Cork, who each received one shilling from the sale to the Ballast Board of Dublin.

At first, perhaps because they were inexperienced in the construction of lighthouses, Messrs. Brash's progress was extremely slow. However, a judicious letter from the Board soon speeded up the work and the tower was ready to take the cut-stone lantern blocking in July, 1849. By March, 1850, most of the construction work was completed and the dome of the tower was being sheeted with copper. The catadioptric apparatus was the first of its kind on the Irish coast at that time; a fixed inner optic and a rotating outer. The outer had eight faces, each with an annular lens, and a set of upper and lower vertical condensing prisms. The resultant effect was an exceptionally powerful beam from each of the eight faces. The light source was a multiple wick oil lamp. The light character was flashing white every ten seconds and was visible at a distance of 18 miles in clear weather. The light was first exhibited, together with the Mine Head light, on 1st June, 1851.

At the time the light was established the tower was a natural stone colour and the compound walls were white washed. In 1892, to prevent any confusion with the unlit beacon on Capel Island, a broad, black band was painted round the middle of the tower, and in 1902, the whole of the tower was painted black.

Fogs were so frequent on this coast that in June, 1856, the Reverend J. Hopkins, incumbent of Ballycotton, fearing some tragedy, wrote to the Board to request a fog bell. The Inspecting Committee, on tour at that time, visited Ballycotton, and recommended the erection of a belfry. Before the end of that year a fog bell was established. This functioned efficiently for half-a-century, until 1908, when an inspection showed the belfry to be unsafe. It was recommended that the bell should be re-positioned in the lighthouse tower, or, alternatively, a reed horn signal should be established. A reed-horn signal, with a character of six blasts every two minutes, replaced the bell on 30th December, 1909. This horn never performed satisfactorily, so, in 1924, it was replaced by an "A" type diaphone.

Fog-bell Tower, Ballycotton

In 1896, it was decided to make Ballycotton, along with several other stations, relieving. Bringing lightkeepers' families ashore from the remote, desolate rock stations, was motivated by the damage caused by a violent storm on the West Coast, on 29th December, 1894. All the West Coast stations took a buffetting, particularly Eagle Island, off the Mayo coast, where the dwellings were damaged beyond repair.

The modernisation of Ballycotton began in 1974, with the establishing of a Radio and Calibration Beacon. In 1975, the light was converted to electric; the original 1851 optic was replaced by an AGA sealed-beam lamp array. Though the island is very near the mainland, in rough weather boat reliefs were difficult, sometimes impossible, so as part of the modernisation, a helicopter pad was constructed. New quarters were built for the keepers and visiting tradesmen, with a watch-tower on the roof. Ballycotton became fully automatic in 1992. An Attendant, who lives ashore, visits twice a month.

Power Head

Power Head, (also known as Poer Head), East of Roche's Point, at the time of its closure in 1970, was the only manned station in the Irish Lighthouse Service, without a light. Established in 1879, as a fog-signal station, it remained just that during the ninety-one years of its existence. Originally built to make safer the approaches to Cork Harbour, it was never deemed necessary to establish a light there; that part of the coast being adequately served by the lights on Roche's Point, Daunt Lightship, and Old Head of Kinsale. But, on a stretch of coast cursed with the most terrible fogs, its powerful fog-trumpet, an irritation to those living in that hinterland, was music to many a mariner, trying to edge his way slowly into Cork harbour, through dense fog.

During its lifetime Power Head was equipped with many different types of fog-signal machinery. Originally it was a Wigham steam siren, but this was replaced in 1892 by Priestman paraffin engines belt-driving Hawthorn Davey air compressors. Around 1909 these Priestman engines were replaced by Petter oil engines. These were changed in 1933, when Petter Diesels, direct coupled to Raevell Air Compressors, were installed. At the end it was a combination of Ruston engine and Atlas Copco compressor.

Roche's Point

Early in the nineteenth century representations were made to the Board to erect a lighthouse at the entrance to Cork Harbour. Ships were being exposed to undue hazard in entering or leaving the estuary because of the absence of any kind of light at its mouth. As there was an old watch tower, Roche's Tower on Roche's Point, in a good state of repair, it was suggested that this be used to house the lantern for a revolving light. This light, the letter of request stated, need not be of enormous magnitude, as long as it was clearly distinguishable from the light on the Old Head of Kinsale. The request was quickly acceded to by Trinity House and a light sanctioned, to be placed atop the old tower. George Halpin Snr. surveyed the site and found the tower to be strong enough to take a lantern. As it then stood, the tower was 35 feet high and its base 46 feet above high water. There was one snag. The owner of the tower, Edward Roche Esq., of Trabolgan, was resident in Italy. It would appear, from contemporary accounts that he was a soldier of fortune and had been detained in Italy as a prisoner of war. The tower, built by either Roche or his father, was described by a local historian of that time as "a banqueting and pleasure house, built by the Roche family to afford them a good view of Cork Harbour and the movements of shipping." During the latter part of the eighteenth century it had been rented, at one hundred guineas per annum, to the Government as a watch-tower. As none of Edward Roche's family had any authority to negotiate a sale in his absence, the process of acquiring the tower was long drawn out. Not until 1815, two years after the project had been sanctioned, was work commenced on the Point. By that time it had been decided to build a new lighthouse proper on the site and a granite tower was designed by George Halpin. The tower was small, with an internal diameter of only 6 feet and an overall height of 36 feet. However, with the elevation of the headland, the lantern was 92 feet above high water. The light was first exhibited on 4th June, 1817. As the years passed and shipping in and out of Cork grew, the tower was considered too small for a major harbour of refuge. It was replaced, in 1835, by the present larger tower, which stands 49 feet high and has an internal diameter of 12 feet. The original tower was carefully taken down, and complete with lantern and all the lighting apparatus, shipped to Duncannon in Co. Wexford, in two small vessels. There it was rebuilt and from 1838 became Duncannon North Light.

Spitbank (Cork Harbour)

The North-East projecting point of Spit Bank, off Cobh, is where the channel turns through just over ninety degrees. The Ballast Board had maintained an unlighted buoy here prior to 1848, when they were requested by the Cork Harbour Commissioners to replace it with a floating light. The Board agreed, after the usual correspondence and inspection, to erect one of Alexander Mitchell's screw-pile structures on the Bank; similar to that which had failed at Kish Bank some nine years previously. However, the Mitchell Pile structure was built successfully in Belfast Lough (1848) and Dundalk (1855).

The light was first exhibited in 1853; a dioptric sixth order, fixed red light, thirty-two feet above high water. In 1895 a fog bell was added to the station. A Principal and an Assistant Keeper were attached to the station and, when off-duty, they lived in rented accommodation in Cobh. A local, Temporary Keeper, was engaged on Sundays and when one of the regulars was sick or on leave. There were two reliefs a day; one at 0900 hours, the other before sunset, so that two men were on duty during the night and one during the day.

On 22nd March, 1942, a new, unwatched occulting red light was established, the fog-signal was discontinued and the Keepers withdrawn. An Attendant, based in Cobh, was appointed. In 1954 the Cork Harbour Commissioners requested the reinstatement of the fog signal, and the bell was re-established , experimentally, on 3rd January, 1956, and permanently the following year. On 17th December, 1978, the mv *Levensau*, dragged her anchor and drifted into the lighthouse, seriously damaging the structure. It was repaired and back in commission within weeks. In 1983, the Commissioner of Irish Lights decided to inform the Cork Harbour Commissioners of their intention to discontinue the Spit Bank Light. After protracted discussion and correspondence, the Pile Lighthouse was handed over to the Harbour Commissioners on 1st Novemenbr, 1985, after the fog signal had been discontinued.

Kinsale: Old Head and Charles Fort

The present lighthouse on the Old Head of Kinsale stands just above the sea, at the end of the promontory. Directly behind it stand the ruins of two older lighthouses, one dating back to the

17th century, the other to the 18th century. And the headland is dotted with the remains of ancient castle, fosse and earthworks; for this place, going back to pre-Christian times was a stomping ground for countless invaders and adventurers. Indeed there are many references to an early pre-Christian beacon lit here. The Spaniards called the Old Head, Capo de Vel, the Cape of Light.

There is a tradition which tells us that the first beacon lit on this Cape of Light was not lit for any altruistic motive, but to lure ships onto the rocks to be pillaged by wreckers. The wreckers in this case being early Celtic settlers, who occupied this land from as early as 100 B.C.

The landlocked harbour of Kinsale provided a magnificent safe haven for mariners. Some used it as a port in transit, others as a base from which to carry on a lucrative trade with various English and Continental ports. Fishing also flourished and to service all this growing sea-traffic, shipbuilding found a vital place. This industry was greatly facilitated by the availability of local timber, grown on Compass Hill and all up-river as far as Shippool. So, from earliest times there was a need for some kind of beacon on the Old Head. There had been a light exhibited from a window in Charles Fort since the 16th century.

In the 17th century, 60 to 80 fishing boats worked out of Kinsale. But even then, there was conflict over fishing rights. French fishing boats were accused of fishing too far inshore. This, coupled with a lack of any kind of expertise or organisation among the local fishermen, caused the industry to decline steeply during the 18th century. Another major determining factor in this decline was the effect of the Penal Laws on fishermen. By the middle of the 18th century there was no large boat working out of Kinsale.

In the 19th century winds of change began to blow and prosperity returned. The fishing fleet grew. In 1829, Kinsale had 5 decked fishing boats, 160 half-decked boats, 45 open sail boats and over 600 row boats. These were crewed by over 4,000 local men and boys. And back-up services ashore provided an extraordinary number of jobs for — 120 coopers, 13 sail-makers, 500 net-makers and 1,282 men, women and children cutting, curing and packing. The boom in the fish industry brought buyers from all over the British Isles, who transported the fish to English and Continental markets by steam powered vessels. So, with all the inward and outward bound sea-traffic the Old Head needed to be well-lighted at all times.

The first lighthouse proper, apart from the open fires lit on the headland by the early Celtic settlers, was a cottage-type lighthouse. This was a simple cottage in which the keeper lived with his family, and which had an open coal-fire in a chauffer on its roof. It was one of six erected round the coast by Sir Robert Reading, who, in 1665, was given the franchise, to build and manage these lights, by King Charles II. It functioned, with relative effectiveness, for the next 15 years. Around 1680-81 it ceased to operate as a lighthouse and for the next twenty years was allowed to fall into a state of disrepair.

On 18th November, 1703, there was a petition sent to the House of Commons, from the "sovereign burgesses and commonalty of Kinsale", requesting the reinstatement of the light, on the basis that it had been "unreasonably discontinued for upward of twenty years". The old cottage and its open beacon were renovated and back in service sometime around 1720. The light continued to be lit, albeit not too regularly, and not too efficiently, for the next 50 to 60 years. But, as this was a time when the Penal Laws had imposed such constraints, there was a real economic depression in the port; sea-traffic had all but disappeared and the fishing industry had slumped. So, the efficient lighting of the Old Head was not of paramount importance.

From the early 19th century there were definite signs of a revival of Kinsale as a fishing port. The economy began to boom again. In 1804, the Revenue Commissioners, who had responsibility for all lighthouses on the Irish coast, except those in the Port of Dublin, instructed their contractor for lighting, Thomas Rogers, to construct a temporary six-foot diameter lantern, with 12 oil lamps and reflectors, to replace the old fire-burning beacon on the roof-top. This was done and the temporary light functioned for the next 8 years. During that time the cottage was used for several extra-mural activities, such as prostitution, smuggling and the making of counterfeit money. For, apart from the fishing industry, there was much naval and commercial activity in the port. Local produce, like corn and livestock, was shipped out of Kinsale to Newfoundland, The West Indies and The Mediterranean. There was a Naval Dockyard situated where the Trident Hotel now stands. So, the constant flux of foreign sailors and fishermen made this a climate ideal for the practice of almost any illegal activity.

When the Ballast Board took over responsibility for the fourteen coastal lighthouses from the Revenue Commissioners, they had their Inspector, George Halpin Snr., report on the state of the lighthouse at Old Head. He found it to be in a deplorable condition, badly maintained and badly managed, and recommended, bearing in mind the importance of Kinsale as a port, that it should be replaced immediately by a new, permanent tower and up-to-date lighting apparatus. His proposal was sanctioned quickly and a new lighthouse, similar to the one just then under construction at Baily, Howth, was sanctioned. It was designed by George Halpin and constructed by the Board's own workmen. The cost was just short of £10,000. A fixed white light was first exhibited on 16th May, 1814 at a height of 294 feet above high water. Twenty-seven Argand oil-lamps were used , each with its own parabolic reflector; in clear weather, the light was visible at a distance of 23 miles. The tower and keepers' dwelling were both white washed, making a clear landmark during daylight hours.

Incredibly, like several other towers built around that time, the Old Head Tower was, after 29 years, deemed to be located at too high an altitude. In July, 1843, the Elder Brethern of Trinity House visited the headland and, seven months later, wrote a very scathing report about its position. It was much too high and very often obscured by fog and low cloud very similar to Cape Clear, Baily and Wicklow Head. Inspector Halpin, who had accompanied the Inspection Committee, agreed with their findings and, at a cost of over £10,000, a new lighthouse was approved in February, 1846. George Halpin designed the new station and it was built on the point of the promontory. The tower was plastered on the outside and painted white, with two red bands, and the light first established in 1853. The old 1814 light was discontinued at that time and its tower reduced greatly in height to avoid confusion for mariners. The stones removed from this tower were subsequently used to build the Horse Rock Beacon in nearby Courtmacsherry Bay.

In 1893 a fog signal was established at Old Head; three cannon were installed, giving two successive reports every ten minutes. A third keeper was appointed to act as fog-signalman and a dwelling was built for himself and his family, at the lighthouse, in 1895.

Sea-traffic continued to grow on this coast, and in 1903 the Mercantile Marine Service Association became concerned about the quality of the light. They wrote to the Commissioners of Irish Lights enquiring "whether they contemplated altering the obsolete and low-powered light at Old Head, Kinsale." Despite the gravity and urgency of this enquiry, the Inspecting Committee took almost two years to report on the matter. They recommended that the light and fog signal should be changed and the proposal was put to Trinity House for their approval. The old lantern and granite blocking were replaced by the present iron lantern; the light changing to double-flashing, incandescent vapourised paraffin. The old, gun fog signal was substituted by a cotton powder charge, with a character of two successive reports every six minutes. This new light and fog signal were established on 17th December, 1907. There was no further change until 1934, when the explosive fog signal was altered to one report every five minutes. Then, in 1972, when, for security reasons, all explosive fog signals on the coast were discontinued, Old Head acquired the siren signal from the discontinued Power Head Fog Signal Station, which had been closed down in 1970.

In 1972 the optic was converted from vapourised paraffin to electric, with a standby generating set should there be a mains electricity failure. When the old Daunt lightship was withdrawn from service in 1974, its Radio Beacon navigational aid was transferred to Old Head and Ballycotton. Old Head, transmitting its Morse identification signal OH (_ _ _ ...), in a character lasting 55 seconds every 6 minutes, is grouped with beacons at Ballycotton, Lundy, Flatholm, South Bishop and Tuskar.

On 1st April, 1987, the Old Head of Kinsale light became unwatched automatic. The Keepers were withdrawn and the station is now looked after by an Attendant, who lives on the premises.

Galley Head

Galley Head lighthouse, with its well-designed compound, containing gas-works and houses for Keepers and gas-makers, is a veritable village. It stands on the Southern extremity of a headland, five miles from Ross Carbery, Co Cork. This headland is known as Dundeady Island, though it is not, in fact, an island, but joined to the mainland by an isthmus, lower than the headland itself. Lord Bandon had, for many years campaigned for the erection of a light here, calling attention to the many ships wrecked off the Head.

The lighthouse, and its out-buildings, were designed by J.S. Sloane, Engineer-in-Chief to the Commisioners of Irish Lights, and the light was first exhibited on 1st January, 1878. Around this period there was a great interest in the potential of gas made from cannel coal as a source of illumination for optics. The suppliers of the lantern, and the French-manufactured optic, were Messrs Edmundson & Co of Dublin, who, together with their Chief Engineer, John R. Wigham, were pioneers in the field of gas-powered lighting. Not surprisingly, they also supplied the gas-making plant. A specially designed gas works was built behind the dwellings to accommodate this. The tower, 69 feet high and at the edge of the sheer cliff, was painted white and that original light could be seen for 19 miles.

Six and a half faces of the lantern have clear glazing, covering a seaward bearing, and nine and a half faces are blanked off toward the land, except for six panes in two faces which have been left clear. The reason for those clear panes in the dark landward arc, local tradition tells us, goes back to an occasion when the Sultan of Turkey was the guest of Lord Carbery at Castle Freke. Shortly after he arrived the Sultan's eye was drawn to the white tower on the distant headland, and he asked his host what it was. Lord Carbery replied that it was a lighthouse that shone out over the sea at night. Whereupon the Sultan wanted to know why it did not also shine out over the land also. Lord Carbery spoke to some friends in high places and certain panes on the landward side were fitted with clear glass.

In 1907, a new light was installed, greatly increasing the candle-power and giving a range of 24 miles in clear weather. The stength of the light was again increased in 1969, on conversion to electric. The candlepower increased from 362,000 to 2,800,000, with an increased range of 28 miles. The station became fully automatic in 1979.

Fastnet

Four and a half miles off the Cork coast, Sou'-West of the forbidding bulk of the cliffs of Cape Clear, lies the even more forbidding Fastnet Rock. And, on this rock stands the most famous of all Irish lighthouses, and one of the great sea-lights of Europe, The Fastnet; sometimes called, pragmatically, 'the eye of Europe'; sometimes, sentimentally, 'the teardrop of Ireland'. It is the land-fall light for all ships inward-bound from the Americas; the first and last light for the transatlantic voyager. So much is resumed, for so many, in the very name — "Fastnet"; it is "hail", or "farewell", depending on whether the voyager is inward, or outward-bound. Thousands of emigrants have watched the great revolving spokes of light dwindle to a yellow pin-prick, far astern, as their ships found new horizons. Others, returning from the New World, have crowded many a ship's rail for hours, waiting to catch their first glimpse of this welcoming light of home. The Fastnet Rock is a jagged pinnacle, comprised of clay slate, of differing degrees of hardness; some containing veins of quartz, others large quartz crystals. It is surrounded by deep water, the tide rising 12 feet, with powerful currents running round the Rock, especially at Spring tides, attaining a velocity of over 3 knots. The water is rarely calm enough to allow men to land directly on the Rock from a boat; no more than ten or twelve tides in a year. For the most part, the Rock is surrounded by white water, in varying degrees of agitation, depending on wind, tide and current. And the fogs that plague this coast are legendary, rolling in like huge puffs of smoke across the water, building into a great, grey, impenetrable wall that obliterates everything, with visibility down to an arm's length. So often, then, the only thing standing between the mar-iner and shipwreck on this treacherous coast, is the guiding light of Fastnet and its explosive fog-signal.

The genesis of the first lighthouse on Fastnet Rock is a par-ticularly tragic story. A story that epitomises the human pro-pensity for failing to act before it is too late, despite numerous exhortations and warnings. On Wednesday, 15th November 1847, the 1,034 ton American liner, *Stephen Whitney,* with 110 pass-engers and crew on board, foundered on West Calf Island, in the channel between the village of Schull and Cape Clear Island. There was a loss of 90 lives, including the Master, Captain Charles Popham, of Cork, and Second Mate, Robert Gill, of Southampton. In the previous four years there had been two other ships wrecked in these waters, the *Sirius,* and the *Lady Flora Hastings;* though not with such a catastrophic loss of life. After each of these tragedies representations were made to the governing body for Irish lighthouses, the Ballast Board of Dublin, to urgently review the location of lights on this coast. No action was taken by the Board. So, the wreck of the *Stephen Whitney* was flashpoint. There was a public outcry. Letters were written to the leading newspapers of the time. Questions were asked in Parliament. The Ballast Board was castigated.

From all the contemporary accounts of the wreck of the *Stephen Whitney* it is certain that the tragedy was caused by the extreme elevation of the lighthouse on Cape Clear. Standing 450 feet above sea-level, it was frequently obscured totally by fog, and was useless to mariners. The attention of the Ballast Board had been drawn to this in 1845, and again in 1846, one year before the *Stephen Whitney* wreck, by Captain Wolf, R.N. He had written a report, after cruising in the area in foggy weather: "I have passed Cape Clear, close enough to see the break of the sea on the shore, but without the light being visible. A ship may, therefore, be lured inside this light, without even knowing it is there, in certain weather."

That is exactly what happened to the doomed *Stephen Whitney*. With poor visibility she was inside the Cape Clear light without even knowing it was there. This caused the officer of the watch to misread the light on Rock Island for that on the Old Head of Kinsale. He, then, with understandable impunity, set a fair Channel course for Cork. Keeping this course he ran aground on the Western Calf, hearing the tremendous roar of white water on the rocks too late to avert disaster.

The 'Cork Examiner' sent their Special Correspondent to the scene. After interviewing some of the survivors he wrote: "The ship was doomed. A brief moment only ensued, and one terrific crash followed, which instantly consigned numbers of souls to eternity. This single encounter stove in the entire side of the vessel, and in less than half-an-hour there were not two planks together, nor a single article of any description that could afford the means of escape to either passenger or sailor."

On the day of the tragedy, a Royal Navy vessel, *Badger*, patrolled the channel to ascertain if it were possible to salvage any portion of either ship or cargo. One of her officers reported: "It seemed as if the *Stephen Whitney* had been ground in a mill, or as if a number of carpenters were employed for months, for the mere purpose of chipping her into fragments of some three or four feet in length."

One of the most eloquent letters was that published in the London Times, on 24th November, 1847. It was generally considered to be the work of an experienced ship's captain, but was simply signed — "A Sailor". It was devastating in its condemnation of the Ballast Board of Dublin: "Thus, there has perished a noble ship, with her gallant commander and eighty-nine passengers, victims of the incompetency and apathy of the Ballast Board of Dublin, who have the administration of £55,000 a-year of public funds, for the maintainance of proper lights on the coast of Ireland. Time would fail me and the patience of your readers would be exhausted, were I to adduce the multiplied proofs which crowd on me as to the incompetency of the Board in question, for the important duties they have undertaken. The uselessness of the Cape Clear light, owing to its frequently being obscured by fog, is notorious among sailors, and the attention of the Ballast Board has been directed to this ill-chosen site by the London Trinity Brethern. The Cape Clear light should be removed, forthwith, to the Fastnet Rock. This rock lies four miles South-West of Cape Clear and is the outermost danger, and this rock is, on many accounts, the proper position for the light. Yet, it is to be feared, that not even this last fatal catastrophe, this dreadful loss of life, will rouse the Ballast Board of Dublin from its apathy, and compel it to exhibit the necessary light that the shipping interest and the public have the right to demand."

Happily, 'A Sailor's' fears were not realised. Just two months after that trenchant letter to the 'London Times', the Corporation of Trinity House gave its statutory sanction to the Dublin Ballast Board's proposal for the building of a lighthouse on Fastnet Rock. "The old light, on Cape Clear, should be extinguished, on the representation that it is too far inside the outlying dangers, such as the Fastnet Rock, and at so high an elevation that it is frequently obscured by fog."

The decision was taken in January, 1848, and within weeks, George Halpin Snr., Engineer to the Port of Dublin Corporation, was commissioned to design the new tower. Cast-iron was the material in vogue at that time for all such building, so a tower, 63 ft. 9 ins. high, made of flanged plates, varying in thickness from 1 3/8 ins. at the bottom, to 7/8 ins. at the top, was agreed on. The lantern was an additional 27 ft. 8 ins., making an overall height of 91 ft. Huge 2 ft. bolts secured the base flanges to the rock, and the base was filled solid with rubble masonry to a depth of 3 ft. Lining walls of masonry, 3 ft. 6 ins. thick, were built up to first floor level. The entrance was on this floor, with a cast-iron stairway giving access to it outside the base of the tower. Work commenced on the building in 1849 and was finished in 1853, a remarkable achievement, considering the number of days when, because of tides and weather, it was impossible to work at all. During construction, the workmen lived in a wooden barracks constructed on the Rock.

A light was first exhibited on the Fastnet Rock on 1st January, 1854. It was oil-burning, not particularly powerful, and, except in very clear weather, only visible from a short distance. The flash, of approximately 38,000 candle-power in the centre of the beam, recurred every 2 minutes; the duration of the flash being approximately 15 seconds. A great remove from the 1,300,000 candle-power of today's light. The oil was stored in tanks accommodated on the second floor of the tower and the keepers lived in a single-storied iron barracks, divided into three separate rooms, on the North-East side of the Rock. Three dwellings, to house the lightkeepers' families, were built on the mainland, at Rock Island, near Crookhaven. Because of the difficulty, indeed the near-impossibility, of bringing boats of any size alongside the Rock, a derrick-mast and jib, and a hand-winch, were erected for landing men and stores. The cost of building that first lighthouse on Fastnet was £17,900, the shore dwellings at Rock Island bringing the total cost to over £20,000.

The first Fastnet light, or Halpin's Lighthouse, as it was known, after George Halpin Snr., the man who designed and built it, remained in its original form for ten years. During that time it had been carefully monitored, both by the resident keepers and by visiting engineers. Doubts had arisen about certain aspects of its stability. During North-West, West, and South-West gales, incredibly heavy seas broke right over the Rock, causing the new tower to tremble. Sometimes to such an extent that cups of coffee and tea were thrown from tables in the top room of the tower. And, such was the fury of the seas lashing Fastnet, that large portions of rock were ripped off the top of the South cliff. Huge blocks of stone, often weighing up to 3 tons, were torn out of the rock-face, striking the tower, but, miraculously, not causing any appreciable structural damage. During one particularly fierce gale, a 60 gallon cask of water, lashed to the gallery railing on top of the tower, was carried away by a huge sea. This gallery was 133 feet above high water. The external entrance stair-case was also causing problems; it was often dangerous, and sometimes impossible, for keepers to get from the lighthouse tower to the dwelling, such was the fury of the seas washing over the steps.

As the designer of the lighthouse, George Halpin Snr., had died in 1854, shortly after the light was first exhibited, the Consulting Engineer to the Corporation of the Port of Dublin, C. P. Cotton, was given responsibility for whatever alterations and modifications were necessary. He visited the Rock with the Scot, George Stevenson, Consulting Engineer to the Commissioners of Northern Lighthouses, in April 1865. After a joint examination of the tower and the Rock itself, their separate reports differed greatly in the their recommendations as to what changes should be made. In an effort to achieve some consensus, the advice of the Elder Brethern of Trinity House was sought. Their Engineer, James Douglass, visited the Fastnet in the Spring of 1866, and shortly afterwards agreement was reached as to improvements. The tower was strengthened, the better to withstand the incessant buffeting of the sea. As it was found impossible to make the Keepers' dwelling safe and comfortable, the upper part of the tower was fitted out to incorporate bedrooms, a living room and a store. While this work was nearing completion, in 1867, the 'Dublin Port Act' was passed, altering the constitution of the Corporation of the Port of Dublin, and appointing and incorporating the new body — The Commissioners of Irish Lights. All powers relating to the development and maintainance of an efficient Lighthouse Service was vested in this new governing body.

For the next 14 years "Halpin's Lighthouse" on Fastnet was relatively trouble free, apart from the normal wear-and-tear caused by wind and weather and the inexorable pounding of the Atlantic. The new Commissioners had the character of the light altered during that period; from one flash every two minutes to one flash every minute. Other minor alterations were effected and normal maintenance work carried out. Then, on the morning of 26th November, 1881, hurricane winds of over 80 m.p.h. hit this coast. Gigantic waves reached unprecedented height and force, and the lantern on the Fastnet tower was smashed, one lens being badly damaged. Just 26 miles away, West-North-West of Fastnet, a similar, George Halpin-designed cast-iron tower on the Calf Rock, was swept away by the heavy seas. It was broken off above the level of the strengthening casing round its base. Miraculously,

no one was injured, as the keepers were all in the lower part of
the tower when the sea hit. Now, even though the Fastnet suffered
no more damage than the broken lantern and damaged lens, that
November storm raised many doubts as to its long-term durability.
Yet, it was to be another 10 years before a more modern and
substantial tower was mooted.

As maritime trade grew, toward the end of the 19th century, the
sea-lanes round our coasts became busier. The major ports flourished, particularly the ports of Cork and Cobh. Because of its
strategic position, as the principal landfall light on the South -
West coast, the Fastnet light was of enormous importance, not just
to transatlantic traffic, but to coastal traffic as well. The Commissioners of Irish Lights decided, in November 1891, that because of
its strategic position, the light on Fasnet Rock must be improved.
To achieve this the old dioptric apparatus would have to be
replaced by a more sophisticated biform light, of the most powerful
type; the new light retaining the characteristics of the old. This
imperative, together with the continuing worry about the stability
of the old tower, would necessitate building a new tower. Such a
mammoth undertaking required the statutory sanction of the
Elder Brethern of Trinity House. This was sought on 23rd
November, 1891, and accorded on 7th December, 1891;   the
alacrity with which the decision was made reflecting the urgency
in replacing the old cast-iron tower. William Douglass, Engineer
-in-Chief of Irish Lights, designed the new tower; his draughtsmen
were J.T. Middleton and S.W. Nugent.

Yet, it was to be four years from then before the preparatory work
began on the Rock for the construction of the new granite tower.
In that interval there was the slow, very necessary surveying of
the site to be completed; the drawing up of detailed plans, and the
changing of those plans many times, before consensus was
reached; the contracting for, and preparation of, the granite
blocks; the establishing of a shore working-base at Rock Island,
Crookhaven; the building of wharves, the assembly of plant,
stores, blacksmiths' shops, carpenters' shops, offices and shore
quarters for the workmen in the yard. All this had to be put in
place before work could start on the Rock. And, a specially designed work-boat, the steamer *Ierne*, was built to carry the stone
and other materials to the Fastnet. She was a twin-screw craft,
126 ft. long, 23 ft. beam, drawing 10 ft. aft and 9 ft. for'ard, when
fully loaded with 90 tons of cargo. She had a specially designed

longitudinal centre bulkhead, with two tiers of rollers on each side of it, on which to load the granite blocks. Her engines were of 700 indicated horse-power, and her speed approximately 10 knots.

The building of the Fastnet tower was a slow process; the days when men could work on the Rock being dictated by the caprices of wind, weather and tide. So much time was spent confined to barracks, waiting for a relatively calm spell to get on with the work, that all-important morale might have been adversely eff-ected, had it not been for the magnificent leadership qualities of the foreman, James Kavanagh, of Wicklow. He inspired all who worked with him and earned their total respect; at all times putting the well-being of his workers before his own. He was a strict, but fair-minded disciplinarian who, in addition to being a man for all seasons, was also a man for all functions, combining the duties of medical inspector and welfare officer with his official duties as foreman. In the seven years it took to build the light-house, he seldom took shore leave. And, on the odd occasion when he went home to Wicklow to visit his family, he would grow restive after a few days, especially if there was a spell of fine, calm weather. He would pace around restlessly, saying, over and over, as he looked out to sea: "They'll get a lot of work done on the Rock today!"

Considering the basic, often primitive methods and machinery available when work commenced on the new Fastnet in 1896, the building of the great, granite tower was an heroic, near miraculous achievement. For the seven years it took to complete there was a constant resident colony of workers on the Rock; as many as twenty-two most of the time. Bad weather inhibited work, but it also often delayed shore leave, as the relief ship could not get anywhere near the Rock. Still, morale remained high, there was little incidence of serious injury or illness and work progressed to schedule. James Kavanagh's charismatic presence seemed to in-spire the men, even the squad of Cornish quarrymen, brought over specially to prepare the rock for the foundations. James Kavanagh was taken ill, on Fastnet, in June 1903 and was immediately brought ashore, to Crookhaven, for medical attention. He died there, on July 6th, of apoplexy. He lived to see the building of the tower itself completed; the internal fitting-out and the putting in place of the lantern took another year.

There was a total of 2,074 granite blocks, or stones, used in the building of the Fastnet tower; their total weight being 4,300 tons. It is on record that, with his own hands, James Kavanagh set each separate stone. Truly an herculean feat. This love of his work, his dedication to it, and the fact that he took so few holidays, must have contributed to his tragic death. To some, Fastnet is known as the William Douglass Tower, after the Irish Lights Engineer-in-Chief who designed it. To many others it will always be remembered as Kavanagh's Tower, after the man who, in a sense, gave his life to, quite literally, build it.

James Kavanagh was an excellent mason who had been in Irish Light's employ for several years, when it was decided to send him to Fastnet, in August 1896, to be foreman on the building of the new lighthouse. Initially, his principal tasks were to build a proper landing place at the East end of the Rock, and to prepare the foundation for the new tower. But, first, to accommodate the resident workmen, a barrack had to be erected and, to protect the various building materials, a weatherproof stores.

Simultaneously, on the mainland, work commenced on the preparation of a site for the shore Depot, comprising stone-yard, stores, accommodation for workmen, and a deep-water jetty, where the granite and other building materials could be loaded for shipment to Fastnet. Being the terminus for the nearest railway, Schull was considered to be the most suitable place for this development. Ground, there, was only to be had at exorbitant rents, so the Commissioners had to search for another location. Eventually they decided on their own property; the land surrounding the Fastnet shore dwellings at Rock Island. This was in Crookhaven Harbour and there was an adequate depth of 3 fathoms, even at low-water of Spring tides. In the Spring of 1897 F. R. Foot was appointed Resident Engineer on the project. His capabilities were well-known and appreciated by the Commissioners, as he had done an outstanding job for them as Resident Engineer on the building of Mew Island lighthouse, off Belfast, and Bull Rock, off the South-West coast. As the specially designed steamer, *Ierne*, was still being built, a steam tug, *Knight of The Cross*, was chartered for a six month period in 1897. A Junior Officer from one of the Commissioners' other steamers, H. Maunders, was given command of her.

Mew Island, Belfast Lough

Cromwell Point, Valentia Island

Black Rock, Co. Sligo

Inishgort, with Croagh Patrick in background

Metal Man, Rosses Point

Rockabill

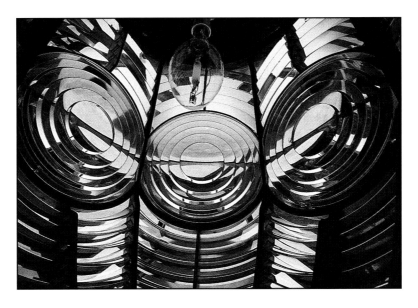

A lighthouse lantern

Spiral stairs, Ferris Point

Ultra-modern tower, Ferris Point

Ballincourty Point, Dungarvan Bay

Old Head of Kinsale

Maiden's Rock

Fasnet Rock

Last Watch leaving Fastnet Rock on its automation.
From left: Dick O'Driscoll, Principal Keeper,
Mick Culligan, Kevin Magner (both Assistant Keepers),
Captain Mick Hennessey (Pilot, Irish Helocopters).

Bull Rock

Peter Duggan (Principal Keeper; centre) with workmen

Helicopter landing, Skellig Michael

Skellig Michael

Haulbowline, Carlingford Lough

Eagle Island

Ballycotton Island, Co. Cork

Tuskar Rock

Roche's Point

Tarbert

Blacksod Bay

Hook Head

Pile Light, Dundalk

"Granuaille", Irish Lights Flagship

Kish Bank

Inistrahull

Christmas, Baily, Co. Dublin

Tory Island, Co. Donegal

The sea was so consistently rough during that Summer of 1897, that the squad of men out on the Rock with James Kavanagh, were seldom able to do any serious work on the foundation of the new tower. They did, however, succeed in completing the building of the masonry store, the barrack for workmen, and the water-tanks. Work on the pier and tramway was inhibited by the heavy seas, and the completion of this had to be left until the following Spring. During 1897 the masonry for the tower was ordered, for delivery to the stone-yard at Rock Island. Small blocks of Dublin granite, each 18 ins. by 12 ins. by 6 ins. were to be used in building the landing pier and platforms, and as filler for the weak spots in the foundation of the tower. These cost £1. 12s per ton for 170 tons. The granite for the tower itself was ordered from John Freeman & Sons, of Penryn, Cornwall, and was made up of two separate orders. The one order for stone where colour and fineness of grain were unimportant, as it was to be used in the lower part of the tower, which would quickly be covered with green weed. The other was for a superior stone, fine-grained, hard and uniform in colour; free from all blemishes or defects, very finely dressed on the external face, and on the inside face where it would form the walls of the rooms.

From the foundation to the top of the tower there were 89 courses to be set in place. To reduce the amount of cutting to be done at either Rock Island or Fastnet itself, all 2,074 stones were prepared in Penryn. As the various courses were ready, the entire Fastnet tower was erected, in sections of 6 to 8 courses at a time, in the contractor's yard in Penryn. There they were inspected by either William Douglass, C.W. Scott, or F.R. Foot, immediately before shipment to Ireland. The top course of each setting was retained to form the bottom course of the next setting. So consistently high was the standard of the Penryn product that, though no stone was finally accepted until it had been examined on delivery to Rock Island, it was not necessary to reject even one of the thousands delivered.

*Commissioners' launch approaching Fastnet
Rock - pre-helicopter*

The Summer of 1897 was bad, and in order to speed up progress on the preparation of the Rock for the foundation, a squad of Cornish quarry-men and stone-cutters was brought over and billetted on the Fastnet Rock. They did most of the heavy quarrying and cut the 'beds' for the lower partial ring courses. During the Summer of 1898 the tramway and pier were also completed, the steam landing-winch and boiler were erected, and the work on the boat-landing was well advanced. On shore, at Rock Island, progress was satisfactory. A steam wharf-crane was erected, gantry and buildings completed, and 'courses' 1 to 13 of the Penryn granite unloaded and stacked in the stone-yard.

After severe Winter gales work on the Rock was started again at the end of March, 1899. The new work-boat, *Ierne*, had been delivered before the end of 1898, and Captain D.P. Fleming given command. All the components were in place now and hopes were high for an early start to setting the first big foundation stones of the tower. But, the great imponderable factor of the weather, once again, as so often before, upset plans and dashed hopes. The bad spell lasted until the end of May and the cutting of the rock to clear the way for the laying of the lower courses was held up. Not until June 8th was the foundation ready for the first course. The weather was fine and the *Ierne* was able to moor close to the Rock. During the day she tested her new landing-gear by off-loading small granite blocks, sand and water. On the morning of the 9th, two huge granite stones, weighing nearly 3 tons each, were landed and set. Then, in the afternoon, a fault developed in the landing-gear and work had to be suspended until the 13th. This, ironically, was one of the very few mechanical breakdowns; thereafter, stoppages were invariably due to bad weather.

How great a factor the weather was, in inhibiting work on the Rock, can be seen by looking at the log kept to record the number of stones set each day; from 9th June, 1899, when the first stone was set, to 2nd May, 1903, when the last stone was set. On only two occasions in that four years was it possible to work for five consecutive days; in July, 1900 and in May, 1902. For most of the time it was two or three day runs, with, occasionally, a four day run. The same log shows that there were spells of ten to fourteen days when it was not possible to work on the construction of the tower at all; the Rock being pounded by heavy seas, and swept by high winds, rain, sleet, and sometimes snow. There were also long delays arising from problems about the contract for the granite. There was great difficulty in getting quality stone of the correct colour. With all of the best quarries demand far exceeded supply. So, the contract with Messrs Freeman was cancelled. A new contract, at the same prices, but containing a penalty clause, was then drawn up with them. Delivery dates were agreed and heavy penalties imposed if these dates were not strictly honoured. This tougher approach to their contractor seemed to work for the Commissioners and work progressed steadily enough after that, weather permitting. On 11th August, 1902, course 86 was completed. This left only three courses to set, and they would have to wait until the temporary light was erected. Meantime, the light from the old cast-iron tower would continue to be used; to raise the level of the new tower further would partly obscure that light for ships approaching from a Westerly direction.

The weather in March of the following year, 1903, was good, and it was possible for the Ierne to land all of the apparatus for the temporary light. This was erected immediately and the light exhibited on May 19th. The way was now clear to finish the three remaining masonry courses, but again the weather changed for the worse, a continuous enormously heavy swell sweeping the Rock for five days, preventing the landing of any stone. By May 26th the sea had calmed and work recommenced, the last stone being set on June 3rd, by the foreman, James Kavanagh, just three weeks before he became fatally ill.

Given the exposed Rock, the total lack of shelter, the vagaries of the weather, the relatively primitive equipment, the man-handling of 2,074 stones, it seems almost miraculous that not a single stone was lost or damaged. On completion, every course was checked carefully, and the maximum variation from the figured dimensions on the drawings on any course was no more than 1/4 in. in the diameter. A plumb-bob was hung from the top of the newly-completed tower, to check any variation from the vertical; again, the tolerance was minimal — 3/16th in. The Fastnet tower is considered to be among the very finest examples of near faultless masonry, a perfect example of the ancient art of pharology.

The optical apparatus and the lantern for the new tower, designed by C.W. Scott and constructed by Messrs. Chance of Birmingham, arrived at Schull in July 1903. Bad weather plagued the erection of this, at one stage causing so much damage to some parts that they had to be shipped back to Birmingham for repair. Other parts, ready for assembly, were washed away by high seas and had to be replaced. Eventually, after several minor mishaps, the work on the lantern was succesfully completed, and the light exhibited, for the first time, on the night of 27th June, 1904. Ironically, after all the bad weather experienced during the years of building, that night was magnificently fine; there was a full moon and a long, mid-Summer twilight that merged with dawn. Not a night for the new light to show to best advantage. The official observers, among them C.W. Scott, Engineer to the Commissioners, were disappointed.

They had not long to wait, however, to see the great lantern at its best. Next night brought alternating driving, thick mist and squalls of scudding rain, and the light was spectacularly penetrative; illuminating the unhomogeneous mist in the most effective way. That superb penetration, the intensity and compactness of the beam, derived from the new incandescent burner, and the flotation of the lens in mercury.

The official Irish Lights Inspecting Committee, aboard the new Irish Lights steamer, *Alexandra*, sailed out of Crookhaven on the night of July 21st, three weeks after the light was first exhibited. They spent several hours that night viewing the light from different approaches. The following day they landed on the Rock to inspect the new tower and lantern, and were totally satisfied with the work. Sir Robert Ball, F.R.S., the Commissioners' Scientific Adviser, in his report to them, dated 24th July, 1904, written aboard the *Alexandra*, off Fastnet, had this to say: "As to the beams of the Fastnet during all the time of our return to harbour, I cannot describe them otherwise than by saying they were magnificent. At ten miles the great revolving spokes of light, succeeding each other at intervals of five seconds, gave the most distinctive character possible. Almost before one spoke had disappeared the next came into view. But the effect was doubtless in part attributable to the haze. It was a most beautiful optical phenomenon. Each great flash, as it swept past, lighted up the ship and the rigging like a searchlight. After the ship entered Crookhaven Harbour, and the direct light from the Fastnet was, of course, cut off, the glow of each successive beam showed in a most striking manner over the highland that bounds the harbour. It is a matter of congratulation to everyone concerned that the Fastnet is now, at length, provided with a monumental tower and a superb light, well worthy of the position of this lonely Rock as being, from the navigator's point of view, the most important outpost of Europe."

That there was no fatal accident, no serious illness, during the building of the tower is due mainly to the watchfulness of James Kavanagh; his caring for the men and his strict discipline. Each workman was required, when coming on to the Rock, to bring with him certain basic, personal provisions, essential to maintaining good health. If anyone was found to have ignored this golden rule of Kavanagh's, he was sent back to the mainland on the next boat. And with the barracks so crowded, it was very necessary to have strict rules in relation to hygiene, both personal and general. The men were wakened at 5 a.m. every morning and compelled to wash themselves thoroughly, and then wash out their barracks. As many as three men often shared one bunk, so cramped were the quarters. It was, therefore, necessary, on fine, sunny days, to lay all the bedding out in the open and let it have a good airing. Jeyes Fluid was used liberally, and from his well-stocked medicine chest, James Kavanagh ministered personally to the basic medical needs of his men.

Only three serious accidents were recorded. Two workmen each lost an eye, and a rigger broke his leg; ostensibly a very bad injury. His claim for compensation was seriously looked at as he was deemed to be "totally and permanently incapacitated." On those grounds he was awarded "substantial compensation" of three hundred and fifty pounds. Some few weeks later, a coal boat came out from the mainland to unload at the Rock. The "totally and permanently incapacitated" ex-rigger was aboard, as an active member of the crew. The workmen who each lost an eye were awarded compensation also; one of them receiving "as much as forty-five pounds". At the time the average labourer's wage was 2s. 6d a day when working ashore at Rock Island Depot, with an extra shilling a day when working on Fastnet Rock.

From the building of the new tower until 1920 Lloyds used the Fastnet as a regular signal station. Flag signals were received from, and given to, passing ships, and messages were telegraphed ashore to Brow Head signal station. The lightkeepers performed the signalling and telegraphy duties involved; Irish Lights being paid an equitable fee by Lloyds.

When the giant transatlantic liners were still plying between Cobh and America, their passing, inward, or outward-bound, was a highlight for the keepers on Fastnet. John Noel Crowley, now Principal Keeper on Baily, and one-time Principal Keeper on Fastnet, worked there as a Supernumerary, in the '50's. He remembers the great liners — *Mauritania, France,* and the various *Queens*, coming and going. "They looked like huge floating castles, or hotels," he said, "and we watched them into harbour, or over the horizon. Sometimes, in calm weather, they would pass very close to the Rock. So close we felt we could almost reach out and touch them. They were like old friends and we'd be watching for them long before they were really due." Very understandable on a bare Rock where there was so little to do, so little excitement. And, this was before the helicopter was deployed to effect reliefs for the keepers. Sometimes the weather was so bad that the launch from the mainland could get nowhere near the Rock, and reliefs could be, quite literally, weeks overdue. The great liners are, alas, gone from those sea-lanes now, as the keepers are from Fastnet.

After 135 years of being "kept" by keepers, the Fastnet light was automated on 3rd April, 1989; Dick O'Driscoll being the last Principal Keeper on the Rock. At the end of March I drove down to Castletownbere, to record Dick and his wife, Maura, for a Radio

Documentary I was making for RTE, called 'The Last Man On The Rock'. I was to fly, by the relief helicopter, to Fastnet next morning, but, as so often happens on this coast, the weather called the tune, and I had my first lesson in long-distance waiting. For three days the fluorescent orange wind-stocking above the heli-pad remained stiff; horizontal in a relentless Force 10 gale. Fog off the sea, and scudding rain, made a tattered curtain through which could be seen, intermittently, the vague bulk of Bere Island. In the safe anchorage of the Roads a dozen sheltering trawlers pitched and rolled, their lights projected, like out-of-focus haloes on the moving screen of mist. In the Depot Control Room men gathered anxiously around the transmitter-receiver. Donie Holland, ex-Fastnet keeper, now Depot Supervisor at Castletown Lights, was in constant contact with the Rock. It was the last relief for Fastnet. There were keepers, stone-masons, electricians, and a solitary carpenter waiting to be lifted out. And, incredibly, the carpenter was James Kavanagh, from Wicklow, a grand-nephew of the legendary James Kavanagh who had been foreman on the building of the Fastnet tower.

From the Control Room the helicopter pilot, Sean Oakes, contacted his base at Cork Airport. The weather forecast was bad. There was no possibility of flights to Fastnet that day. Perhaps tomorrow; but who could tell, with such weather. So, stoically then, with a resignation born of long experience, the men waiting round for news, good or bad, drifted downstairs to stow their boxes of food in the Depot fridges. With each man taking his own provisions to the lighthouse, there was a lot of perishable food about. Hopefully they would be lifted out tomorrow. Meantime, they were faced with a long wait in a wet and windy sea-town; in a limbo between the families they had just left and the job waiting to be done.

Disconsolately they drifted off into town. Some to the guesthouses they had just vacated, to book in for at least another night; others to the pub, to play darts, or cards. Fastnet's Principal Keeper, Dick O'Driscoll, rang his wife, Maura, in Eyries, four miles over the mountain, to ask her to come and collect him. For him there was the bonus of an extra day and night at home. I was invited to go with them, and we made our recordings for the Radio programme that afternoon. Sitting in their house above the sea, we watched the huge Atlantic rollers rush the broad mouth of the Kenmare River, and I talked with Maura. I asked her what it was like being married to a lighthouse keeper; a man who had spent half their married life away on a rock. It had, she admitted, been very difficult at times .... "Especially with the children, when they were sick, or maybe had an accident. I'd be on the 'phone to Dick, but wouldn't, out of consideration, want to bother him by telling him. Sure, what could he do, out there on the Rock? So, I'd keep it all to myself, and then, afterwards, I'd feel badly for not sharing with him. But, the shore leaves were great. The homecoming was marvellous, every time. Every shore leave was like another honeymoon!"

But, one couldn't always count on the homecomings being on schedule. Very often, before the days of helicopter reliefs, Dick O'Driscoll told me, men could be ten, or fourteen days overdue. The cutter used then for reliefs might not be able to put to sea at all. And, sometimes, when she did risk it, she would have to stand 200 fathoms off the Rock, before coming in, in the lull of a huge swell, to attempt to pick up the waiting keepers. Westerly gales, with an accompanying heavy swell, could often confine keepers in the Fastnet tower for up to 12 days, battened down, while the big seas broke incessantly across the entrance door.

For three days the radio message from Fastnet to Castletownbere was the same: "The wind still high. Fifty-two. And the sea gone mad." Useless to argue with a Force 10 gale and a sea gone mad. So, we waited, our sole consolation that if there is one thing worse than waiting to get on to Fastnet, it must be waiting to get off. During the third night the gale blew itself out and the wind shifted to the East. Next morning the helicopter made its first run to the Rock, in a light wind over a choppy sea. From the air the first view of the lighthouse was staggering; the granite tower gleaming in the early morning sun, like a great shining pencil stuck into the jagged black rock. Coming in to land the heli-pad looked frighteningly small, but we were set down without a bump.

Landing supplies - pre-helicopter

Now, if the view of Fastnet from the air was staggering, then the view of the tower from the heli-pad was positively intimidating. Everything was dwarfed by the granite colossus rising nearly 200 feet directly above. There was no space to move around on this Rock, to stand back, to get an alternative perspective. The eye was forever drawn, as if by some subtle hypnosis, upward along the lovely contour of the tower, marvelling at how it had remained impervious to the onslaughts of wind, rain and sea, for almost 100 years. The mind was trying to visualise it after automation; still lit, at the requisite times, still spreading the great spokes of light across the darkness, like some ghost ship, some *Marie Celeste*, riding the seas forever. Ironically now, it would no longer be occupied by man, who, against incredible odds, had risked life and limb to build it, fighting his fear every day.

And, the men who have kept the light there over the years have also known fear; helped only by their trust in Providence and the mammoth granite tower protecting them from the buffeting of wind and sea. Dick O'Driscoll told me that they always had absolute confidence in the construction of the tower, in its ability to withstand the elements. The system of dovetail joggles totally bonds the entire tower into a virtual monolith. No stone can possibly be shifted until all the stones above it have been removed, and, even then, the joggle of the course directly below it would have to be broken off. This is most unlikely, as the cement used in the bed flows into, and completely fills, the cavity between male and female dovetails.

But, in heavy seas there can be a frightening vibration. Dick remembers "a particularly heavy sea striking the tower. The vibration was incredible. My cup of tea was filled to the top and the surface tension was such it spilled into the saucer. The lens oscillated and spilled two and a half pints of mercury out of the vat. The same sea knocked all the delph from our kitchen dresser and tins of food from the shelves in the larder. And the heavy spray came cascading through the vent in the dome. And, if you stood with your back to the inside of the granite walls, you could feel the vibration running right through your body, when the big sea hit the tower."

The Fastnet has given its name to the Blue Riband of Yacht racing — The Fastnet Race. This is a bi-annual event, held in August, starting at Cowes and running round Land's End to turn at Fastnet Rock for the last leg to Plymouth. Each race attracts around 300 yachts and was, for the keepers on Fastnet, a gala occasion; to see the fleet, under full sail gybe, and tack, and turn, right under the lighthouse. John Noel Crowley, who spent many years as Principal Keeper on the Rock, described his grandstand view: "Looking down on them from the tower, with their multi-coloured sails, was like watching dozens of butterflies wheeling round in a circle."

But, the 'butterflies' ran into serious trouble in the 1979 race, when a freak storm devastated most of the yachts; boats were dismasted, capsized, sunk; whole crews went overboard and 15 competitors drowned. Hugh Coveney, of Cork, a Commissioner of Irish Lights, took part in that race, and was airlifted to safety. He marvels that so few crew members actually drowned in such atrocious conditions; with over 2,000 people crewing the 300 or so yachts, the incidence of fatality was relatively small.

Part Three

South-West Coast:
Crookhaven to Loop Head

Crookhaven - Mizen Head - Copper Point - Sheep's Head -
Ardnakinna - Castletownbere - Roancarrig - Bull Rock - Skellig
Michael - Cromwell Point - Valentia - Inishtearaght - Little
Samphire Island - Scattery Island - Beeves Rock - Tarbert -
Kilcredaun - Loop Head.

*"James looked at the Lighthouse. He could see the white-washed rocks;
the tower stark and straight; he could see that it was barred with black
and white; he could see the windows in it ; he could even see washing
spread on the rocks to dry. So, that was the Lighthouse, was it? No,
the other was also the Lighthouse. For nothing was simply one thing.
The other was the Lighthouse too. It was sometimes hardly to be seen
across the bay. In the evening one looked up and saw the eye opening
and shutting, and the light seemed to reach them in the airy, sunny
garden where they sat."*

Virginia Woolf: "To The Lighthouse".

Erecting a radio mast

Cape Clear, Sherkin & Crookhaven

Clear Island and Sherkin Island guard the Southern approaches to Roaring Water Bay, and are strategically situated as sites for navigational aids. Sherkin still has its lighthouse on Barrack Point. A light was first exhibited here in December 1884, using a small lantern loaned by Irish Lights to the local Harbour Board. A local priest, Fr. Davis, seems to have been the motivating force behind the push to establish a more permanent light. The permanent light was established in January, 1886, using the same loaned lantern. The following year Fr. Davis asked the Commissioners for the loan of a fog bell, and they agreed. By October, 1894, this bell was broken, but, undaunted, the Harbour Board applied for the loan of another bell. The Commissioners, after some delay, supplied another bell, which in turn was also broken within a few months. A third was requested, but, this time, the Commisioners gave an emphatic "no". In March, 1914, the Skibbereen Harbour Board requested that Irish Lights should take over Sherkin Island Light, but the Board replied that they could not comply.

Clear Island had its first light exhibited in May, 1818; a revolving light with 12 Argand burners and reflectors. It was a George Halpin designed tower, built near the old, then unoccupied, Admiralty Signal Tower. Two years later there was trouble involving some of the keepers. Inspector Halpin, acting on a tip-off from the local Parish Priest, investigated the matter. He found the station neglected and dirty and found that the Principal Keeper had been selling some of the oil in his charge. The same Keeper was also a great trouble maker. The Board ordered that both the Principal and his Assistant be tranferred from the Island and their conduct investigated. Some months later the Principal was dismissed and the Assistant sent to Old Head, Kinsale. About the same time there was grave concern about smuggling activities on this coast, and the Admiralty requested that a flag-staff should be erected at the Lighthouse, to alert cruisers on patrol in the vicinity. The request pointed out that, as the locals were quite hostile toward preventive measures, the mast would be safer inside the Lighthouse compound. The Ballast Board turned down this request on the basis that it would "take up the Keeper's attention and be an apology for neglect of his light-keeping duties."

Over the first 20 years of its existence the position of the Cape Clear Light had been a bone of contention; Trinity House considering it to be built at too high an elevation, at 450 feet above sea level; George Halpin maintaining that such altitude gave visibility at a greater distance. Yet, in a report in 1844, Halpin had, reluctantly, admitted that a "lighthouse positioned at the Western point of the island, 100 feet lower, would be less liable to fog". The argument and prevarication went on regarding the re-siting of the light, until, tragically, the decision was taken out of the hands of the various protagonists. In November, 1847, the American liner, *Stephen Whitney*, was wrecked on Western Calf Island, between Schull and Cape Clear, with a loss of 92 lives. In heavy fog, the light on Cape Clear had not been visible. This, then, was the deciding factor in terminating Clear Island Lighthouse and building the first Lighthouse on Fastnet Rock. Cape Clear light was discontinued on 1st January, 1854, when the Fastnet Light was first exhibited. The Crookhaven Light, on Rock Island, near the Western extremity of Roaring Water Bay, had but recently been established at the time of the *Stephen Whitney* tragedy. As far as could be ascertained at the time, no one on board the doomed vessel was even aware of its existence. Therefore, they mistook it for the Old Head of Kinsale Light, and steered their last, fatal course accordingly. Ironically, Rock Island at Crookhaven, was to be vital in the building of the second Fastnet Lighthouse at the end of the 19th century. It was rebuilt at that time to make it a service depot for the building of the great granite tower. A stone-yard was created there to prepare the various courses of granite to be shipped out to Fastnet Rock.

Mizen Head

Mizen Head, better known as 'The Mizen', is, from a navigational point of view, one of the most strategically placed lighthouses on this coast. Originally built and established as a Fog Signal Station, in 1909, it was not lighted for just half-a-century. The light was first exhibited in 1959 and was only automated early this year, 1993, when the Keepers were withdrawn. A prefabricated, reinforced concrete bridge links the rock on which the Lighthouse stands with the mainland. When this bridge was built, around the turn of the century, it was reckoned to be the first of its kind in Europe, and is still a unique example of engineering.

Copper Point

In May, 1860 Lord Bandon wrote to the Ballast Board in Dublin, enclosing a letter with many signatures, asking for "a conspicuous beacon on the East end of Long Island." Long Island lies off Schull in Roaring Water Bay, and was an accepted and well-frequented harbour of refuge for ships trading along that coast. The letter was referred to Trinity House and they instructed Captain Roberts to survey the area. He recommended that two beacons were necessary; one on Goat Island, the other on Long Island, at Copper Point. He also recommended buoys at the Amelia Rock and Cush Spit. Both unlighted beacons were completed in late 1864.

Not until 1955 were any representations made to have the area lighted. In that year local fishermen requested that a light be established at Copper Point. Again, in 1959, the Schull Parish Guild of Muintir na Tíre, suggested that lighting was necessary. But, it was not until 1972 that the Inspecting Committee on Tour recommended that the old Copper Point Beacon be lighted. Schull Harbour Board took responsibility for the erection and maintenance of leading lights and the Commissioners of Irish Lights went about converting Copper Point to be a lighted beacon. The Schull Harbour Leading lights and Copper Point quick-flashing light were established on 1st June, 1977. In February 1981, Copper Point was designated as a Lighthouse proper.

Bantry Bay Lights:
Sheep's Head, Roancarrig, Castletownbere, Ardnakinna

Castletownbere on the Northern shore of Bantry Bay has been an especially busy place since the advent of the helicopter relief for the lighthouses on the South-West coast islands. For, in addition to the Directional Light in Castletown itself, there is the helicopter base, from which the reliefs were carried out. And, with the work of automation taking place on the islands, it was also the scene of the frenetic comings and goings of tradesmen, electricians, electronic experts, and the army of people necessary to automate the lights.

In addition to the Directional Light, there has been a light at Ardnakinna Point, since November 1965. Before that, the Point, at the Western tip of Bere Island, was marked, since 1850, by an unlighted beacon. There has also been a lighthouse on Roancarrig, at the eastern entrance to Bantry Bay, since 1847. This location was chosen by George Halpin, in preference to the suggested location at the Eastern end of Bere Island. He also designed the tower.

The most recent addition to the efficient lighting of Bantry Bay is the light at Sheep's Head. This was built to ensure safe passage, in and out of the Bay, for the giant oil tankers using the newly built Gulf Oil Terminal on Whiddy Island. The unwatched light was first exhibited Monday, 14th October, 1968, at a time when the oil boom in Bantry Bay was just beginning. Unfortunately, the mid-seventies brought problems; recession, cutting down Gulf's through-put by 50%, and a strike at the Terminal. In the Summer of 1974, tankers were to be seen, quite literally in their dozens, lying at anchor along the 12 mile length of the buoyed channel in Bantry Bay. Any chance of recovery was severely inihibited by the exp- losion of the *Betalgeuse,* at Whiddy, on 8th January, 1979. Gulf Oil had assumed the cost of the construction of the lighthouse at Sheep's Head and the navigational aids in the Bay itself.

The Calf Rock and the Bull Rock

Off Dursey, the long, narrow island at the tip of the Beara Peninsula, is a group of four Rocks, or, rather, a family of Rocks. They are known as The Bull, The Cow, The Calf and The Heifer, and are as strange a family as you are ever likely to come across. Differing in size from the bulk of The Bull, over 300 feet high and 600 feet in diameter, to the pimple of The Heifer, so low that it seems to be barely managing to keep its head above the water, these Rocks are a major hazard to shipping. Atop The Bull, the lighthouse and the fog-signal station look like toys, doll's houses, placed there by some giant hand; and, running through the Rock is a tunnel, large enough to accommodate the passage of a large trawler. The Calf lies low, like a crouching lion, only 78 feet above sea-level, with the incongruous stump of the ruined cast-iron lighthouse tower on his back.

This place is steeped in legend and mystery and tradition. Tradition that goes back to Don, the son of Milesius, who, approaching the Beara Peninsula from the sea, with a war party, was wrecked with all his followers on The Calf Rock. And, there is a wonderful legend, where the suspension of one's disbelief is greatly facilitated by perceiving these siren rocks as members of some odd kind of family circle. This legend relates how, quite early every

Mayday, before the rising sun has dispersed the sea mist, the Fastnet Rock sets out on a twenty mile journey to visit its relations — The Bull, The Cow, The Calf and The Heifer. Having cruised round them and paid its respects, it returns home for another year.

These rocks were unlighted until the middle of the 19th century when pressure was brought to bear on the Ballast Board "by merchants, shipowners and local landed gentry", to build a lighthouse. Calf Rock was surveyed and George Halpin Snr. drew up plans for the new lighthouse. These, together with a detailed estimate for the cast-iron tower, floors of Valentia slate, lantern and optics, were presented to the Board in March, 1858. Halpin had noted in his presentation that, due to the exposed position of The Calf Rock, and the consequent difficulties for the contractor, the tenders would be higher than his estimate. Tenders were slow to come in; the interested contractors finding it very difficult to land on the Rock. However, after re-advertising, four tenders were received, and in December, 1860, Henry Grissell, Regents Canal Iron Works, London received the contract. His estimate for the lighthouse was £11,360, and £6,151 for the lightkeepers' dwellings to be built on the mainland. Halpin's estimate for the same had been £18,000, so his fears that the actual tender price might be much higher were not realised; at least not at that stage. There is one anomaly, however, that is worth considering. Halpin had estimated £2,000 for the dwellings and this had been queried by the Board of Trade as being "ridiculously high". Similar dwellings, they argued, had been built at Land's End, at half that cost. And yet, Henry Grissell's tender for £6,151 seems to have been accepted without demur.

Bull, Cow, Calf and Heifer Rocks

Though the contract was awarded in December, 1860, Grissell spent all of 1861 and most of 1862 in argument with the Board about drawings and modifications. He even expressed the opinion that, having spent considerable time on the Rock, he believed it was the wrong rock on which to build the lighthouse, and that, almost certainly, it would one day be washed away by the sea. This sparked off a three-way correspondence between the Ballast Board, The Admiralty and the Board of Trade, resulting in a very peremptory letter being sent to Grissell. This instructed him to get on with the job, as it was considered very undesirable for a contractor to raise objections in areas which were clearly beyond his province. He proceeded with all speed and the tower was completed by August, 1864. It appeared a very solid construction, made of cast-iron plates bolted together and was 102 feet high from ground level to vane. The entrance door was 9 feet above ground level, with access by an outside, cast-iron spiral staircase.

Though Grissell had completed the tower in 1864, the lantern and lighting apparatus gave some trouble and the light was not exhibited until June, 1866. The tower weathered those two Winters very well, except for three broken plate glass windows. These were smashed by high seas, because the storm shutters had, incredibly, been placed inside the tower, instead of outside.

After all the arguments, all the delays, all the prevarication, there was a lovely, final irony in the final amount paid to Mr Henry Grissell for building the lighthouse on Calf Rock. Having added expenses, the amount was £30,463.16s.9d, almost twice the original quote.

The new light functioned well for over two and a half years, the tower withstanding some bad Winter gales and fierce Atlantic seas. Then, on the night of 30th January, 1869, a storm of great ferocity hit that coast. The Calf had eight feet of the tower's balcony and rail washed away, and the shed, used as a stores, destroyed. The Irish Lights Engineer-in-Chief, J.S. Sloane, went down immediately to inspect the damage, but found he could not get out to the Rock, as the seas were still running high, whipped by gale force winds. While waiting on the mainland for the storm to abate, it was his sad duty to have to write an on-the-spot report to the Commissioners, detailing an appalling tragedy. On Friday, 12th February, at the height of the storm, the Assistant Keeper, Richard Howard, on shore leave, saw what he took to be distress flags flying from The Calf. Worried for the safety of the men on duty out there, he quickly got together six local boatmen and they rowed him, through mountainous seas to the lighthouse. Howard had misread the flag signal and, to his surprise, the light keepers on The Calf were all safe. Turning the boat to return, it was caught broadside by an enormous wave and capsized. The seven men were drowned.

On receiving Sloane's report the Commissioners instructed him to distribute £28 among the families of the drowned men, seven widows and twenty-two children, as an interim relief for the bereaved, pending the Board of Trade decision regarding pensions. However, that body decided that it had no power, under the Merchant Shipping Act to grant pensions, but, in the circumstances, gratuities should be paid. The following once-off payments were made: £30 to the wife of the Assistant Keeper, £25 each to the widows of the six boatmen, £5 to each child and £5 each to the widowed mothers of two of the boatmen. Even in relative terms these sums were paltry and totally inadequate for the loss of breadwinners, but such was the near-feudal system obtaining at the time that the families, though aggrieved at such treatment, were powerless to even attempt to achieve any kind of equitable settlement.

So bad was the damage to the tower that James Douglass of Trinity House was requested to vist The Calf and make his recommendations. This he did in May and a major strengthening job was started immediately, to include the replacement of the balcony. The work was contracted to Oxmantown Foundry, Dublin and took two years to complete. The light functioned efficiently for several years after that and the tower withstood the buffetting of sea and wind. Then, on 27th November, 1881, a particularly violent storm destroyed the lighthouse, beyond repair. The cast-iron tower was severed, just above the strengthening casing, by a huge wave. Fortunately, the keepers and two workmen were in the bottom part of the building when this wave struck. The Royal Navy ship H.M.S. *Salamis* was in the area at the time, and her Commander reported that they had seen, through the sheets of scudding rain and spume, five men on the Rock. The men were waving frantically and had written in red on the one remaining white band of the sheared-off tower — "NO ONE HURT WANT TO LEAVE THE ROCK". Henry Grissell's warning, nearly twenty years before, that the tower was being built on the wrong rock, and would be washed away by the sea, had come true.

So bad was the weather that no boat could even approach The Calf for two weeks after that sighting of the men by H.M.S. *Salamis*. Eventually they were rescued by John O'Shea, a boat attendant under contract to Irish Lights, helped by H.M.S. *Sea Horse*. Six men were taken off, two keepers, a helper, and two masons and a labourer. To help them recover from their traumatic experience the keepers and their helper were granted three weeks paid leave. There is no record of how the others fared. The Commander of the H.M.S. *Sea Horse* spoke so highly of the bravery of John O'Shea and his boatmen in effecting the rescue, that the Board of Trade paid Mr. O'Shea a gratuity of £25 and £5 to each of the others. Relatively, they fared better than did the dependents of the unfortunate boatmen who had drowned 12 years before.

After the destruction of the tower on The Calf there was never any question of where the light should now be placed; on Bull Rock, where its elevation would protect it, to a great degree, from the sea, and yet not have it obscured in fog. Meantime a temporary light was erected on the Western extremity of Dursey Island, using an old lightship lantern, taken out of moth-balls at Kingstown stores. It is ironic that the strengthening carried out to the Calf Rock tower in 1872 was, ultimately, the cause of its breaking in two. This changing of the wall thickness was a major blunder in structural engineering, especially at a time when some of the best engineering talents of the century had accumulated so much experience — the Stevensons, Rennie, Telford and Brunel.

The decision was made and work commenced immediately on Bull Rock. With the elevation of the Rock and the difficulty of landing building materials, progress was slow. But, eventually, at the end of 1888, the tower, keepers' dwellings and an oil-gas works were completed, and a fog signal in place. The light was first exhibited on 1st January, 1889, and the temporary light on Dursey Island discontinued. The station functioned extremely well, and the first major alteration was not made until April 1902, when the explosive fog-signal was replaced by a siren with three trumpets, operated by air compressors. A further alteration in 1910 saw the conversion from gas to vapourised paraffin. The candle-power was greatly increased while continuing to use the same optic.

The relatively flat top on The Bull made it a good spot for a helicopter landing pad and this was constructed and reliefs have been made by helicopter since 1969. The candle-power of the light was further increased by changing to electricity in August, 1974. Bull Rock went automatic in 1991 and has been unmanned since.

The following is the 1993 Census of Birds on the Rock. Fulmar - 34 pairs, Kittiwake - 350 pairs, Herring Gull - 4 pairs, Great Black-backed Gull - 2 pairs, Razorbill - 50 individuals at nest sites, Guillemot - 423 individuals at nest sites. The latest on the Storm Petrel is that from the 1970 Census - 1000 pairs. In the 1970 Census 5 pairs of Lesser Black-backed Gulls and c. 200 individual Puffins were recorded, but none were seen during the 1993 count.

Skellig Michael

George Bernard Shaw visited Skellig Michael in 1910; being landed on the Rock on 17th September by row boat. It was a calm, clear day and Shaw was immensely impressed at the boatmens' skill, by the two towering rocks and also by the keeper he met there. The keeper asked only for newspapers and literature to be sent out to him; this, Shaw thought, spoke eloquently of the man's character.

Shaw wrote of that visit: " .... *but for the magic that takes you out, far out of this time and this world, there is Skellig Michael, ten miles off the Kerry coast, shooting straight up, seven hundred feet sheer out of the Atlantic. Whoever has not stood in the graveyard on the summit of that cliff, among the beehive dwellings and their beehive oratory, does not know Ireland through and through.*"

Thousands visit Skellig Michael every year. But, for most people on the Ring of Kerry run, the Greater Skellig — Skellig Michael and the Lesser Skellig, are usually viewed from some vantage point on the mainland; a crossing ruled out by the vagaries of the weather for some, and fear of water for others. Looking out into the Atlantic, there seems to be a perpetual suggestion of fog on the sea, as if the accumulated spume and spray of centuries has left a residue, a pale patina of blue-grey mist hovering just above the restless, heaving waters. And, rising out of this magic mist are the two great rocks — the Skelligs — submerged mountain peaks from another age; great gothic cathedrals carved by nature out of slate and old, red sandstone.

There is no permanent human presence on Skellig Michael now. Since 1987, when the lighthouse on the Rock was automated, the keepers have gone; so ending 160 years of permanent residence. Long before that, from the sixth to the sixteenth century, Skellig Michael was the home of a large monastic community, founded by Saint Finian. The beehive dwellings, remaining from that time, are still in a remarkable state of preservation. Walking on this, now deserted, Rock, the ancient, abraded stones seem to possess a tongue of their own that speaks across the centuries. They seem to carry a special 'charge', a dynamic that creates a very special synergy. I talked with several lighthouse keepers who had served on Skellig Michael, and several of them testified to this extra-ordinary 'climate', this spirit that pervades the place. One, in particular, told me that his two years of duty on the Skellig had changed his whole life. "I'm not a religious man," he said, "but something happened to me there. It happened slowly. It's very hard to describe, really. Just this very strong feeling that I was in touch with something, something very old, something good. And it changed me. Changed my outlook, my attitude. Those few years on Skellig certainly made me a better person."

And, outsiders, like George Bernard Shaw, just visiting the Rock, have been greatly effected too. Dom John Main OSB, the Benedictine monk, and founder of a worldwide Mantric Meditation movement, visited Skellig Michael in 1932. He was then only six years old, holidaying from London and staying with his cousins at Main's Hotel in Ballinskelligs, on the mainland. The memory of that experience stayed with him all his life. It was, he said, in large part, responsible for his becoming a monk many years later. And another famous Benedictine, Dom Bede Griffiths, visited the Rock in the early 1930's, and was also greatly moved by the experience.

There is no evidence that the early monks who settled there, at any time lit beacons to guide passing ships; as Dubhan had done at Hook Head. This may have been because the threat to ships was not quite as great here as on the Wexford coast. But, it was great enough for the Grand Jury of the County of Kerry, about 1796, to request the Government for a lighthouse on Bray Head, Valentia. This was granted, but, as on so many other occasions, nothing was actually done. Over twenty years later, after the Ballast Board had been given responsibility for lighthouses, the Knight of Kerry, Maurice Fitzgerald, reminded the authorities of this. He also cited two recent wrecks, one in Dingle Bay, the other in Ballinskelligs Bay; both due to the absence of any light between Cape Clear Island and Loophead. Eighteen months later, Inspector George Halpin Snr., having made a tour of that coast, made his recommendations to the Board. Great Skelligs Rock was his choice for a lighthouse, not Bray Head. And, he saw a need for two lights, one at a much higher elevation than the other. Trinity House, at first, queried the decision, largely because of the size of the Rock and the difficulty of building there. However, in November 1820, sanction was given for the building of both lighthouses.

There then followed a year of protracted negotiation with the owners of the Rock, the Butler family of Waterville, Co Kerry. The Ballast Board wanted to lease, in perpetuity; the Butlers preferred to have an annual rent of thirty pounds. This rent was not just a notional figure, they explained, it was based on the 'rent' they had got heretofore for Skellig Michael - 16 to 18 stone of puffin feathers — which enabled them to rear 100 sheep in Summer and 50 in Winter. Eventually the dispute was settled after an 'Inquisition', held in Tralee. A value of £780 was placed on the Rock, and that amount was paid to the Butlers in November 1821.

George Halpin designed the buildings and the roadways. The landing places, built centuries before by the monks, needed only some modification. It was, wisely, decided to use as little imported stone as possible; only granite for the lantern 'blocking', tower floors and stairways, window sills and some wall coping stones. The towers and keepers' dwellings were built of rubble masonry, with slate cladding on the outside walls. Extensive rock-blasting was necessary to clear a way for road-making and to procure slate for the cladding. This, unfortunately, greatly eroded, beyond repair, a large part of the lower part of the old path and steps leading up to the Eastern end of the beehive settlement. Rock blasting operations are always dangerous; particularly so in the confined space of such a Rock, and on such precipitous cliffs. On 16th November, 1825, one of the workmen, Peter Cane, was killed during a 'blast'. His wife was awarded a pension of £6 per annum, with an additional £3 per annum for "each child by her husband, under the age of sixteen years." There was a less serious accident during the building of the towers, when a sloop, the *John Francis,* went on fire off Port Magee. She was being used to carry building materials to the Rock, and her owner, a Mr Hill, claimed compensation from the Board. His claim was unsuccessful.

Because of the necessarily slow pace of the blasting, work on the road-making and construction of the towers and dwellings fell behind schedule. By January 1826, the lower tower was at last ready to have the lantern installed, but the upper tower had not even been commenced. George Halpin was determined to have both lights exhibited before another Winter set in, but realised that everything now depended on good weather during Spring, Summer and Autumn of 1826. For once, the weather was consistently good and the second tower was ready to take the lantern before the onset of the Winter gales and fogs. Both the upper and lower lights were first exhibited on 4th December, 1826; though finishing work on the upper tower continued for almost a year after that.

The lights were fixed, first order catoptric, using Argand oil lamps and parabolic reflectors. The upper light was 372 feet above high water and was visible at a distance of 25 miles, in clear weather; the lower light was 175 feet above high water and was visible at 18 miles. The two towers were the same height, approximately 48 feet, and each was painted white. Sperm oil continued to be used in the lamps until the late 1840's, when it was replaced by rape seed oil, which proved much more efficient and economical.

When one considers the hazards of building lighthouses on wave-washed rocks and reefs, and exposed, precipitous cliffs, the incidence of serious accident, or fatality, has been relatively small.

And, there has been a similarly small incidence of any kind of personal vendetta, or even animosity, between lighthouse keepers. This, despite the fact that they live together, in the confined space of a lighthouse, for several weeks on end; a situation where all the normal little quirks, foibles and idiosyncrasies could be, quite easily, magnified, and tempers consequently frayed and exacerbated. But, miraculously, for the most part, there has been very little trouble; even in the 1850's, when several families lived in a very limited space, like Skellig Michael, rearing young children, and still managing to maintain good relationships with each other. One of the few exceptions was an incident which occurred on Skellig Michael in April 1865, when the Board received an extraordinary complaint from the Principal Keeper of the upper station. He claimed that he had been assaulted and badly beaten-up by one of his colleagues, the Principal Keeper of the lower station. The matter was thoroughly investigated and the keeper from the lower station was discovered to have a drink problem. He was duly dismissed from the Service.

In 1880, the Commissioners of Public Works had become aware of the fact that the beehive dwellings and the remains of the oratory on Skellig Michael needed some kind of "caretaking". They looked around for the most efficient and economical way to do this and decided to appoint certain, more mature, keepers as custodians, or caretakers. This worked extremely well for nearly ten years, until a "man who invented sin" situation arose out of the un-Christian and discriminatory action of a local Catholic priest. Toward the end of 1889, the Parish Priest of Cahirciveen wrote to the Board demanding that, in the best interests of the Roman Catholic Church, the keepers selected for these "caretaking" duties should be "of the Faith", that is Roman Catholics. He requested the Board that all Protestant keepers should be replaced in doing this work. The Board, without prevarication, informed the Reverend gentleman that they could not accede to his request, but assured him that the monuments were in no danger whatever, and that every care would be taken of them.

In times when medicine was still relatively primitive, and health services practically non-existent, families living in such isolated places were very much at risk. Cut off as they were from the mainland, even the minimal medical services then in place, were not available to them, especially during prolonged spells of bad weather, when a boat could not approach the Rock. Minor illnesses and infections left, perforce, untreated, could easily become aggravated and quickly become chronic; especially with children.

121

In March 1869, the Principal Keeper of the lower light on Skellig, William Callaghan, had a double tragedy befall him. Two of his children died, within a few months of each other, and another lay ill. He requested that the Board transfer him to another station, on the mainland, explaining that he had just buried two of his children on the Rock, and was fearful for the safety of the third. The minutes of the next Board meeting, on 3rd April 1869, merely record that his request was noted by the Inspector. He was not, however immediately transferred. There is a small grave in the medieval chapel on Skellig Michael, reminding us of these unfortunate deaths; Patrick, aged 2 years, who died in December 1868, and William, aged 4 years, who died in March 1869.

On 1st May, 1870, a light was established on Inishtearaght, the most Westerly of the Blasket Islands, 22 miles due North of Skelligs. The establishment of this light was to have immediate, and long-term, effects on the little community on Skellig Michael. The upper light on Skellig was discontinued, that same day, reducing the work-force of keepers on the Rock by half. Over twenty-five years later, after many years of requests, and demands, the keepers on Inishtearaght succeeded in convincing the Board that both stations — Skellig and Inishtearaght — should be made 'relieving'. A terrace of eight well-designed, two-storey houses was built behind Knightstown, on Valentia Island, and toward the end of 1900 the families of the keepers on both rock stations "went ashore" to a new, more civilised way of life; a way of life where they could enjoy the improving social and medical benefits of the time, where the children could have a proper education, and where all could grow in a larger, caring community, far from the stultifying isolation of Skellig and 'Tearaght.

In 1904 there was a proposal by the Engineer-in-Chief, C.W. Scott, to build a new, more powerful light on a projecting spur of rock, just below and to the West of the disused upper lighthouse. However, after two years of surveying, reports and general prevarication, it was decided to improve the light in the lower tower and build an explosive fog signal on the Western spur. On 22nd December, 1909, the new light was established; a flashing 3rd order light, with a character of 3 quick flashes every 10 seconds. The fog signal took longer to establish; five years to be exact. Indeed it seemed to be jinxed from the start, for, having been established on 13th June 1914, it malfunctioned almost immediately and had to be temporarily discontinued just a month later. It was re-established on 9th December, 1914, and would appear to have functioned reasonably efficiently for the next five years.

Then, surprisingly, the machinery was removed and the signal operated manually until 1940, when after the outbreak of World War Two, it was again discontinued, until 1948. It was eventually silenced, for the last time, by two severe rock falls in 1953, and as there were no requests forthcoming from mariners over the next few years, for its replacement, it was discontinued permanently in 1960.

For centuries, lighthouse keepers all over the world, have, in addition to 'keeping the light', doubled as coastguards, lifeguards and paramedics. In the tradition of the lighthouse keeper, William Darling, and his daughter Grace, who in 1795, rescued nine people from Big Harker Rock, after their ship had foundered in a storm, keepers have been vigilant and brave beyond the call of duty. In November 1916, three keepers from Skellig Michael rescued two boatloads of survivors from the ss *Marina*. They were awarded £1 each from the Board of Trade and one guinea each from the owners of the *Marina*. In another incident, during the Second World War (1939-1945), an aircraft crashed in flames into the sea off the North side of the Rock. Keepers joined in a long search for survivors, but found neither survivors nor wreckage.

Two keepers have lost their lives on Skellig Michael. The first was the unfortunate Michael Wisheart, who was transferred to Skellig in 1821, from Tuskar Rock, where he had been Principal Keeper. He had been demoted to Assistant on Skellig after his involvement in smuggling brandy and other contraband. After eight years service on Skellig, he fell to his death, while cutting grass for his cow near the cliff's edge. Over a century later, 22nd August, 1956, Seamus Rohu was reported missing on the Rock. An extensive search of the Rock and the surrounding sea by his fellow-keepers, the Valentia lifeboat and the Irish Lights steamer *Valonia*, proved fruitless. His body was never recovered.

Before the radio telephone was installed, keepers on Skellig had, for many years, used their own unique form of semaphore signalling; deploying a pair of long-handled bats. They signalled to the Bull Rock, 16 miles away, the signaller positioning himself in front of a large white-washed vertical rock. The keeper on duty at Bull Rock read the message through a telescope and then semaphored it to shore via Dursey Island.

After the 1962 Tour of Inspection the Committee recommended the modernisation of the lower lighthouse. The old 1826 tower was demolished, and a new reinforced concrete tower built on the same spot. The dwellings were completely re-designed; the whole operation taking two years to complete, at a cost of £49,000. The Engineer-in-Chief A.D.H. Martin was responsible for the design of the new tower and engine room and the modernisation of the dwellings. A further phase in the modernisation was the building of a reinforced concrete landing pad to accommodate the helicopter which came into service in November 1969. Since then the fortnightly reliefs have been effected from Castletownbere.

To make it effective in all weathers, the lower lighthouse was built at a height of only 175 feet above sea level. This makes it very vulnerable, especially when the wind is in the South and huge seas run directly at that side of the Rock. On 27th December, 1955, during a Southerly storm, one gigantic wave ran so high it flooded the lantern and extinguished the light. A keeper, attempting to mount the stairs in the tower, was pushed back by the downward rush of water, but, other than shock and superficial bruising, he was unhurt. The light was out for 24 hours, while the keepers carried out running repairs. In 1950, before the modernisation, certain facilities on Skellig were still somewhat primitive, like the earth-closet in a small building on the South side of the tower. This closet had become choked and Brendan McMahon, Acting Principal Keeper, decided to clear it, quickly and effectively. Not for him slopping about with a shovel and bucket. He placed a few fog signal charges in the choked drain and detonated them, sending part of the slated roof of the closet cascading into Seal Cove, 170 feet below. So, washing the bespattered walls clean, and finding enough spare slates to repair the roof before the Principal Keeper returned from shore leave, took more time than if Brendan had gone about the task in a more orthodox way.

For almost two hundred years, until the early 1950's, the scurrilous 'Skellig List' was published annually, on Shrove Tuesday, at the beginning of Lent. This was the publishing, in the form of satirical verses, of the names of eligible bachelors and spinsters, paired for an imaginary wedding on Skellig Michael, on Shrove Tuesday night. Weddings were not permitted during Lent, but the monks on Skellig observed a later date for Easter than Christian communities on the mainland. It all started with the reluctance of England and Ireland to adopt the Gregorian calendar in the 16th century, and there resulted a two hundred year gap in which there was confusion as to when Lent began. When, eventually, mainland communities did come into line with Roman practice, in 1782, the off-shore communities, such as Skellig Michael, often held out, observing the old date for Easter. So, from that date on, the 'Lists' began to appear, lampooning in the most savage and derogatory way the 'paired' couples; giving endless fun to some, and great offence to others. The practice was so popular in the early 19th century that professional printers were employed to produce broadsheets and these became the basis for a boisterous carnival on Shrove Tuesday night. So much offence was given, to so many innocent parties, that Church and State combined to stop the practice. The 'List' compiled in Loher, near Waterville, in 1952, was, as far as can be ascertained, the last.

The white water around the base of the cliffs of Skellig Michael is a favourite playground for grey seals. Other sea mammals frequently seen in the waters round the Rock include Summer schools of white-beaked dolphins, and groups of porpoises. Less frequent visitors are white-sided, common, and bottle-nosed dolphins. Small herds of killer whales and Risso's dolphins also hunt the rough seas off the Skellig for grey seals, porpoises and squid, with the minke whale and 60-foot fin whale also making an occasional appearance.

Large numbers of rabbits, many of them black, swarm over the Rock. The result of inbreeding and little or no predation, all effort to cull them has proved useless. Over the years keepers have tried many methods, but to no avail. At one time it was considered introducing myxomatosis, but this was quickly abandoned, and ferrets were brought onto the Rock instead. But, the ferrets simply disappeared and the rabbit population continued to increase. Goats, and the occasional cow, have also been kept on Skellig Michael over the years.

Both Skellig Michael and Little Skellig are renowned for their sea-bird colonies. The Little Skellig has such a huge colony of gannets, over 20,000 pairs breeding, that there is, quite literally, little space left for other species. There is just a small colony of fulmars, puffins and razorbills breeding there, and spread along the cliff ledges, about 1,000 pairs of kittiwakes and 500 guillemots. Little Skellig is reckoned to have the second largest colony of gannets in the world. Skellig Michael has very large colonies of storm petrels, Manx shearwaters and puffins, with smaller colonies of kittiwakes, fulmars and razorbills. Oddly, few gulls nest on the Rock; they feed on the garbage from the lighthouse and prey on some of the other, smaller, sea-birds, also raiding their nests for eggs in breeding season.

The following is the 1993 Census of birds on Skellig Michael. Fulmar - 821 pairs, Shag - 1 pair, Kittiwake - 1085 pairs, Herring Gull - 7 pairs, Great Black-backed Gull - 20+ pairs, Razorbill - 235 individuals, Guillemot - 1038 individuals. The latest figures on Manx Shearwaters - c. 5000 pairs, and Storm petrels - c. 10000 pairs, are from the 1973 Census. The Puffin count - 3055 individuals, is from the 1991 Census.

Apart from rock pipits, a pair of peregrines, a pair of choughs and some wheatears, on Skellig Michael, there are few land-birds resident on the Skelligs Rocks. However, in May-June and again in August-October, there are large migrations of land-birds off the Kerry coast — waders, corvids, warblers, flycatchers and redstarts. Many of these spend short periods resting and sheltering around the monastery and lighthouse. And there are regular Winter visitors — thrushes, finches and buntings; so, there is never a time, even in mid-Winter, when Skellig Michael is without visiting land-birds. Indeed, these islands are not only important breeding grounds, they also serve as staging posts for migrants right through the year.

Like most outlying islands, exposed to searing wind and incessant sea-spray, there is a limited flora on Skellig Michael. The 38 species recorded tend to be types that are hardy enough to withstand the buffetting to which they are constantly exposed; varieties that have adapted to growing in these conditions. And they are helped to rapid growth by the concentration of nutrients — nitrogen and phosphorus — deposited by the large colonies of sea-birds. A huge area of the Rock is overlaid with tussocks of sea pink, but, on the Southern slopes, these tussocks are now dead and overgrown with a healthy sward of rock sea spurrey. This seems to thrive around the countless puffin burrows. In other places sea campion dominates. Close to the small gull colonies, near the sea, scentless mayweed and common sorrel grow in healthy profusion. And, on the fulmars' nesting ground, is a dense growth of common orache and common scurvy grass. Scarlet pimpernel, hyper-sensitive to humidity, wind and sea-spray, grows in the shelter of the old monastery walls, a vivid carpet interwoven with highlights of English stonecrop and common pearlwort.

The light on Skellig Michael, manned continuously for over 160 years, became unwatched automatic on 22nd April 1987. The last lighthouse keepers departed the Rock, leaving the beehive dwellings and monastic ruins to the restive bird colonies and the swarming rabbits.

Valentia Island

Valentia Island lies close to the tip of the Iveragh Peninsula; so close, in fact, that it was joined by bridge to the mainland, at Portmagee, in 1970. The island, about six miles by three, is home to the most Westerly settled community in Europe; a community that has evolved, over a century and a half, from the coming together of people from many different parts of Ireland and England, and sometimes Spain. Indeed the Spanish influence started as far back as the 16th century, when "skins, tallows and beeves" were regularly exported from the island to various Spanish ports. The main imports would appear to have been wine, and salt from Andalusia. The Spanish ships would anchor in the narrow channel between Portmagee and the island, where the bridge is now built, and auction their wine; the Revenue Officers, who, obviously, did not go thirsty, keeping a discreet distance until the local gentry had collected their purchases. There was also a local fishing fleet using the harbour.

In 1828, the Knight of Kerry, Maurice Fitzgerald, owner of most of the island land, petitioned the Ballast Board for a "harbour light to guide vessels from the sea, and lead them through the Northern entrance past Harbour Rock." It was not until 1837 that Inspector Halpin visited the island and recommended that a light be placed on Cromwell Point. Work began on the site that same year, using the walls of an old fort and making as few alterations as possible. The light was exhibited on 1st February, 1841, a year before the building work was complete.

In 1865 the first Transatlantic Telegraph Cable was laid, linking Valentia with Heart's Content, in Newfoundland; the shortest distance across the Atlantic. In the beginning most of the staff were English, many of them having been trained by the Post Office as telegraph clerks. They integrated very well with the local community, marrying and settling on the island.

In January, 1891, two unlighted beacons were established above Glanleam, to guide vessels, during daylight hours, past the dangerous Harbour Rock, at the Northern entrance to Valentia Harbour. These beacons were lighted on 1st May, 1913, and it was part of the duties of the keeper on shore, from either Skelligs or Inishtearaght, to clean and charge the generator, periodically. The front light was converted to electric in 1967 and the rere light discontinued at the same time. This was re-established on March 9th, 1977.

At the turn of the century, when lightkeepers families were withdrawn from desolate stations like Skellig and Inishtearaght, they were settled in houses specially built for them, by Irish Lights, at Knightstown, Valentia. Many lighthouse keepers still in the service, were born on Valentia Island, their fathers, and very often their grandfathers having been in the Service before them. In the early days of the relieving stations, the wives of the keepers had very lonely lives indeed; their husbands being away from home for six weeks out of every eight, and more if the weather was bad. The little community of lighthouse keepers and their families were very much Irish Lights people, Irish Lights maintained the excellent houses in fine style, both inside and outside, and expected the residents to play their part in keeping everything "shipshape and proper". There were regular inspections of the dwellings; the Inspector quite likely to run his finger along a window ledge or the top of a cupboard or door, checking for dust. There was a flag-pole in the compound contiguous to the houses and, Navy fashion, a flag flew every day and was lowered at sunset.

But whatever the small drawback of such minimal regimentation, it was worth it all, for the wives and children of the keepers, to be settled in comfortable houses, to be part of a caring community, to be close to schools, churches, shops and medical services. After the long years spent, for many of them, in the isolation of remote rock stations, with their relatively primitive accommodation and amenities, it was joy to have come, at last, back to normal civilisation.

Inishtearaght

The lovely fjord-like inlets of the South-West coast of Ireland, Bantry Bay, Kenmare River and Dingle Bay, all remind us of a time when, aeons ago, these bays were filled with a soft and soluble soil, eroded by the ceaseless movement of the sea, until only the rock remained. And, beyond the rocky promontory of Slea Head, for almost ten miles out to sea, some of the rock still remains, in the form of islands — the Blaskets, Inishvickallane, Inishtearaght and, beyond them the Foze Rocks. These rocks are the outermost of all these large and small islands; the most Westerly land in Europe. The lighthouse on Inishtearaght, built 1865-1869, could have been built on the Great Foze Rock, had it not been for the persistent opposition of the Ballast Board of Dublin to Trinity House. In March 1846, Captain Wolf, of HM Coastguard had surveyed the South, South-West and West coasts of Ireland and had recommended that lights be placed at certain places, among them the Great Foze Rock. There was very little reaction of any kind to this until, in 1849, the Cork Harbour Commissioners began to pressure the Ballast Board on the matter. At that time Inspector Halpin agreed that lights should be placed at the stations recommended by Captain Wolf, but, consistent with policy, nothing further was done, until 1857. In that year The Board of Trade, having requested the information in 1853, received a "statement of contemplated works". They duly questioned some of the locations, among them the Great Foze Rock and the query was referred to the Inspection Committee. The Committee considered that Foze would present too great a difficulty in the building, and also in the maintainance, as the Rock was low lying and would suffer a lot from the huge Atlantic seas. They recommended Inishtearaght as a much better location for the new lighthouse. Trinity House was also informed of this latest recommendation, but they continued to prefer the Foze Rock location.

After much three-way discussion, and correspondence, between the Ballast Board, the Board of Trade and Trinity House, the Foze Rock was again inspected by all three parties. Trinity House was adamant that Foze was the better location; they had, they pointed out built lighthouses on equally exposed and wave-washed rocks. The Ballast Board was equally adamant that Inishtearaght was the correct site. In the end the Board of Trade made the decision that the new light should be on Inishtearaght, and in September 1863, directed the Ballast Board to proceed with the construction. However, another year was to pass before legal possession was obtained; the island belonging to the Earl of Cork and a Miss Hussey.

Eventually, work started on the preparation of the site in late 1864. The rock was so uneven that a large quantity had to be removed to make a platform for the lighthouse and keepers' dwellings. This necessitated so much blasting that the Officer Commanding the Royal Engineers, General Sir John Burgoyne, offered the assistance of his Sappers in the operation. This was gratefully declined by the Board's Inspector, Captain Roberts, due to lack of accommodation on the rock for so many men. In January 1865, the ex-Trinity House steam tug, *Bishop*, was repaired and deployed to ferry men, materials and provisions from Dingle to Inishtearaght.

Work progressed slowly, because of the weather and the fact that the rock-blasting was so difficult. During the Winter months it was found to be more economical to lay-off the workmen, suspending all work until Spring. Economising was very essential, as expenditure on clearing rock had gone way over estimates. Then, in 1866, the men threatened to strike, in support of their demand for an increase in wages. Masons and stonecutters wanted 4d per day added to their 5s per day and plasterers 6d to their 3s 6d. The Board agreed with alacrity to this, presumably having had too many delays already, for whatever reason, to risk another by having a strike.

By 1869 the work had advanced to the point where the lantern and apparatus could be installed. This was the latest state-of-the-art equipment. The first order holophotal light, showing a flash every one and a half minutes, had just been exhibited at the Paris Exhibition. The lighting of Inishtearaght was planned to coincide with the discontinuance of the Upper light on Skellig Michael, on 4th May, 1870, but the light was lit three days earlier on 1st May. Thirteen years later this optic was replaced by a first order double-flashing light, manufactured by Edmundsons of Dublin, to improve the strength of the beam.

Unloading supplies at Rock Station — pre-helicopter

From the start, the familes of keepers had lived on the Rock. The new dwellings were comfortable, but the many ramifications of living in such isolation must have been heartbreaking. Especially for young mothers trying to rear children. On a Rock where mobility, in terms of access to the mainland, was totally dependent on the vagaries of the weather, there must have been many practical problems. Cut off, as they often were, for several weeks on end, illness, pregnancy, schooling, proper fresh food, must all have been a worry. By 1896, the keepers on Inishtearaght requested Irish Lights to make the station relieving, with accommodation for their families on the mainland. This request was granted in 1896, and the keepers families from both Inishtearaght and Skellig Michael were lodged at the Commissioners' expense, on the mainland at Valentia. Towards the end of 1900 houses were built for them at Knightstown.

The Commissioners encouraged the keeping of goats, wherever feasible, as they were sure footed on the sheer rocks on which many of the lighthouses were built, and produced an adequate supply of fresh milk. Unfortunately the keepers were not quite as sure-footed as the goats and on 12th September, 1913, one of the Assistant keepers on Inishtearaght, fell to his death from the sheer cliff, while rounding-up goats for milking. Compensation was paid to his family, eventually, but the Commisioners re-marked, at the time, that the goats were the property of the Board and it was really part of the keeper's duty to look after them!

On the business of keeping goats on lonely, isolated Rocks such as Inishtearaght, a memo was sent from Head Office to all light-keepers, dated 25th September, 1918, and signed by the Secretary to the Commissioners of Irish Lights, one Hubert G. Cook. It was headed 'Goatkeeping at Lighthouse Stations' and read: *"In view of the difficulty experienced at many lighthouse stations in obtain-ing supplies of fresh milk for young children, the Commissioners desire to draw the attention of their Lightkeepers to the desir-ability of keeping goats wherever practicable. Lightkeepers may, in some cases, have been discouraged in the past by the poor results obtained by keeping the ordinary Irish breed of goat, whose average yield of milk is small and of comparatively short duration.*

Goats of the Anglo-Nunian and Toggcuberg breeds, and crosses of these types with Irish goats, give from two to four quarts of milk a day, and remain milking for nine or ten months in the year, while, by keeping two or more goats, it would by good management be possible to maintain a supply of milk all the year round.

Keepers should, however, note that goats of the better class are by no means as hardy as the ordinary goat, and that they require reasonable care and shelter from cold winds and rain during the Winter months especially. At very exposed stations it would pro-bably be advisable to stall feed them, and goats well-housed and adequately fed in this way will, as a rule, well repay the extra trouble entailed.

In cases where difficulty is experienced owing to the lack of a good stud goat in the vicinity of the station, Keepers should write for information to the Honorary Secretary of the Irish Goat Society, Trillick, Co. Tyrone (enclosing a 1 1/2d stamp for reply).

The society has been formed with a view to improving the breed of goats in Ireland. It has started a goat farm but the supply of good milch goats is still inadequate to meet the demand. It also endeavours to supply good stud goats to the centres in the diff- erent counties, and so to gradually improve the existing breed of goats in each district.

A leaflet issued by the Society, entitled "Hints to Goat- keepers", is forwarded herewith for the information of each lightkeeper at the station, and it may be mentioned that a weekly article on goat-keeping is contributed by the Secretary of the Irish Goat Society to the weekly Irish Times."

For some years after that exhortation keepers did have goats on various isolated rock stations. Eventually, however, the withdrawal of families to dwellings on the mainland as stations became relieving, and the advent of the fridge and deep freeze, made the goat obsolete. And, as the goats' usefulness was eroded, they were left to roam the cliffs and crags untended; some died of old age, others —t he better class we presume — from exposure. The few remaining became feral, staying away from humans, roaming the highest, most inaccessible crags; gaunt, windblown, remote silhouettes seen fleetingly against the sky. Few, if any, survive today.

Until the advent of the helicopter, and the building of a heli-pad on the Rock, Inishtearaght was one of the most difficult stations for landing. The hoist, or derrick, was invariably used, as the combination of the outward-sloping wall at the landing stage and the considerable scend, made stepping-off directly from a boat, too hazardous to even attempt. Usually one would step-off at the crest of the wave, but here, the slightest hesitation could be fatal, because the boat moves away, outward, as it falls, leaving an ever-widening gap. And there was the added distraction of all that water, incessantly cascading from the rock ledges.

The most recent Census of the bird population on Inishtearaght is that of 1988. Manx Shearwater - 800 to 1200 pairs, Storm Petrel - c. 15000 pairs, Leach's Petrel - 3 individuals, Fulmar - 225 pairs, Shag - 1 individual, Kittiwake - 516 pairs, Herring Gull - 3 pairs, Great Black-backed Gull - 2 pairs, Lesser Black-backed Gull - 35 pairs, Razorbill - 120 individuals, Guillemot - 135 individuals, Puffin - 2516 to 3365 individuals.

Little Samphire Island

About half-a-mile West of Fenit, and half-a-mile from shore, lies Little Samphire Island, strategically placed to lead vessels to the entrance to Tralee Bay, past the dangerous outer rocks. With the growth of imports and exports, and the increase in sea-traffic, in the middle of the 19th century, the influential ship owners and merchants of Tralee petitioned the Ballast Board of Dublin, for the erection of a lighthouse on the island. The Board passed the matter to their Inspector, George Halpin Snr., who promptly investigated, stating in his report that he considered one light on Little Samphire might not be sufficient to fully light the passage of ships from outside the Bay up to the canal. This canal connected the Bay with the town of Tralee. That report was written in July, 1846. The Inspector was asked to look at the situation again, and did this in September of the same year.

As a result of this second report, the Ballast Board decided it was expedient to build a single lighthouse on the island, and Trinity House approved this decision, but not until February, 1848. Then, due to terrible weather conditions, work was not started on the new lighthouse until March 1849. Having started, progress was slow and by early 1852, though the outer work on the tower had been completed the internal work had not. The Tralee Harbour and Canal Committee and Management were now pressing for a speedy completion of the work, as several ships, inward bound had complained about the absence of a light and the danger of the outer rocks. But, the light took another year to complete, and was exhibited for the first time on 1st July, 1854; a fixed light, with red and white sectors. The tower was built of a very attractive, natural bluish limestone, with a seperate dwelling house for the keeper and his family. On Little Samphire the Principal Keeper's wife acted as Female Assistant Keeper, a not too unusual arrangement in those days.

During the latter part of 1910, the Fenit Pier and Harbour Commissioners complained about the ineffectivness of the light. In an effort to remedy this the Commissioners of Irish Lights had it changed from fixed to occulting. A clockwork, hand-wound occulting machine was installed, giving a character to the light of an 11 seconds flash, 3 seconds dark, 3 seconds flash, 3 seconds dark. Not until 1931 was there another change; on this occasion the request coming from the Imperial Merchant Service Guild for a change in the sectors. A green sector was added, on 29th May, to cover Mucklaghmore Rock and other rocks to its East. Finally, in December 1954, with a view to the ultimate automation and demanning of the station, the light was converted from oil to acetylene; the character being changed from group occulting to a single flash of one second every five seconds. On 2nd January, 1956, the keepers were withdrawn from Little Samphire and it became fully automatic.

The Tralee and Fenit Harbour Commissioners, during the late 1960's, began to receive complaints from many ships' captains that the Little Samphire light was showing an appreciable drop in brightness. The Commissioners of Irish Lights were appraised of this and immediately had the mantle burners and apparatus overhauled. The light showed very little improvement, so, early in 1972, the Deputy Engineer-in-Chief went down specially to study the problem. He came to the conclusion that, with increased development in Tralee and its environs, there had been a marked increase in shore background lighting, and this, for the inward-bound mariner especially, was swamping the light from the island tower. Conversion to electricity was the answer.

Scattery Island

The light on Scattery Island has been tended by three generations of McMahons, since it was first exhibited 120 years ago. That is, until 1993, when the last McMahon retired from Irish Lights, and Gary Griffin took over as Attendant. That last McMahon was Patricia, who had been born on the island and had been Assistant Attendant to her father, Austin, all of her adult working life. Austin had been born on Scattery too, and had, in his time been Assistant Keeper to his father, also Austin. He had then succeeded his father when he retired. Scattery, which once had a community of over a hundred people, is uninhabited now. Patricia, and her brother Austin were among the last to leave in October 1978. They had just settled on the mainland when Austin, then aged 55, was tragically killed by a car, in January 1979. Since then Patricia has been Attendant to the Scattery Island light, until she retired this year.

Patricia went by boat to the island every two weeks, until her retire- ment. She remembers that, although Scattery is just an estaury island, the Shannon in one of its angry moods could cut off any travel to the mainland for two weeks sometimes. She also remem- bers the great life on the island when 120 people lived there; every family self-sufficient on its small-holding. Now, in her retirement, she still, through the habit of a lifetime, looks across the Shannon every night to make sure it's lighting. Scattery and its light have been, and always will be, her life.

Scattery light was first established on 1st December, 1872, after many years of pressure from Limerick Harbour Commissioners and the Chamber of Commerce. They had long advocated the need for a light to lead vessels to the safe anchorage of Scattery Island, and also to guide up-river, because of the Narrows between the island and Rinanna Shoal. Some difficulty arose in constructing the lighthouse. At the time there was a British War Department Battery on the island, with a large, much-used firing range. The best position for the light, if it was to be of maximum help to shipping, was on the firing range. So, an ingenious design was made; a lantern and apparatus, housed on top of an iron frame-work, which would be mobile, enabling it to be moved out of the line of fire during practice. A Keeper's dwelling was constructed just beyond the boundary of the firing range. The construction of the mobile iron 'tower' was well advanced when, on the night of 29th October, 1868, a severe gale blew it away. The tangled mess finished up against the glacis of the old fort. It was decided not to attempt to reconstruct this iron trolley and an elegant, small, stone tower was built near the Keeper's dwelling. The Keeper was withdrawn in 1933 and an Attendant took charge of the light.

Scattery is a place rich in history, tradition and ancient archaeo-logical remains. The ruins of churches, monasteries, a castle, a round tower and a cathedral are extant. The most conspicuous building for many miles is the round tower, 120 feet high, and very unusual in that its door is at ground level. The monastery was ravaged by Vikings in the 9th century, and probably occupied by them well into the 10th century. It was then recaptured by Brian Boru. There are scant remains of a castle built on the island in the 16th century. Tradition has it that newly launched boats, on their maiden voyage, cruised round Scattery, 'sunwise', as a mark of respect, and sailors going on long voyages, took pebbles from the island's shore to sea with them "to help avert danger and return safely home." Scattery is a 'magic' island, deserted now, full of ghosts and memories. The ancient stones have a language of their own, a quiet, insistent voice that is very audible if we take the trouble to listen.

Beeves' Rock

In the wide, upper reaches of the Shannon Estuary, near the entrance to the River Fergus, stands a unique lighthouse on Beeves' Rock. It guides shipping up and down the main channel, to and from the Port of Limerick, and also into the entrance of the river. Approaching it from whatever side, it has the appearance of a large, stone lightship, riding at anchor in the perpetually lively waters of the estuary, with backdrops of gentle, rolling hills and verdant pastureland.

The light was established in 1855 and has undergone many changes in design, layout and appearance over the past century. For almost forty years before that, the Rock had been marked by an unlit beacon; this having been proposed by the Limerick Chamber of Commerce. They had actually proposed a perch, but after much deliberation it was decided, on the advice of George Halpin, that a beacon which could be converted into a lighthouse, with accommodation, would be best. This first 'tower' was completed in 1816. Two years later, there was a proposal, by a Philip Doyle, to fit a gas-light to the top of this 'tower', but nothing came of this. So, not until 1846, was there any further suggestion of change. In that year Lord Mounteagle of Mount Trenchard, Foynes, began to campaign for a lighthouse on the Northern tip of Foynes Island. The Ballast Board immediately enquired of Limerick Chamber of Commerce as to where they considered the best location for a light in that vicinity. They replied that Beeves' Rock was the best position, and added that shipping would be willing to pay a farthing per ton 'light dues'. Trinity House sanctioned the building of a lighthouse proper on Beeves' Rock in 1847, and George Halpin went to work on the design.

Because the Rock was completely submerged at high tide, work progressed slowly. The contractors were James & William Burgess, also responsible for the building of Loophead and Rockabill, and they completed the contract within three years. The lantern, dome, 3rd order dioptric apparatus and general tidying-up took another four years. The end result is the unique edifice we know today, which is automatic and unmanned, and under the authority of the Limerick Harbour Commissioners.

Tarbert

Tarbert is a harbour light, the tower standing on a tidal rock off the North side of Tarbert Island in the Shannon Estuary. It is a navigational aid to vessels inward or outward-bound, helping them clear the Bowline Rock, and guiding them, when necessary, into the safe anchorage of Tarbert Roads. Over the years it has been known as Tarbert Rock, Tarbert Island, or just Tarbert. It was built in 1831-1832, at the behest of Limerick Chamber of Commerce, at a time when over 200,000 tons of shipping had used the Shannon Estuary in a three year period. In advance of the tower being built mariners agreed to pay a sum of one farthing per ton in addition to their Port dues, so imperative was it that the spot should be lit.

Inspector George Halpin designed the lighthouse, but suggested that the building should go to outside tender; the contract going to Henry Baxter. However, before the contract could be signed Baxter died and the contract then went to Robert Howard. Work commenced in early 1831 and the light was established on 31st March, 1834. The original fixed light could be seen at a distance of 12 miles. The tower was built of cut limestone and was painted white. Conspicuous for many years at a height of 74 feet, it is now dwarfed by the gigantic twin chimneys of the nearby E.S.B. generating station. The delicate cast-iron footbridge to the tower was not built at that time, but about seven years later. The builder's name is not on record. George Halpin reported, to a meeting of the Board, on 11th November, 1841: "The approach bridge has been of much service and the attendance and risk of boatage have been thereby dispensed with." A Buoy Depot was located at Tarbert in 1916, to service the large lighted buoys in the Shannon.

In January 1981 there was an agreed rationalisation of Shannon Estuary lights between the Commissioners of Irish Lights and the Limerick Harbour Commissioners. All navigational aids, East of, but not including, Scattery Island, were transferred to the Limerick Harbour Commissioners. Tarbert is one of these, but the Buoy Depot remained under Irish Lights. The Attendant at Tarbert is in the unusual position of wearing two hats, so to speak; being employed by two separate Boards of Commissioners.

Kilcredaun

In January 1819, the Limerick Chamber of Commerce applied to the Ballast Board for lights at Scattery Island and Kilcredaun Point. It was decided at that time that one lighthouse would be sufficient, and that should be at Kilcredaun, 10 miles East of Loop Head, on the Clare coast. This, it was felt, would benefit mariners most, by marking the mouth of the Shannon Estuary, and also leading vessels to safe anchorage at Carrigaholt. Kilcredaun light was established on 1st September, 1824; Scattery would have to wait nearly fifty years for its lighthouse.

The lighthouse and keeper's dwelling were built to George Halpin's design; the tower being of solid stone, painted white, with a height of 43 feet, the lantern 136 feet above high water. It was then, and still is, painted white, and connected to the keeper's house by a short corridor. Ironically, shortly after two vessels had gone aground on Beal Bar in October 1930, and there was general agreement that a second light was needed, the Inspecting Committee decided that Kicredaun should be demanned. In 1941, a new, truncated lantern, with a Chinaman's hat dome, was fitted to replace the 114 year old lantern which was in very bad condition. A new house was built for the Attendant in 1966, and in 1979, the light was converted to electricity.

Loop Head

On the Clare shore, at the mouth of the Shannon stands Loop Head lighthouse. There has been a light, of one kind or other here, at this strategic location, since the middle of the 17th century, guiding ships into the Shannon Estuary. The first lighthouse on Loop Head was built around 1670 and was similar to the cottage-type light built at Howth Head and Old Head of Kinsale, by Sir Robert Reading. These cottages accommodated the keeper and his family, albeit in somewhat cramped conditions. They usually had three rooms, with an internal stone stairway running between two of the rooms, leading to a platform on the roof. On this platform was placed the brazier, or chauffer, in which the beacon fire was lit. A small part of the remains of this old structure may be seen near the keepers' dwellings.

As with most such lights of this period, management was not good; there was very little supervision, or discipline, and, especially in remote places like Loop Head, very little attention paid to maintenance. So toward the end of the 17th century the light fell into disuse and the headland was dark for nearly twenty years. Then, in 1770 it was re-established, after repeated demands by the aldermen and merchants of Limerick. It was not replaced by a more modern structure until Thomas Rogers replaced it with a more conventional tower in 1802. This new tower was about the same height as the present tower, with four rooms and a lantern. This 12 foot diameter lantern contained 12 oil lamps. To achieve maximum power the reflected light shone through a 22" diameter convex lense of solid glass. This glass was like the "bottle glass", or "bull's eye" used in mock-Georgian houses.

As shipping increased in the Shannon, the Limerick Chamber of Commerce complained of the poor light at Loop Head, and suggested that a new tower should be built to accommodate a better lantern. This suggestion, made in 1836, was not acted upon until 1844, when George Halpin designed a tower, and the contract for its construction was given to the Limerick firm of William and James Burgess. A few years later the same firm built the Rockabill lighthouse, off Skerries. The new tower at Loop Head was completed in Spring, 1854 and the light exhibited on May 1st. It was a fixed light and functioned well for the next 15 years, when it was replaced by a more modern intermittent light. This gave a more distinctive character; twenty second light, followed by four seconds dark, and was achieved by rotating a screen around the lamp. The screen was rotated by a clockwork machine, which had to be manually 'wound-up' at regular intervals. From 1898 until 1972, an explosive fog signal was in operation.

After several modifications and improvements the light was converted to electric in 1971 and the optic is now driven by an electric motor instead of the old clockwork rotation machine, which served it so well for so long. In 1977, Loop Head's Radio Beacon was grouped with the new Radio Beacon on Slyne Head. In the 70's a watchroom was built into the roof of the keepers' dwelling. But, alas, the keepers have left Loop Head now; it was automated and demanned in 1991.

Calf Rock and Little Calf — Callwell

Part Four

The West Coast:
Black Head (Clare) to Eagle Island.

Black Head - Mutton Island - The Aran Chain - Cashla Bay - Slyne Head - Inishgort - Achillbeg - Clare Island - Black Rock (Mayo) - Blacksod - Broadhaven - Eagle Island.

"Turning, she looked out across the bay, and there, sure enough, coming regularly across the waves, first two quick strokes, and then one long, steady stroke, was the light of the Lighthouse."

Virginia Woolf: "To The Lighthouse".

Black Head (Clare)

Galway Bay is bounded to the South by the Clare coast, where The Burren thrusts its unique, carboniferous limestone head into the Atlantic. There, on Black Head, in the shadow of Slieve Elva (1,134 feet), and Gleninagh Mountain (1,045 feet), stands the squat, square lighthouse, whose beam has guided shipping in, and out of Galway Bay, since 1936. The simple, concrete tower, painted white, is 13 feet 4 inches square and 28 feet high; the focal plane of the light being 67 feet above high water. First exhibited on February 21st, 1936, Black Head light has been indispenable ever since; surviving a threat to have it discontinued, because of financial problems regarding its maintainance, in 1952.

The main reason for the light being built at Black Head was the continuous request being received by the Galway Harbour Commissioners, from mariners plying in and out of the port of Galway, and from passing ships using Galway as a harbour of refuge in bad weather. With the shelter afforded by the Aran Islands against Sou'-Westerly gales, the Bay was an ideal shelter. Among those advocating a light on Black Head were the Captains of visiting transatlantic liners, calling regularly to Galway in the 1920's and 1930's. They would anchor their mammoth vessels off Ballyvaughan, just East of Black Head, with the tender *Dún Aengus* ferrying passengers to vist Galway City and the Aran Islands. A light on Black Head became a necessity.

A formal request was made for the Black Head light, by the Galway Harbour Commissioners on 18th September, 1934. There ensued some intensive negotiations between the Galway Harbour Comm-issioners and Irish Lights, with the London Board of Trade also involved. The Galway interests were so anxious to have the light established that they offered to repay, to Irish Lights, over a short period, the cost of construction. And agreement was reached, whereby the Galway Commissioners agreed to maintain the light, and that no other charge would fall on the General Lighthouse Fund other than the cost of construction. This cost was to be repaid in three stages; five hundred pounds on deciding the project would go ahead, five hundred pounds six months later, and the balance when the light was exhibited. A most unusual arrangement, but acceptable to all parties. So, the tower was constructed by Robert MacDonald, of Galway, and the light, after some difficulty with the fitting of the lantern, was exhibited in 1936. It functioned satisfactorily over the next few years, but, with the outbreak of the Second World War in 1939, the transatlantic liners stopped calling at Galway and, even the coastal traffic declined. In the post-war years, while the coastal traffic returned, the transatlantic traffic never did, on the same scale. Reluctantly the Galway Harbour Commissioners informed Irish Lights that they were considering discontinuing the light at Black Head; it was no longer economically possible to maintain it. After establishing that there was a real need for the light, the matter was submitted to the Ministry of Transport and Civil Aviation in London, whose Advisory Committee recommended that Irish Lights should take over the light. The take-over became official on 13th April, 1955. John Casey, who had been the Attendant Keeper at Black Head since its establishment, was retained, with an increase in wages. He worked on until 1980, when, after a total of 45 years service at the station, he retired. His son, Joseph took over from him, on 1st January, 1981.

Mutton Island

Mutton Island, in Galway Bay, is situated just off Salthill, on the Northern side of the Roadstead leading into the Port of Galway. This low island has always been a source of embarrassment to ship's captains, especially when coming in on the high tide. At low tide, the shingle and the acres of seaweed-covered rocks are clearly visible; at high tide, the sea comes right up to the wall surrounding the lighthouse compound, on occasion breaching it. At low tide, winkle pickers from Salthill walk right out to the island on the natural causeway of weed-covered rocks; at high tide, inward-bound vessels, helped by a Sou'-Westerly wind, have often run too close to the North side of the channel and gone aground. Most have been refloated; unlike the Dutch coaster mv *June*, which became a write-off in 1962.

As far back as the 17th century, when pirate hoardes infested Galway Bay, there was some form of watch-tower and a crude beacon on Mutton Island; probably a coal, or peat fire lit on top of the tower, as in the old 'cottage' lighthouses. But, it was not until the beginning of the 19th century that merchants and shipowners of Galway sought a proper lighthouse on Mutton Island: and, not until 1817, was the tower built and the light established. In that same year, towers of similar design were built at Fanad Head, Donegal, and Roche's Point, Cork. Mutton Island was one of the very few lighthouses where a Keeper, Walter Walsh, was appointed shortly after the construction work began, and sixteen months before the light was exhibited. Because of the easy accessibility at low tide it was deemed desirable to have a 'watchman' on the site, and his constant presence probably had the psychological effect of speeding up the actual work. He reported, in August, 1817, just a few months before the light was first exhibited, that a certain seaweed collector was also removing stones for ballast. The Galway hookers, because of the weight of mast and sail they carried, used stones for ballast, and the stones from the island foreshore were ideal for this. Notices were quickly painted, and sent to Walter Walsh for erection, stating that anyone found removing stones would be prosecuted.

Though so close to shore, with a strong Sou'-Westerly wind blowing, it could take nearly an hour to tack out to the island. The inward journey could take as little as seven or eight minutes. Weather was a big factor in the life of a Keeper with a family, living on Mutton Island; getting them to school in Galway was a permanent problem. In 1923, the Keeper received permission to keep a small boat at the lighthouse, to take his children to school, when weather permitted. But, often, high winds and rough seas would cut them off for days. So, later that year, the Irish Lights Board granted him an education allowance to educate and board three of his children in Galway.

The light became unwatched in September 1958; the new Group flashing light replacing the Group occulting light. A sun-valve, mounted on top of the dome ventilator, controlled the light, turning it on at dusk, and off at dawn. Then, with the rapid expansion of Galway in the 1960's and '70's, with increased industrialisation, and the new suburban sprawl, the brighter background lighting along the coast tended to swamp the Mutton Island light when approaching it from seaward. The answer was to abolish the island light and improve buoyage in the immediate vicinity. Two new lighted buoys were established; one, called 'Mutton Island', South-East of the actual island, on the North side of the Roadstead; the other, called 'Tawin Shoals' on the South side of the Roadstead, North-West of the actual shoals. After 160 years of continuous service Mutton Island's light was extinguished on 13 December, 1977. The island is now in the jurisdiction of the Galway Harbour Commissioners.

The Aran Chain:
Inisheer, Straw Island, Eeragh, Cashla Bay, Inishmore

When the light on Inishmore was found to be ineffective in foggy weather, due to being positioned at too high an elevation, alternatives were looked at in an effort to find the best way to light the 'chain' of the Aran Islands. It was decided to replace it with two lights; one on Inisheer, at the Southern end of the 'chain'; the other on Eeragh, at the Northern end. These two lights were established on the same day, 1st December, 1857 and the light on Inishmore was discontinued.

Both towers, and adjacent dwellings, were built of the local hard, crystalline limestone, and were subsequently marked with distinguishing coloured bands. The fixed optic for Inisheer was supplied by Chance Bros., of Birmingham; the flashing optic for Eeragh, by Wilkins, of London. The Inisheer light was changed from fixed to occulting in January 1913. A new optic was installed on Eeragh in 1904. Both lighthouses were automated and the keepers withdrawn in 1978.

With the extinguishing of the Inisheer light, local fishermen, both from the islands and from Galway, suddenly found Killeany Bay and Kilronan unlit. A light was necessary at the entrance to Killeany Bay and they actively campaigned for a new light on Straw Island. Their campaigning was to go on for fourteen years before sanction was given by the Board of Trade, and, even then, they waited another seven years before the Straw Island light was established, in 1878.

In 1983, a Directional Light, known as Lion Point, was established at Cashla Bay, on the Connemara mainland, just under Rossaveal Hill and seaward of the entrance to Rossaveal Harbour. Cashla Bay is directly opposite the Northern end of the Aran chain, and the light was established in direct reponse to repeated requests from mainland and island fishermen; the fishing fleet in this area having increased greatly since the 70's. It was also considered a very necessary light to guide the Aran Island Ferry in and out of Rossaveal.

Slyne Head

Slyne Head lighthouse is built on one of a chain of small islands which form an archipelago, 10 miles South-West of Clifden. The station is located on an island called Oileanaimid; the largest of the islands forming the group, low lying, and composed of a metamorphic type of rock known as gneiss. It probably got its name — 'island of wood' — from the large quantities of flotsam and jetsam, mostly wood, washed up there and collected by local mainlanders in their currachs. On the nearby mainland is the spot where the aviators, Captain J. W. Alcock and Lieutenant A. Whitten-Brown, crash-landed their Vickers Vimy in a bog, near the Marconi Wireless Station, on the morning of June 15th, 1919. They had flown, in just under sixteen hours, from St. John's, Newfoundland.

In the early 19th century, with increasing trade in and out of Galway Port, the Corporation, Harbour Board, Merchants and Shipowners of that city, together with HM Coastguard, made many requests for proper lighting on the West coast; especially on the approaches to Galway Bay. The Aran Islands were lit, and Mutton Island, but Slyne Head was left in abeyance; indeed, at one time it was considered "wholly unecessary" by Trinity House. However, after years of constant badgering, by various public bodies, and the inhabitants of Roundstone and Clifden, it was agreed that George Halpin should inspect that part of the coast. His report recommended, not one, but two lights at Slyne Head, to help mariners distinguish it from Clare Island to the North and the Aran Islands to the South. Incredibly, after so much stalling, Trinity House agreed and sanctioned two towers at Slyne Head.

George Halpin designed and supervised the building of the two lighthouses, the work being done by the Ballast Board's own workmen. Two dwellings were built for each tower, together with storehouses and general outhouses. Stone from the island was used extensively in the construction, with some granite and sandstone brought over from the mainland. During the building two fatal boating accidents occurred; one early on, the other a few months before completion. In 1832, a boatman called Hallam was drowned while ferrying stores to the site; and, on 27th March, 1836, another workboat overturned and eight men were drowned. Again, even relative to that time, paltry "compensation" was paid to relatives; six pounds per annum to widows, one of whom lost a husband and a son; three pounds per annum to children under sixteen years of age; and a once-off "donation" to three sisters who were supported by one of the men.

Both towers were painted white, and, except for minor internal differences, were identical. They stood 142 yards apart and were 79 feet high, from base to vane. One light was revolving, the other fixed. They were both exhibited for the first time on 10th October, 1836, though much work remained to be done, largely to the inside of the towers. Both towers were finished off with copper domes; the work on these being done by a well-known master-coppersmith of the time, called John Smith.

The seas that wash the rocks and islands of this archipelago can be treacherous in the extreme, with huge swells and strong cross-currents. Ferrying stores and people to and from the light-houses was a perilous business. With families living on the island, and the constant traffic to and from the mainland, lives were in constant hazard. On 22nd October, 1852, one of the Keepers, who had been transferred to Kilcredaun, in Clare, went ashore to make arrangements to transport his wife and five children to their new station. When returning to the island he was drowned, together with the boat-crew of six local men. Three of the six were of the same family, named King. The boat contract remained in that family until the advent of the helicopter in 1969.

The twin lights served mariners and fishermen well for over half-a-century. Then, in 1887, Trinity House granted statutory sanction to discontinue one of Slyne Head's lights, and to introduce a red landward sector in the other. But, it was to be another eleven years before the necessary alterations and improvements were made on the island and the light extinguished. The darkened tower had its lantern, granite blocking and apparatus removed to prevent obstruction of the new light to the South. Slyne Head became a relieving station in April, 1898, when the Keepers and their families were accommodated in temporary, rented dwellings at Bunowen, pending the building of new dwellings in Clifden. The new houses were ready for occupation in 1906.

Changing from car to cart at "End of the Road"

For many years, before being automated and demanned in 1990, the relief of Keepers on Slyne Head was effected, very efficiently, by helicopter; the journey, from Clifden to the lighthouse, taking no more that six or seven minutes. At the turn of the century it was a much slower journey, and the decision as to when exactly the relief would be carried out was totally at the discretion of the boatmen, the King family. As close to the scheduled day as weather permitted, they would place a 'bat' against the wall of their cottage on the mainland. This informed the anxious Keepers on the island that the relief was 'on'. The boat contractor then went to Bunowen, three miles away, and despatched the (horse-drawn) cart contractor to pick-up the Keeper in Clifden. The cart took the Keeper and his belongings, mostly food supplies for his month on the lighthouse, back to the boatman's cottage. From here everything was tranferred to creels carried by donkeys for the rocky trek to the boat slip at Slackport. After that it was a three mile journey by currach through the minefield of little rocks and islands to the lighthouse. In 1963 the track from the boatman's cottage to the slip was surfaced by Michael Keane, one of the Irish Lights coast tradesmen, and it became known locally as "The M1". This allowed the motor-van, which had replaced the horse-drawn cart, to make a straight-through journey from Clifden to the boat slip at Slackport.

In those days, before lighthouses became relieving, several families lived, in close proximity, on small islands and rocks. Often weather-bound for several weeks, it seems extraordinary that, for the most part, they lived in great accord, and such little tension existed. They would appear to have been very philosophical about their situation, and to have done their best to live together in reasonable harmony. But, human nature being what it is, occasionally tension built up and spilled over into acrimonious feuding, sometimes with tragic results; as in two instances on Slyne Head, toward the end of the last century. In September 1859, a newly-arrived Assistant Keeper on Slyne Head was drowned. His death is referred to in the Board's minutes of that time as, simply, 'a drowning', but there were more sinister aspects to the case. The dead Keeper, John Doyle, had been sent to Slyne Head to, temporarily, stand-in for Principal Keeper Gregory, who had fallen ill. Gregory's wife, Anne, took great umbrage at this appointment, as she considered that her son, who had, albeit unofficially, been assisting his father with his duties, should have been officially deputised to look after the light during her husband's illness. Shortly after his arrival on the rock, she is alleged to have put poison in John Doyle's tea. He, feeling ill, went out of the house to get some fresh air, and, unsteady from the chronic pain caused by the action of the poison, fell into the sea and was drowned. But, while the Board, in its minutes, described the death as "drowning", the Coroner's Court Jury later returned a verdict of "death by poisoning". Anne Gregory was named as the poisoner and committed to trial. She served many months, on remand, in prison, but, as far as I can establish was never actually convicted of the alleged murder. The Ballast Board's Inspecting Committee was convinced that she had been wrongly indicted by the Coroner's Jury, and were sympathetic to the fact that she was mother of a large, mostly young, family. A land station was found for them, and they were transferred from Slyne Head.

Changing from cart to donkeys at Contractors House

The second incident on Slyne Head was in 1894 when the wives of two Keepers, Harris and Harrison, lodged a complaint against the Ballast Board, claiming that their husbands had been wrongfully dismissed from the Service. The Board had deemed them guilty of insobriety and also for leaving the station in a boat and going to the mainland. The basis of the ladies' complaint was that the two men who had filed the complaint, King (a Temporary Keeper) and Roach (a workman), were men of dubious character, who been before the bench for drunkness and for fighting. The feeling, at Board level, was, that drunkeness and rowdyism was one thing, but dereliction of duty, by going ashore, was another. While transfer, or demotion, or both, would be equitable punishment for the first offence, the second must be punished by dismissal.

During the 1939-1945 War, shipwrecked sailors, came onto the island and took a boat belonging to the contractor to get to the mainland. On another occasion, during the same War, a Liberator aircraft crashed into the Atlantic some miles from the coast. Six of the crew escaped the wreckage in an inflatable dingy and drifted onto the archipelago, near Lough Aillebrack, about four miles North-East of the lighthouse. Unfortunately one of them died in the boat; the others were taken to Clifden hospital. Another four were listed as "missing, presumed dead".

Changing from donkey to boat

As part of their 1973 Forward Policy programme, Irish Lights, over the next few years, modernised the remaining lighthouse at Slyne Head. The explosive fog signal was discontinued, and replaced by a Radio Beacon; the lighting system being converted to electric, in 1977.

Inishgort

Inishgort is a Harbour Light to guide vessels from seaward to the inner channel of Clew Bay. The tower, of coarse limestone, was designed by George Halpin and built at the behest of the Marquis of Sligo and the merchants and shipowners of Westport. The light was first exhibited in 1827, over a year before the building was completed, and is visible at 10 miles in clear weather.

Inishmore

Ironically, the first two lighthouses to be built and established in Galway Bay, on Mutton Island, off Salthill (1817), and on Inishmore, the largest of the Aran Islands (1818), are no longer lit.

Inishmore had, by far, the shorter life of the two, functioning for a mere 40 years, before being discontinued in 1857. Here again, it was a question of having built the tower too high. Inspector George Halpin and Captains Grantham and Cunningham, of Irish Lights, had, in the report following their survey in July, 1813, recommended the highest point on the island, 413 feet above high water, as being the best location for the lighthouse. This was beside the disused Admiralty Signal Tower, and the pre-Christian stone fort of Dun Eoghla.

The tower on Inishmore is a magnificent example of what can be achieved by the use of local stone and high-class workmanship. The limestone used came from a quarry at Kilronan and was cut and dressed by an islandman, Christopher York. All the finished stones were brought up to the site by York's magnificent horse, of over twenty hands, known as Stal York. The construction of the tower was by two masons from the mainland, James Lardner and Michael Bolger. But, this fine tower, proved to be too high in fog, and it did not cover the entrances to the Sounds, North and South of the island.

It is on record, that the tower was used as an observation post in both World War 1 and World War 2; by the British from 1914 to 1918, and by the Irish from 1939 to 1945.

Achillbeg and Clare Island

On 29th September, 1965, after 159 years unbroken service, the light on Clare Island was extinguished, and replaced by a new, unwatched electric light on nearby Achillbeg. Since the establishment of a lighthouse on Blackrock Island, seaward and North-West of Clare Island, 101 years before, there had been intermittent and desultory discussion as to whether the Clare Island light should be discontinued or not. It was accepted that a smaller light should relace it, somewhere in the vicinity of Achill, but agreement could never be reached as to exactly where. Eventually, Achillbeg was selected as the replacement location.

The old Clare Island lighthouse must, arguably, be situated in the most picturesque location on the whole Irish coast. Perched near the edge of a high, sheer cliff, it commands a grand-stand view of one of one of the most rugged and beautiful stretches of sea-board. In the late 16th century the island was the stronghold of the powerful O'Malley clan, wild and fearless mariners, whose piratical activities made life a misery for Spanish and English merchant ships, and greatly embarrassed the British Government. These forays were led by Grainne O'Malley, or "Granuaile" as she became known. The pirate princess eventually reconciled with Queen Elizabeth and lived out the end of her life in peace on Clare Island, where she founded a monastery and is, reputedly, buried. The present Irish Lights tender, and flagship, *Granuaile*, is called after this turbulent lady.

The lighthouse was first established on the island in 1806, built by the Marquis of Sligo. It was taken over by the Dublin Ballast Board in 1810 and was the subject of a report by their Engineer, George Halpin Snr., in 1811. He found it to have "a tower, with two apartments and a small house attached." The lighthouse functioned satisfactorily for the next two years, until a fire, on 29th September, 1813, destroyed the lantern and part of the tower. This fire was caused by the practice of throwing the snuffings of the used oil-lamp wicks into a tub, for disposal later. Some wicks, still smouldering, fell out of the tub and ignited the lantern. A temporary light was set up until a new tower and Keeper's dwelling were built; the new light being exhibited for the first time toward the end of 1818. The ruins of the old tower and the original Keeper's house are still visible on the site.

The lighthouse on Clare Island had a long, and relatively trouble-free, century and a half of service. There were occasional incidents, like the tower being struck by lightning in 1834. When this was reported to the Ballast Board they asked Trinity House how English lighthouses were protected, and got an unexpected reply. Proper lightning conductors were rarely fitted to lighthouses; the usual practice was to place a small tube of glass, closed at the upper end, on the point of the spindle of the vane on top of the lantern tower. This had been found to work as a reasonable protection, because of the non-conducting properties known to be in glass.

Black Rock, Mayo

Black Rock, a small island off the Mayo coast, with high, precipitous cliffs, almost constantly fringed with white water, presents a forbidding aspect, no matter how one approaches it. It is reputed to be the most difficult Rock on which to land; totally inaccessible at times, either by boat, or by helicopter. Three generations of lighthouse keepers will attest to this, having waited for several weeks, sometimes months, to be taken off, at the end of their stint on duty there. It is a bleak, barren, inhospitable place, wracked by prevailing Westerly winds, pounded by huge Atlantic seas. For, this rock is near the edge of the Continental Shelf, and lies directly in the path of the enormous swell that sweeps inexorably landward. There is rarely respite here from either wind or wave.

The light, in the fifty-feet high circular tower, was first exhibited on 1st June, 1864. At 282 feet above high water, it is the second highest, in elevation, of all our lighthouses; Mine Head, Dungarvan, being 3 feet higher. The tower was built of stone quarried from the rock on which it stands; the keepers' dwelling is contiguous. It is difficult to imagine now that the keepers' families actually lived on this rock for twenty-nine years, until dwellings were built at Blacksod, on the mainland, and the station made relieving, in 1893. Difficult to appreciate how, before the turn of the century, the wives and children of the keepers, lived out their lives here, in relatively primitive fashion. Children were born here, often, in bad weather, without benefit of midwife. Children were reared here; again, often without benefit of such necessities as fresh milk, or fresh vegetables. For even goats, hardy, adaptable, did not thrive here. Any attempt to grow vegetables was doomed to failure; plants blackened and blighted in infancy by the scorching wind and flying salt-spray. And there was the insurmountable problem of schooling. Yet, I have met men and women, octogenarians, nonagenarians now, who were born on Black Rock and similar rocks, and are long-since settled on the mainland. And they, invariably, have some special, indefinable quality, a kind of quiet dignity, no doubt attributable to their origins in such remote and wildly wonderful places.

The water is deep here, even close to the rock, and many ships have come in close to seek some little shelter. During the Second World War, the ss *Macville*, lying close under the rock, was attacked by a German bomber. The lighthouse lantern had panes shattered by gunfire and some damage was caused to roof tops, but the keepers were unhurt.

In the early 1970's, when Irish Lights were experimenting with nuclear powered lanterns, Black Rock was considered as the trial station. It was however decided not to use it, mainly because of its height above sea level. The modification necessary for the proposed new optic, in order to divert some of the light downward, would have reduced the candlepower of the horizontal beam too drastically. It was decided to use Rathlin O'Birne instead; its lantern being less than half the height of Black Rock above sea level. The station was automated in 1974, the keepers finally withdrawn in November of that year. An Attendant, accompanied by an assistant, makes regular monthly visits to the lighthouse. Travelling by helicopter, they usually stay overnight on the rock, to carry out a thorough check.

Blacksod

Blacksod lighthouse is picturesquely situated at the South-East corner of the Mullet Peninsula; the centre of a sort of natural amphitheatre of water and hills, low-lying to the North and East, with the sheer cliffs of Achill Island rising to the South. The building itself is unique among Irish lighthouses; a squat, two-storey, square tower, with the lantern on top, built over the centre of a single-storey building. It was built in 1865, by Bryan Carey, of local reddish-grey granite. The lantern was then fitted and the light first exhibited on 30th June, 1866. It was intended that the light at Blacksod would, in conjunction with Black Rock, lit two years before, make Blacksod Bay a safe anchorage, on a coast where safe achorages were so very necessary. How well such a navigational aid would have served the Spanish Armada Commander, Martin de Berthendona, when he steered his galleon, *La Sancta Maria Rata Encoronda*, into the Bay 273 years earlier only to run aground under Fahy Castle.

A Keeper resided at the station with his family until the light was made unwatched in 1931. After that, the Relief Keeper, ashore from his duties on Black Rock, looked after the light, until the 1st November, 1933, when Ted Sweeney was appointed Attendant at Blacksod. That was to be the beginning of a "dynasty" in the Lighthouse Service, as Ted's three sons followed him into Irish Lights. Vincent, since his father's retirement in 1981, has been Attendant at Blacksod; Jerry is Attendant on Eagle Island; and Ted Junior is an Engineer on the Irish Lights tender *Gray Seal*.

In addition to being Attendant Lighthouse Keeper Ted Sweeney was also local Postmaster. During the late 1960's the old cottage where the Post Office was located was pulled down and a new bungalow, with Post Office attached was planned. While this was being built, between 1969 and 1972, with the permission of both Irish Lights and the Department of Posts and Telegraphs, the

Blacksod Post Office was accommodated in one of the rooms under the lighthouse tower; the first and only time a Post Office formed part of a working lighthouse.

In 1944, the weather forecast that decided the British to make the D-Day landings in France, came from the Blacksod Point Meteorological Station report made by Ted Sweeney. Ted could not possibly have guessed at that time that his forecast would help make a decision that was to change the course of a World War.

Ted was in the news again in 1969, when together with his son Vincent, he appeared as a guest on the Television Show "This Is Your Life". The Show was to honour the achievement of Tom McCleane in rowing single-handed across the Atlantic. Ted and Vincent were the first people to assist McCleane when he made landfall at Blacksod Bay.

In 1967 Blacksod light was converted to electric and, in 1969 a helicopter landing pad was built in the lighthouse compound. This is now used as the base for the monthly visits of the Attendant Keepers to the automated lights at Eagle Island and Black Rock.

Broadhaven

Broadhaven light is at the Northern tip of the Mullet Peninsula; a harbour light, it guides vessels from seaward clear of a sunken rock on the Western side of Broadhaven, and into safe anchorage. Unlike its exposed and weather-beaten neighbours, Eagle Island and Black Rock, it enjoys comparative peace and quiet, out of the real swing of the sea, nestling on Gubbacashel Point.

It was first established on 1st June, 1855, a fixed third order dioptric, supplied by W. Wilkins of London, 87 feet above high water and visible for twelve miles in clear weather. The fifty foot high tower was built of grey stone and originally intended to be only an unlit beacon, that might, at some later date be converted into a lighthouse proper. However, during its building strong representations were made for a lit tower with buoys marking the channel right up to Belmullet. By the time the building was completed the Ballast Board decided, on the advice of their Inspector, George Halpin, to accede to these requests and fit up the new tower as a proper Harbour Light. It functioned, unchanged, until 1924, when the light was improved and modernised, changing from fixed to occulting. In 1931 it was converted to unwatched acetylene and, finally, in 1977, made electric.

Eagle Island

A little to the North of Black Rock, and closer to the Continental Shelf, is Eagle Island; a high, exposed rock, which originally had two lighthouses, but now has only one. This station has the reputation of suffering more storm damage than most in the 158 years of its existence. It is almost as if the elements here have conspired to let man know in what contempt they hold his puny efforts.

I once visited the island shortly after a severe Spring storm, when wind and wave had caused great damage. Windows had been shattered, ironwork twisted beyond recognition, doors and gates ripped from their hinges and flung across rocks and into the sea. And, incredibly, the three foot thick storm wall had been breached in several places by the sea; whole segments of it had been lifted by the waves and flung across the miniature golf course. This course, so lovingly constructed and cultivated by the keepers, had been ruined overnight. It was as if the elements, the demented wind and the wilful sea, were screaming "futile! futile!", in a great show of contempt for man's handiwork.

Two towers were originally built to help guide ships past all the dangers from Blacksod Bay to Broadhaven. By keeping the twin lights in line at night, or the twin towers by day, ships could steer a safe course, avoiding all hazards, including the notorious Stags Rocks. But, even in the building of the towers the weather played its destructive part. When the West tower was partly built, two courses high, it was swept away by a huge sea, together with much of the building materials stacked nearby. Eventually, though certain work was not yet completed, the two lights were exhibited for the first time on the night of 29th September, 1835. The cut stone used in the towers was all quarried on the island.

Four months after being lit, the island was hit by a particularly severe storm. On the night of 17th January, 1836, the lantern in the West tower was hit by a flying rock. This shattered one of the panes of glass and extinguished the light; but, within an hour, the intrepid and resourceful keepers had the light working again. On this occasion the dwellings were badly damaged and the families of the keepers suffered great hardship. A violent gale on the 5th and 6th of February, 1850, caused very severe damage to both lanterns, putting both lights out of commission. Seas remained so rough that the workman designated to go out and repair the damage could not make the passage until the 14th. In the interim the keepers worked in shifts to repair the lights and they were back in commission on the night of the 11th. It only remained for the workman to replace the broken glass when he arrived.

On 11th March, 1861, at mid-day, the Eastern tower was struck by a freak wave. This shattered 23 panes of glass and washed some of the lamps down the stairs. The reflectors were damaged beyond repair by the broken glass. In spite of the best efforts of the keepers to effect emergency repairs the light was not lit that night, but it was exhibited on the following night, March 12th. This was truly an incredible wave to have risen 220 feet and retained enough force to inflict such damage. So much water cascaded down inside the tower that the keepers found it impossible to open the door, and had to drill holes in it to let the water out.

But, the ultimate storm struck Eagle Island, and many other West coast stations, on the 29th December, 1894. The East tower dwellings were damaged beyond repair and the terrified women and children took refuge in the tower itself. But, their ordeal was prolonged there as the sea broke the lantern glass, put out the light and cascaded down inside the tower. Immediately the storm had abated the women and children were brought ashore and housed temporarily in Belmullet, pending the building of new mainland dwellings at Corclogh. The East tower light was discontinued on 1st November, 1895, when the new, improved dioptric 1st order light came into operation in the West tower. Eagle Island continued to be a relieving station until 1988, when it became fully automatic and was demanned.

Slyne Head - Callwell

Part Five

The North-West Coast:
Black Rock (Sligo) to Tory Island

Black Rock (Sligo) - Sligo Lights - St. John's Point (Donegal) -
Rotten Island - Rathlin O'Birne - Aranmore - Ballagh Rocks - Tory
Island.

*"...... and pausing there she looked out to meet the stroke of the
Lighthouse, the long, steady stroke, the last of the three, which was her
stroke, for watching them in this mood, always at this hour, one could
not help attaching oneself to the thing one saw; and this thing, the
long, steady stroke, was her stroke. Often she found herself sitting and
looking, with her work in her hands, until she became the thing she
looked at - that light, for example."*

Virginia Woolf: "To The Lighthouse".

Lighthouse Keepers' children, Fanad Head, 1904

Black Rock, (Sligo) and Sligo Lights

On the stretch of North-facing Mayo coast, from Broadhaven to Black Rock (Sligo), there is no lighthouse proper; just a buoyage system. There had been a beacon on Black Rock since the 18th century, strategically placed to help sea traffic using the ports of Killala and Sligo. This had been washed away during a storm in the Autumn of 1814, and despite immediate appeals from the merchants of Sligo, Killala and Ballina for its re-establishment, nothing was done until 1816. In that year some very inadequate restoration work was carried out by a local contractor. Then, in 1819 a new, more substantial unlit beacon was erected. This was built of solid limestone, by Thomas Hamm of Ballina, and was 51 feet high. It was proposed, at that time, to place a 'Metal Man' on top of this beacon, identical to that on Newtown Head, Tramore. The shipowners of Sligo, however, requested that this 'Metal Man' should be placed on Perch Rock, off Oyster Island, in Sligo Harbour, and the Black Rock Beacon converted into a lighthouse proper.

While the 'Metal Man' was erected on Perch Rock in 1821, Black Rock had to wait for its lighthouse until 1835. The old beacon tower was used as a fine, solid base for the new tower; an outside spiral staircase being built to the entrance door well above the high-water mark. The light was established on 1st June, 1835. Not until 1863 were the panniers added. The outside staircase and the panniers made Black Rock unique among our lighthouses. The panniers were added to give additional, and very necessary storage and living space in the cramped tower. Originally oil fired, the light was converted to acetylene in November 1934, at which time the station was made unwatched and had its lantern truncated, and the unique panniers removed. Both the main light and the auxiliary were converted to electric in September 1965.

Two towers were originally erected on Oyster Island, the lights being first exhibited on 1st August, 1837. Intended to form leading lights from Sligo Bay into the Channel leading to Sligo Port, they were found to be not quite accurate and were replaced by a single temporary light in February, 1891. Two years later the discontinued towers had been removed and a new tower was being constructed toward the North-West point of the island. This, eventually, became a rear leading light, with the 'Metal Man' in 1932. The 'Metal Man' had been established on Perch Rock in 1821, when it was decided to convert Black Rock Beacon to a lighthouse proper. In October 1908, an acetylene light was established beside the figure of the sailor and was converted to propane in October, 1979. The lighted beacon, on timber piles, in the sand off Lower Rosses Point, was established in October 1908. At the same time two leading lights were established on Coney Island, but these were subsequently moved to give a different lead in 1951. The rear light was discontinued in September, 1965, but the structure was left in place to give a daytime lead. The front light was discontinued in June, 1977, at which time both structures were removed. A light on Bonmore Point, established at the same time as Lower Rosses and Coney lights, was moved onto the edge of the Golf Course in August, 1951, and eventually discontinued in June, 1964.

St. John's Point & Rotten Island:
Donegal Bay

As early as 1825, the merchants, traders, and fishermen of Killybegs had looked for the establishment of a light on St. John's Point on the North shore of Donegal Bay. This harbour light was very necessary to mark that side of the Bay, to guide traffic to Killybegs Harbour, from entrance up to Rotten Island. It was later considered important to have a second light, to help passage from St. John's Point to the inner channel, and past rocks to safe anchorage in Killybegs Harbour. Mr Drury, the Inspecting Commander of the Coast Guard, recommended a light on Drumanoo Point, but George Halpin, the Ballast Board Inspector, while agreeing that a light was necessary, recommended Rotten Island instead.

The St. John's light was first exhibited on 4th November, 1831, while the buildings were still unfinished. The tower was designed by George Halpin and was built of cut granite, painted white. The light was a first order catoptric fixed, 98 feet above high water. The original lighting set lasted just over 100 years and was then replaced by an occulting light. The station was converted to unwatched in the early 1930's, and in July, 1942, the light was changed from occulting to flashing.

The Rotten Island lighthouse was also designed by George Halpin, and was also built of cut granite, painted white. The original light, first exhibited on 1st September, 1838, was a third order catoptric, fixed white. During the building of the tower, three workmen were drowned, on 15th September, 1836, while returning from work on the rock. The light was changed from fixed to flashing in

December, 1910. When the station was made unwatched in 1959, the lighting apparatus was changed. The new system, using dissolved acetylene from a battery of cylinders, gave a candle-power of 2,600 white, and 500 red, but was not found to be as efficient as the old. Many complaints were received from mariners using the harbour. Electricity was laid on by overhead cable and the light converted in February, 1963; this increased the candle-power to 13,000 white and 2,600 red. The character remained the same; one flash every three seconds. The character was altered, in February, 1965, to one flash every four seconds.

Rathlin O'Birne

Rathlin O'Birne, off the North-West coast of Donegal, became our first, and probably the world's most powerful nuclear-powered light, when it converted to an Isotope generator on Thursday, 15th August, 1974. This was the result of nearly ten years discussion between Irish Lights and the Atomic Energy Research Establishment, Harwell, Buckinghamshire. In 1964, that body had asked for Irish Lights views on the possible use of isotope powered thermo-electric generators in the area of marine lighting and navigation. Black Rock, Mayo, was originally the lighthouse chosen for this experiment, but it proved to be at too high an elevation, and Rathlin O'Birne was selected instead. Though the Isotope generator continued to be used for remote navigational aids, such as lighted buoys, it was not developed for use in other lighthouses.

Raughley Bourne, or Rathlin O'Birne as it is now known, is a small, relatively flat island, separated from Malinmore on the Donegal mainland, by a narrow strip of sea. But that narrow neck of water is very deceptive and can be impossible to cross, by boat, for much of the year, depending on tide-rip and wind. The island has had a lighthouse since 1856 and two fine dwellings. Keepers and their families lived here for over fifty years after the light was first exhibited; the families moving to new shore dwellings at Glencolumbcille, in 1912.

The lighthouse on Rathlin O'Birne was built as a direct result of constant pressure from the wealthy and influential merchants and shipowners of Sligo. Since 1841 they had been petitioning the Ballast Board of Dublin, which body eventually agreed to build the lighthouse; Trinity House insisting that it be on condition that tolls be only levied on local shipping and not on Atlantic vessels.

The George Halpin designed tower and dwellings were constructed by James Aiden, being completed in 1846, with the fitting of a copper dome to the tower. Incredibly, there is no record of why ten years elapsed before the lantern was fitted and the light exhibited on 14th April, 1856. The tower, 65 feet high and 116 feet above high water, was originally unpainted grey limestone from Sligo; the lantern and dome were painted red. Subsequently, in the late 1860's, the limestone was painted white. The red lantern and dome remained the same until 1935, when the whole building was painted white.

There is, on Rathlin O'Birne, what appears to be at first a "folly"; two 6 to 7 feet high parallel cut stone walls. They are about 12 feet apart and run from the beach up to the edge of the lighthouse compound. The space between them is covered with a lush, deep carpet of untrammelled grass, so that, at first view, one doesn't think of it as being a roadway. It was the original roadway from the strand to the lighthouse, used a lot by the keepers and their families at one time. The wall was built as a protection against the scorching Atlantic wind and spray and is a thing of rare beauty, so well was it constructed.

When I visited the island in the late Summer of 1989, I followed the course of this wall and it led me, eventually, to a little fresh-water spring, protected by a canopy. On the grassy area surrounding this spring, I came across, at every second step, dead or dying seagulls. They were victims of botulism, the dread disease which effects the central nervous system, causing paralysis; an occupational hazard for all scavengers. Having become infected on the mainland the birds had returned to the island to die. I was shocked to find the little spring piled high with their dead bodies. They had, in a last effort to assuage their suffering, been drawn to the fresh-water, but too many had piled in together and they had become jammed under the canopy.

Rathlin O'Birne has a large population of sea-birds. For some it is a permanent home; for others a temporary one. It is an important Wintering-place for a colony of Barnacle Geese. The following Census of the bird population was taken in 1987. Storm Petrel - 500/1000 pairs. Leach's Petrel - 15 ringed (probably breeding). Shag - 10 pairs. Common Gull - 1 pair. Lesser Black-backed Gull - 7 pairs. Great Black-backed Gull 45/60 pairs. Herring Gull - 460/550 pairs. Black Guillemot - 8 pairs. Barnacle Geese (wintering) - c. 300 individuals.

Aranmore

The island of Aranmore lies to the North of Rathlin O'Birne and had a lighthouse as early as the end of the 18th century. This first light was established in 1798 and functioned until 1st August, 1832, when Tory Island light was established. Presumably it functioned efficiently, because, in the years after its closure, many requests were received from master mariners and shipowners, engaged in trade on the North and North-West coasts, for its re-establishment. Eventually the Ballast Board of Dublin acceded to these requests and George Halpin Junior designed a tower and dwellings. These were constructed by Daniel Crowe & Sons of Dublin, and the cast iron balcony and lantern supplied by Messrs. Edmundson of Dublin. Much of the masonry from the old tower and dwellings was used in the construction of the new station, the tower of which is 76 feet high. The new light, a second order dioptric removed from Rathlin O'Birne in 1864, was exhibited for the first time on 1st February, 1865.

Over half a century ago, the Commissioners, on their annual tour of inspection, would land below the lighthouse, making the steep, 233 foot climb, on foot. The inspection made, they then walked the 4 1/2 miles to rejoin the ship at Aran Roads. That procedure was reversed with the coming of the internal combustion engine to the island; the Inspecting Committee being transported by tractor and open trailer from the village to the lighthouse. Now, with the advent of the helicopter, they are transported, in a matter of minutes, from mainland to island.

Ballagh Rock

The channel between Aranmore Island and the Donegal mainland at Burtonport is known as the Aran Roads. At the Northern end of this stretch of water is Ballagh Rock, the largest of a group of rocks known collectively as the Blackrocks. These rocks are very exposed to huge seas from the North and the North-West and a grave danger to shipping on that coast. Indeed, one of the first recommendations made by the Inspecting Committee, in 1867, after jurisdiction had passed from the Ballast Board to the newly formed Commissioners of Irish Lights, was that an unlit beacon should be erected on Ballagh Rock.

Even though approval was given immediately, both by Trinity House and the Board of Trade, almost eight years elapsed before the beacon was completed, sometime in the Autumn of 1875. The conical shaped stone tower was 30 feet high and 15 feet diameter at the base. Mariners sailing in these waters instantly testified as to how great an aid it was to navigation. Sometime in 1928 a black band was painted on the white beacon, and in this form it functioned well for over 50 years. Then, with the advent of the I.A.L.A. Buoyage System 'A', Ballagh Rock, or Blackrock, as it had become known, came into the second phase in 1981, and was recommended for conversion to lighted 'West Cardinal' beacon. This, however, presented a problem to the engineers it — being impossible to get a 'West Cardinal' character, nine quick flashes every fifteen seconds, with propane gas. Using the acetylene necessary for this would involve heavy, long-distance transport and possible long delays. So, it was decided to re-character the new light as a lighthouse, using the more easily obtainable pro-pane, which was available on the local mainland. A lantern was placed on top of the old beacon, and a store constructed to house the propane gas containers and equipment. During the course of this construction, in the Summer of 1981, the contract Bolkow 105 helicopter, EI-BDI, had to ditch when flying between Arland's Point and the Ballagh Rock. She was carrying an underslung skip of concrete, and the pilot was fortunate to get clear of the sinking chopper. He swam to the nearby rocks and was picked up by the attending boat, which happened to be at Ballagh just then, and taken to Burtonport. The new light was first exhibited on 21st May, 1982, with a one second white flash every two and a half seconds. From that time, it was decided by the Inspector, that the light should be known again as Ballagh Rock, not Black Rock; there were already three other "Black Rocks" marked by the Service round the coast. In May, 1983, the light source was converted to electric batteries.

Tory Island

North of that part of the Donegal coast known as The Bloody Foreland, out past the smaller island of Inishbofin, half-seen in the mist and spray of the forbidding North Atlantic, lies the island of Tory; a prehistoric, ridge-backed monster, now visible above the heaving face of the sea, now lost in the great, grey maw of restless water. North of Tory the nearest land is the Hebrides. Over the centuries the great cliffs of the island have been eroded, by North Atlantic wind and wave, into a serried line of enormous "tors", or pillars. And, from these the place gets its name Tory, or, as the islanders call it "Torry".

And the inhabitants of Tory are a unique people; a people who have never seen themselves as "Donegal" or even "Irish", but as "Torry Islanders"; a people who have, over several generations, lived a spartan life on this most barren of islands where there is very little vegetation, where the thin layer of sub-standard soil, in which something might have grown has, for the most part, long been cut away and used as fuel for simple domestic uses, like cooking and heating, and sometimes the making of poteen. This is a community that, because of its location, survived the Great Famine rather better than most mainland, or indeed off-shore, communities. Because the prevailing winds here are parallel to the coast, the small and delicate spores by which the potato blight was spread, did not survive the journey in sufficient numbers to infect the Tory crop. Consequently, 140 people still survive on the island. Survive is the operative word; for life here is hard; a ceaseless struggle against the forces of nature, and other forces more difficult to combat, like unemployment.

Most families subsist on Social Welfare and minimal, seasonal earnings from fishing and tourism. There could, conceivably, be a better, albeit still seasonal, income from tourism, but the remoteness of the place, the difficulty of access, has always been a difficulty in developing this. However, since July 1992, there has been a regular ferry service to the island — daily in Summer season, and three times a week off-season. A hotel is also being built on the island and is scheduled to open before the end of 1993. And, there is much to attract the tourist here; the peace and quiet, the excellent fishing, history and mythology. The round tower, in the main street of the village, is over one thousand years old. And there are the celebrated "cursing stones", last used in 1884, to invoke a curse on the gunboat, *HMS Wasp*, sent to the island to forcibly collect overdue rates, after the islanders had refused to pay them. The *Wasp* was wrecked and all but six of her crew drowned. But, the principal figure in the island's mythology is Balor of the Evil Eye, the God-Chief of a pirate race which terrorised the Irish coast in pre-historic times.

Since a light was first established on Tory in August, 1832, the George Halpin designed lighthouse, with its large compound, has been very much a part of island life. Lighthouse keepers, from all over Ireland have served here, some have married here, reared families here. They have always integrated well with the islanders and I have met many who, though now serving on other stations, go back every Summer for a holiday. The original source of the light was oil, but in 1887 a small gasworks was built at the lighthouse and coal gas was used from then until 1923, when there was a change over to vapourised paraffin. In 1972 there was a further change to electricity. Tory Island was automated in 1990 and demanned.

There is quite a movement of bird-life on Tory; again, some permanent residents, some temporary. The 1987 census gave the following count. Fulmar - 240/260 pairs. Shag - 5/10 pairs. Black-headed Gull - 2 pairs. Common Gull - 30 pairs. Lesser Black-backed Gull - 6 pairs. Great Black-backed Gull - 34 pairs. Herring Gull - 43 pairs. Kittiwake - 500/530 pairs. Little Tern - 20 individuals. Guillemot - 600/650 individuals. Razorbill - 600/630 individuals. Black Guillemot - 5 individuals. Puffin - 600/700 individuals. At a time when the corncrake has become all but extinct in many mainland areas, it is interesting and important that the meadow on the landward-facing side of Tory Island is a breeding area for corncrakes; 8 to 10 pairs being counted in recent years.

Inishtrahull - Callwell

Part Six

The North Coast:
Lough Swilly to St. John's Point (Down).

Fanad - Buncrana - Dunree Fort - Inishtrahull - Inishowen - Rathlin East - Rathlin West - Rue Point - Chaine Tower - Maidens - Ferris Point - Black Head (Antrim) - Barr Point - Mew Island - Donaghadee - South Rock - Angus Rock - St. John's Point (Down)

"When darkness fell, the stroke of the lighthouse, which had laid itself with such authority upon the carpet in the darkness, tracing its pattern, came now in the softer light of Spring mixed with moonlight gliding gently as it laid its caress, and lingered stealthily and looked and came lovingly again.."

Virginia Woolf: "To The Lighthouse".

Building new lighthouse, Inishthrall

Lough Swilly Lights:
Fanad, Dunree, Buncrana

The oldest of the three lighthouses in Lough Swilly is that at Fanad Head, on the Western shore. It stands at such a strategic point, facing the open North Atlantic, and also lighting the entrance to the Lough, that it is, in effect, a dual purpose light; both sea light and harbour light. Officially it is listed as a sea light, and was first exhibited on Saint Patrick's Day, 1817. The tower, similar to those at Mutton Island and Roche's Point, was designed by George Halpin, and that first light was a fixed catoptric, showing red to seaward and white toward the Lough. It can be seen for fourteen miles in clear weather.

As so often happened in those days, it took the wrecking of a ship and the loss of human life to bring about the building of a lighthouse on Fannet Point, as the headland was known in the early 19th century. The *Saldana* ran aground on the treacherous rocks below the Point, with a total loss of life. The only survivor was the ship's parrot, which wore a silver collar with the name *Saldana* inscribed on it. Captain Hill, of the Royal Navy, stationed in Derry at the time, and with vast experience of patrolling the North-West coast, from Lough Foyle to Blacksod Bay, wrote to the Dublin Ballast Board, recommending a lighthouse on Fannet Point. He stated, categorically, that, in his opinion the *Saldana* would not have been lost had there been a light on Fannet.

Commissioner on tractor

The good Captain's advice was taken seriously and the building of a tower at Fannet sanctioned. For the next half-century the lighthouse at Fanad Head was to be the only light in Lough Swilly. In that period traffic in and out of the Lough had greatly increased and there was pressure for at least two more lights in the area. Eventually, it was decided, to build lighthouses at Dunree Head and Buncrana Pier. At first it was thought that one of the Martello Towers, at Macanish and Dunree, could be converted, but that was not found to be feasible. The lights at Buncrana and Dunree were both exhibited on the same day, 15th January, 1876.

In the early 1880's it was decided to give Fanad Head Light a major overhaul. A new, larger, higher tower was built, close to the old tower, and an additional dwelling. The new light went into operation on 1st September, 1886. In December 1916, the station was struck by lightning, but there was very little damage caused. In 1969, with the advent of the helicopter, Fanad Head became the land base for Tory Island and Inishtrahull.

Inishtrahull

Even further North than Tory is the island of Inishtrahull. Seven miles off Malin Head; on calm, clear days looking very much closer than that; on dark days lost in the North Atlantic mist and the enormous swell sweeping in off the Continental Shelf. This, the geologists reckon, is the oldest piece of land in Ireland. I first visited the island in the Summer of 1989 and spent a few days there in the company of Roddy Muir, a young Scottish geologist, working at the University of Wales in Aberystwyth. He had flown out with me by helicopter, a guest of Irish Lights, who have a great tradition of generosity in making transport available to geologists, naturalists and such.

Now, in technical terminology, any rock formation that doesn't match, geologically speaking, with its immediate vicinity, is called "suspect terrain" and, since around the turn of the century Inishtrahull has been considered to be in this category. McCallion, in a geological survey at that time, found that the basement rock on the island did not match that of the Irish mainland. His initial feeling was that the gneiss rock of Inishtrahull was similar to that of the Outer Hebrides This augen gneiss, so called because of the little pink 'eyes' (augen) in it, is a crushed granite and attracts a lovely, blue-grey luminous lichen. In time McCallion came to doubt his own theory; leaving no evidence to either prove or disprove it.

In early 1989 Roddy Muir began work on a project funded by the National Environment Research Council. His brief was to discover the origin of the basement rock found in the islands of Islay and Colonsay. In the course of his research he discovered the McCallion Report, and subsequently, in his Paleographic reconstruction (the reconstruction of past environments), he became convinced of the geological links between Greenland, Islay, Colonsay and Inishtrahull. By a careful study of the Theory of Plate Tectonics (the constant movement of the earth's face), and visits to all four locations, Muir confirmed his beliefs. His visit to Inishtrahull enabled him to fit into place the last piece in this intriguing geological jigsaw. The island of Inishtrahull is really part of the Southern tip of Greenland and is not, geologically, related to the Irish mainland at all.

The Earth's crust, the rigid outer layer, called the lithosphere, has an average thickness of approximately 75 km. Below this is a semi-fluid layer, called the asthenosphere. This layer varies, in places, from 100 km to 200 km in thickness. The semi-fluid mass can flow vertically, or horizontally, thereby allowing the outer crust to subside, rise, or undergo lateral movement. By the associated processes of continental drift and seafloor spreading, the Earth's continents are constantly moving over the surface of the planet on this substratum of hot molten rock, know as magma. Roddy Muir, in our many conversations, referred to this as the "great heat engine in the Earth". And this "heat engine", 1800 million years ago, was responsible for Inishtrahull, Islay and Colonsay breaking free of the Southern tip of Greenland. Islay and Colonsay "anchored" off the coast of Scotland, while Inishtrahull drifted further South, finding "berth" off the Donegal coast, over 800 miles from Greenland.

Ironically, this island, this "oldest land in Ireland", has got the most modern lighthouse tower, built by Collen Brothers and established on 8th October, 1958. Built at the West end of the island, it replaced the old lighthouse, the ruins of which may still be seen at the East end. That was the first lighthouse to be built and lit (17th March, 1813), by the Ballast Board of Dublin to George Halpin's design. It was built largely at the behest of the Royal Navy, whose ships were using Lough Foyle as a base for their North Atlantic operations. The first light was a revolving light, which reached its full brilliance every two minutes, and it served shipping well until the 1860's when Inspector Halpin considered it should be replaced by a more up to date first order dioptric apparatus and a new lantern. The new light came into operation in September 1864, with a character of one flash every two minutes. This was changed, early in 1873, to one flash every minute, only to discover, a few months later, that it was identical to Skerryvore, 61 miles to the North, off the Scottish coast. It was again changed to one flash every 30 seconds.

Around 1900, it was decided that a fog signal was required somewhere near Malin Head. After the usual lengthy discussions and consideration of various sites, it was decide to construct the fog signal station at the West end of Inishtrahull. This station became operational in 1905. This meant that the lighthouse was at one end of the island and the fog signal at the other. So, in 1952, when the Commissioners of Irish Lights were considering the replacement of the fog signal machinery and the modernising of the lighthouse, it was decided to group all the elements together at the West end, by building a new tower beside the fog signal station, and abandoning the old East Station. The new tower, built of reinforced concrete, is modern and novel in design, having the fog signal, or diaphone, built into the tower, above the light. The new light was first exhibited on the night of 8th October, 1958. It is 1,700,000 candlepower and can be seen over 30 miles away in clear weather. However, because of the curvature of the Earth, its geographical range is only 20 miles.

Now retired, one of the best-loved Keepers in Irish Lights, D.J. (Danny) O'Sullivan, served for nine years on Inishtrahull as Principal Keeper. Published poet and short story writer, naturalist and newspaper columnist, his accomplishments reflected great glory on the Service to which both he and three other generations of his family gave such loyal service. This dynasty of lighthouse keepers began with Danny's grandfather, Daniel, who served, in the second half of the 19th century, as a gunner' on Rathlin Island. In that time the fog signal gun, an 18-pounder, was looked after by a specially designated Keeper called the 'gunner', as distinct from the Keeper who tended the light. Danny's father followed the 'gunner' into the Service, and was serving as a Keeper on the Bull Rock, when he was accidentally drowned there in 1917. His body was never recovered. Danny then entered the Service, and his three sons, Eugene, Hugh and Donal followed him in due course.

Danny loved Inishtrahull and, having worked nights and days there for nine years, came to know the island in all its moods. His poem, "Dawn In Inishtrahull", captures perfectly a dawn mood; it also shows the Naturalist's hyper-sensitive observation at work. The poem has been much anthologised, both in Europe and America.

"The moon shines on the isle of Inishtrahull,
Bejewelling nuptial tinted herring gull;
May-fly dancing in the balmy air,
And moth returning to its daylight lair.

A shoal of herrings breaking out at sea
Sparkle like hoar frost on an aspen tree.
Spindrift in the shady rocky cleft,
And raised-beach quartz that the ice-ages left.

The droning beetles seek the crevassed walls
To dive into when hungry lapwing calls;
Earwigs, likewise, into earthed homes,
And red ants under scarred lichened stones.

An otter seeking rest on rock remote
Glistens with phosphorescence on his coat;
The snail Arborum, with his watery glue,
And bunch of pearlworth in a crystal dew.

The flaming sun ascends o'er Cantyre's Mull,
Flings out his arms; day breaks on Inishtrahull!"

I had not yet read that poem when I first went to the island. Waking very early on my first morning there, I went up into the tower. There was a cloudless sky and a lively sea running from the North-West. In the white, pre-dawn light, there were little wisps and cusps of mist, low over the sea. The sunrise was, as yet, the faintest blush in the East, but the enormous bulk of The Mull of Kintyre stood against it like some great blue whale, towering above the sea-mist. And, in that rare, illusory moment, it looked so near, I felt I could reach out my arm and touch it.

Inishtrahull is now uninhabited. The last islanders moved to the mainland over half-a-century ago. For several decades the familes of the lighthouse keepers lived there, until the station became relieving and they too went ashore. The three Keepers on duty were the last to live there, and they are now gone since the light was made automatic and demanned in 1987. There is a small, safe anchorage, big enough for yachts and fishing boats, on the North-

East side of the island, and beside the landing-place, a clear spring well. In Summer, passing yachts put in there to anchor for the night and replenish their water tanks. The little pier is used by fishermen from the mainland to stack their lobster-pots. Sea grass and wild roses, once cultivated, grow up around the ruins of the long-abandonded houses, and sea gulls, dying from botulism, stagger dementedly about, searching for fresh water. But the spring well is protected, unlike the one at Rathlin O'Birne, and they cannot get to the water there.

At the East end of the island, down below the old lighthouse, is a graveyard. The simple headstones, their inscriptions somewhat eroded by wind and rain and sea spray, are still legible enough to tell a terrible tale of infant mortality; the scourge of a time when the very basic medical and social services available rarely reached such remote communities in time. Dead and dying seagulls litter the grass between the headstones.

In the 1992 Wildlife Census Inishtrahull's bird population was quite healthy. Eider - 150 pairs. Fulmar - 250 pairs. Shag - 400 pairs. Common gull - 30 pairs. Herring Gull - 500 pairs. Great Black-backed Gull - 30 pairs. Lesser Black-backed Gull - 50 pairs. Black Guillemot - 20 pairs. The island is considered to be a very important Wintering place for about 300 Barnacle Geese, and about 30 pairs of Arctic Terns occasionally nest.

Inishowen

The first half of the 19th century saw a huge increase in the volume of sea-traffic up and down the Foyle, as the Port of Derry grew. The Tuns Bank, a spit of sand, just North-East of Magilligan Point, on the Derry shore, was a grave danger to shipping and the Ballast Board of Derry and the Derry Chamber of Commerce requested that a light be established on the Donegal shore at the entrance to Lough Foyle, to lead shipping clear of the Tuns Bank. George Halpin, the Dublin Ballast Office Inspector of Light-houses, surveyed the area and recommended that, to achieve the desired result, two separate lights would be needed. The request was made in 1832, and statutory sanction given in 1833 by Trinity House. George Halpin designed the twin towers and the dwellings. James Pettigrew, of Dorset Street, Dublin built the two lighthouse towers, while the Ballast Office workmen built the rest of the station and the dwellings. The twin towers, of cut stone, bearing East and West, stood 153 yards apart; the overall height of each tower being 49 feet. They were painted white, with fixed white lights 67 feet above high water, and they were both established on 1st December, 1837.

It took four years for mariners using the Port to realise that the lights should each have some distinctive character. Numerous requests were forwarded to the Dublin Ballast Board. In addition to these complaints from mariners the Admiralty was not very happy with the twin towers either; suggesting that they were ill-adapted for the purpose of clearing the Tuns Bank, due to their being at the same elevation. The suggestion was that the West tower be raised. This received the approval of the Inspecting Committee in June 1861. But, incredibly, the arguments for and against this seemed to go on interminably; there were various experiments with a second light being exhibited in the East tower. This failed; the two lights appearing as one from even a short distance. Other alternatives were tried; all equally non-viable.

So the trial and error went on; a process of elimination, rather than of illumination, until, in January 1941, a fire in the fog signal engine-room, caused serious damage to roof-timbers, and destroyed an oil supply tank. The cost of repairing the damage caused yet another re-think. But, not until 1957 was a decision taken to abandon the front light and auxiliary light. Eventually, the lantern on the East tower was removed. The station was automated in September 1979, and the Keepers withdrawn.

Rathlin Island, East & West, Rue Point

Off Fair Head, in Antrim, the island of Rathlin is, relatively speaking, almost in the shadow of the Mull of Kintyre. Being so close to Scotland there has always been a Scottish influence here among the families that make up the still vibrant community inhabiting the island. Even before Robert Bruce came here and encountered the spider in the cave, there had been a lot of coming and going across the stormy, narrow North Channel. Rathlin is unique among Irish islands in that it has three working light-houses; one, Rathlin East, still manned, with Rathlin West and Rue Point unwatched automatic.

The first lighthouse on Rathlin was the East tower, in which two lights, an upper occulting and a lower fixed, were exhibited on 1st November, 1856. The upper light was in the tower itself and 243 feet above high water; the lower light was a lantern placed close to the base of the tower. This two-light set-up was designed to obviate confusion with other lights for shipping approaching and passing through the North Channel. The tower and other buildings were designed by George Halpin Snr., after nearly twenty-five years of prevarication between the Commissioners of Northern Lights, in Edinburgh, and the Corporation for Improving the Port of Dublin (The Ballast Office). The tower was built of stone quarried on the island. Ten years later a fog signal was established, which consisted of an 18-pounder gun, fired every twenty minutes in foggy conditions. This was only discontinued in 1972, for security reasons, together with similar fog signals round the coast. The lower light was discontinued in July, 1894, when the tower light was intensified. In 1912 a completely new optic was installed. The East tower light is due to be automated and demanned in 1994.

Again, in the selection of the best location for the second lighthouse on the island, there was much difference of opinion, this time between Trinity House and Irish Lights, who had now taken over from the Ballast Board as the governing body for Irish lighthouses. Two headlands were being considered, Bull Point and Crockantirrive, and it was even mooted, at one stage, that the light might be placed on one and the fog signal on the other. Crockantirrive was finally selected as the location for both light and signal and work progressed, albeit slowly. This can be appreciated when one sees the amount of concrete that had to be poured and set against the cliff face. And, to facilitate the transporting of the building materials for the new lighthouse, an inclined railway had to be built at Corraghy. Then, the new lighthouse was quite different in design. C. W. Scott, the Engineer-in-Chief, of Irish Lights, was determined that he would not make the error some of his predecessors had made and place the lantern at too high an elevation. He designed and built this lighthouse upside-down, so to speak. The huge concrete glacis was built at a 45 degree angle to the cliff. Living quarters are incorporated in the building, and it is by entering through the 'attic' and descending through the various levels that one comes to the lantern. The diaphone fog signal is situated at the top of the concrete slope. The Light went into operation on 10th March, 1919.

Though there was a recommendation for an unwatched light at Rue Point in July 1914, the six-sided concrete tower which stands there today was not built until 1920-1921. A temporary light was erected on the Point in November 1915 for the Admiralty, without any notice to Mariners being issued. However, during the following year, the high cost of maintaining this temporary structure led the Inspecting Committee to recommend that a permanent light should be erected. The Board of Trade refused to sanction such expenditure during the War. The acetylene fog gun, proposed by the Inspecting Committee at the same time, was sanctioned, and went into operation on 12th April, 1917. In November of that same year the temporary light was wrecked by a severe storm. The fog gun trestle remained undamaged and so the light was transferred to this, and functioned in this makeshift way until the new tower was built, incorporating the fog gun on its roof.

Chaine Tower

Most of the 10th to 12th century round towers in Ireland were built contiguous to monastic settlements and in inland locations. Where, occasionally, they were near the sea, they served, in those early days before lighthouses were built on our coasts, as very effective sea-marks and navigational aids. The tower on Scattery Island, in the River Shannon, the only such edifice with its entrance door at ground level, was one. There were others at Killala, Ardmore and Tory Island, which were, no doubt, useful to mariners over the unlighted, pre-lighthouse centuries.

The lighthouse on the Western arm of the narrow entrance to Larne Lough, Chaine Tower, is a round tower, but one with a difference. It was built, not in the 10th, 11th or 12th century, but in the 19th century, and is an exact replica of an ancient Irish round tower. Called after James Chaine, Esq., M.P. for North Antrim in the early to mid-19th century, it was built, by public subscription, to commemorate his memory. He had been one of the pioneers in the development and improvement of Larne Harbour, and well-loved of the local community. He had been buried, in an upright position, overlooking the lough, near Sandy Point. Mr. Dixon, a prosperous Merchant of Belfast, and Chairman of the Memorial Committee, wrote to the Commissioners of Irish Lights, enquiring if they would assist in the building of such a tower, which might, advantageously, be used as a lighthouse. Failing assistance with the actual construction, it was suggested that the Commissioners might consider maintaining such a memorial lighthouse. The Board considered the matter a local one and regretted that they could comply with neither request.

That was in June, 1885, and the Memorial Committee, nothing daunted, quickly trimmed sail and came up with an alternative suggestion that was acceptable to Irish Lights. They would build the replica round tower, without a light, at Sandy Point Bay, opposite Ferris Point, where there had been a lighthouse since 1839, if the Commisioners did not object to such a beacon. So, Chaine Tower was completed in January, 1888, with full approval from Irish Lights and the Board of Trade. It was even given the 'imprimatur' of a Notice To Mariners. The Larne Harbour authority undertook to maintain the unlit beacon. There were various suggestions as to whether the tower should be painted or not, it being eventually agreed that it should remain its natural stone colour.

Just eight years later, in April 1896, the Larne and Stranraer Steamship Joint Committee wrote to the Commissioners, complaining of the inadequate marking of the treacherous Hunter Rock, just off the entrance to Larne Harbour. They suggested that a light should be attached to the round tower on Sandy Bay Point. Two months later the Inspecting Committee granted that this should be done and the trustees of the tower were approached with a request to hand Chaine Tower over to the Commissioners of Irish Lights. This request was granted, provided the outside was not altered, the causeway maintained and the building used solely as a lighthouse. There was no objection to making an extra opening so that a light could cover Hunter Rock. The work of conversion went ahead without delay and the light, a fifth order condensing lens, with occulting mechanism, giving a white and red flash every five seconds, was established on 1st July, 1899. An extra Assistant Keeper was sanctioned for the Maidens Lighthouse, with the specific function of being responsible for Chaine Tower, a house being rented for him in Larne.

The light was made unwatched from 5th October, 1905, and converted from oil to coal gas from the Larne mains gas supply. The extra Assistant Keeper was dispensed with and the Principal Keeper at Ferris Point, across the Lough, was given responsibility for the Chaine light. The light was converted from gas to electric in September, 1935, the second conversion to electric on the coast; the first being Donaghadee, twelve months earlier.

The Maidens

As far back as 1819 there was a concerted campaign by the Merchants and Shipowners of Larne to have the Maidens Rocks lighted. Inspector George Halpin visited the Rocks and recommended that two lighthouses were needed. The twin towers were built 800 yards apart. One, on the Northern Rock, but known as the West Tower, the other on the Southern Rock, but known as the East Tower. The West Tower was 84 feet above high-water, with a visibility of 13 miles; the East Tower was 94 feet above high-water, with a visibility of 14 miles. The lights were first exhibited on 5th January, 1829 and functioned efficiently for 60 years before it was thought necessary to introduce an auxiliary light to cover the nearby Highland Rocks. This light was built into a window of the East Tower.

Despite numerous schemes and suggestions and recommend-ations no further major changes were made until 12th March, 1903, when an improved new light was exhibited from the East Tower and the West Tower light discontinued. On 12th October, 1977, the East Tower light was converted to electric and the station made unwatched at the end of that month.

Looking at the Maidens, with their huddle of buildings close in under the towers, the low Rocks almost submerged at high-water, I remembered Dylan Thomas and the lines from "Under Milk Wood"

>"Our Heron Head is only
>A bit of stone with seaweed spread
>Where gulls come to be lonely."

And I thought of all the men and women and children who had lived on these two Rocks over a century and a half ago. Lived in the cramped quarters on the tiny patch of land that was rarely dry; no room there for children to run, or play, or even hide. Lived, almost within hailing distance of the mainland, and yet were so isolated. For, when sea and wind conspire to batter this coast, the Maidens are inaccessible, often for weeks on end. It was this inaccessibility that caused Irish Lights, in 1899, to decide against installing J.R. Wigham's Quick Revolving Light. The Engineer-in-Chief felt that, should anything go wrong with it, "it might be days before assistance could reach the Maidens."

Ferris Point

Ferris Point, on the Eastern arm of the entrance to Larne Lough, had its first lighthouse built in 1838, and the light exhibited on 1st February, 1839. This was the result of nearly ten years of petitioning and lobbying by the numerous merchants and ship-owners of Larne, who contended that a light was urgently needed either on Sandy Point, or on Ferris Point. The Keepers' dwellings took more time to complete and were not ready until the following year. The light was converted from oil to electric in November, 1957.

The shape of Ferris Point, quite literally, changed drastically as part of the Irish Lights Modernisation Programme; the old station disappearing, the new station we know today emerging. It now resembles an airport control tower complex, with the new lantern located above the watch room; an ultra-modern, space age look. The station is now the nerve-centre for the control of lights, fog signal station and buoys in the area. It is the helicopter base for Northern Ireland rock and island stations and has state of the art buoy workshops and a gas bottle store. The Ferris Keepers control the fog signal Station at nearby Barr Point, the Maidens Light-house since its automation, and Chaine Tower on the opposite shore; together with the various buoys and beacons around the entrance to Larne Lough.

Black Head (Antrim)

A Douglass designed tower was built on Black Head, on the North shore of the entrance to Belfast Lough, in 1901. The tower was built of granite and its light was first exhibited in 1902. A fog signal also came into operation at the same time. Black Head was converted to electricity on 23rd September, 1969 and became automatic unwatched in August, 1975.

Mew Island

Before the lighthouse was built on Mew Island this area of the approaches to Belfast Lough had been lit by a Light on the Lesser Copeland Island, thereafter sometimes called Lighthouse Island. This was established in the early 18th century; one of four 'cottage type', coal-burning lights around the Irish coast. The others were at Loophead, Old Head of Kinsale and Howth Head. Prior to the

Copeland light there had been a lighthouse, probably a 'cottage type' also, on Island Magee, near Carrikfergus, which had a short life of four or five years. In 1796, Thomas Rogers, added a six foot diameter lantern into a corner of the Copeland 40 foot high square tower, and changed from coal to oil.

Lighthouse Keepers coming off duty

In 1810, after the Revenue Commissioners had handed over responsibility for the lighthouses to the Corporation for Improving The Port of Dublin or the Dublin Ballast Board, Copeland Island was one of the first stations to be listed for improvement. The Board's Inspector, George Halpin Snr., designed and built a new 52 feet high tower and lantern alongside the old tower, with a fixed oil-fired light. The light, 131 feet above sea level, was first exhibited on 24th January, 1815. Much later, in 1851, the old lighthouse tower was used to house a huge fog bell, operated by a weight-driven machine. This machine was, periodically, wound up by the Keepers.

Now, as commerce increased, around the middle of the 19th century, the old sailing ships were being replaced by steam-driven vessels. The new ships cost more to build, carried bigger cargoes, and their owners soon began demanding a better positioned light on this part of the coast. The Belfast Harbour Commissioners requested the removal of the Copeland Island light to Mew Island. Irish Lights acceded to this request, but not until 1882 was work commenced on the new station, which was designed by William Douglass, Engineer-in-Chief. The new light and fog signal were established on 1st November, 1884. The tower and dwellings were built of rubble masonry, quarried on Mew Island, with granite dressings, quarried near Newry, and is stuccoed in Portland cement. Until 1928, Mew Island had its own gas-making plant. It was then the last gas-works on the coast and was discontinued in favour of oil. The paraffin, in turn, gave way to electric lamps in July, 1969. Mew Island is scheduled for automation in 1995-1996.

Donaghadee

The lighthouse tower at the end of the harbour wall in Donagh-adee is built of cut limestone, fluted. It was originally unpainted, a natural grey colour. For many years now, the tower has been painted white, with a black plinth. The light was first exhibited in this tower as long ago as 1836, when the little port of Donagh-adee was still the Irish terminal for the "Short Sea Route" to Portpatrick, twenty-two miles away in Scotland. This run had operated successfully since 1662 and only began to be non-viable with the advent of bigger ships, which found Portpatrick difficult of access, and Donaghadee a poor haven in Easterly gales. There was also, until the Belfast and Down Railway reached Donagh-adee in 1861, a great problem with road transport. The development of a new route between Larne and Stranraer proved very successful and this took over in 1871.

A serious fire badly damaged the lantern and optic on May 12th, 1900. A temporary light was shown while the lantern was repaired and a new optic obtained, so the light was back to normal by September of that year. Donaghadee had the distinction of being the first lighthouse on the Irish coast to be converted to electric, on 2nd October, 1934. Chaine Tower at Larne followed in 1935, and Tuskar in 1938. The Donagadee light became unwatched at the time of converting to electric. Much of the service work on the many buoys in Donaghadee Sound used to be carried out at the lighthouse, but these have long since been serviced at Larne Buoy Depot on Ferris Point. In 1950 the Ministry of Commerce asked the Commissioners of Irish Lights for permission to erect a fog signal. This was to aid local vessels, mainly fishing boats, returning to the Harbour during fog. The siren was mounted on the lantern balcony railing, and came into operation in 1953. It is controlled from the Harbour Board Office.

Around the turn of the century, the steamships on the Belfast to Liverpool route were in great rivalry with the Railway steamers on the Heysham and Fleetwood routes. In an effort to outdo each other in getting their passengers to London as quickly as possible, short cuts were made through the Donaghadee Sound instead of taking the longer and safer route round Mew Island. Three of the Belfast Steamship Company's ships, the *ss Magic, ss Optic and ss Caloric*, had struck some "very hard underwater obstruction" when using the Sound. This was thought to be uncharted rocks; afterwards referred to, unofficially, as the Magic Rocks. Captain Dean, the Marine Superintendent, refused to light the buoys in the Sound, as he felt it was a place that should be avoided at nightime by all vessels, as the time saved by cutting through the Sound, rather than rounding Mew Island, was not commensurate with the risks involved. However, after that initial refusal, in 1907, the Engineer-in-Chief, C.W. Scott, submitted estimates for the lighting of the Donaghadee Sound Buoys, but, not until 1910 were they actually lighted.

South Rock

South Rock is situated about one and a half miles off the Ards Peninsula, near the little fishing village of Portavogie, Co. Down. It is now marked by a lightship, anchored three quarters of a mile to seaward of the old, abandoned lighthouse, which was built on the Rock itself. Indeed, the Rock is almost totally submereged, except at low tide, when its jagged pinnacles can be seen, like serrated sharks' fins protruding above the water. It has ever been a danger to shipping on this busy coast. As long ago as 1767 the merchants and shipowners of Belfast were petitioning for a light here, but, though the need for the light was acknowledged by all concerned, it was not until 1797 that the tower was actually built. In that thirty year interim, countless sailing ships had their timbers splintered on the saw-toothed rocks.

It was built by Thomas Rogers, and was known as the Kilwarlin Light, after Lord Kilwarlin, the late Marquess of Downshire, who was the chief petitioner for its construction. It was Thomas Rogers' greatest achievement; the building of it as great a feat of pharology nearly two centuries ago, as was the building of the Kish a mere quarter of a century ago. Before it, only two wave-washed lighthouses had been built; the Eddystone and the Bell Rock, neither of them subject to the same exposure as South Rock. It is reckoned to be one of the great examples of lighthouse engineering; an indestructible edifice, which, despite the fact that it has been without any kind of maintenance since being abandoned 116 years ago, is still in relatively good condition.

The tower was built of mountain granite, solid for the first twenty feet of its height. It originally contained four apartments, which accommodated stores and dwellings. The light was 60 feet above high water, and was visible, in clear weather, at a distance of twelve miles. A white catoptric light of the second order, revolving, it was first exhibited on 25th March, 1797. There was an alarm, or fog bell, which had to be struck, manually, in foggy weather; the keepers working in half-hour spells. Sadly, however, this great masterpiece of the lighthouse-builder's art, was built in the wrong place, otherwise it would still be in use today, as are the Eddystone and the Bell Rock.

When work started on the South Rock tower, in September 1793, the granite blocks were being dressed in Wexford, 180 miles away down the East coast. Two sloops were chartered to transport the first two consignments to South Rock. On their 'maiden' voyage, in convoy, they were hit by a particularly severe storm; one was sunk, with its cargo of granite; the other was driven off-course and eventually made safe harbour in Penzance. This mishap forced Thomas Rogers to look elsewhere for his granite. He found a quarry, not far from Newcastle, and placed his order there. The blocks were transported to Newcastle by canal, dressed there, two courses at a time, and then shipped out to South Rock. Paper templates were kept for the next course. On the Rock, the courses were bound together by eight vertical iron rods, each 4 inches square. These formed a circle, and were then fixed to cast-iron plates at every 8th course. Inside the tower the four floor were connected by ladders passing through holes in the floors.

In 1874 the Glasgow Shipowners' Association suggested that South Rock Light should be located three-quarters of a mile seaward of its present position. It being generally accepted that, unfortunately, one of the noblest towers ever built in Irish waters had been wrongly placed, there was not much difficulty in getting the new lightship sanctioned. The light was exhibited for the first time on 1st April, 1877, and the South Rock lighthouse was abandoned on that same day, and became an unlit beacon. The character of the new light was the same as that of the old, but the fog signal was changed from the bell to a gun, fired once every fifteen minutes in fog. The character of the light was changed to Group flashing (2) every 45 seconds, in 1906, and the gun replaced by an explosive charge, with two reports every 3 minutes. A submarine bell was established in 1923, but was discontinued in 1946.

The colour of the South Rock lightvessel was changed in 1955, from black with a white stripe, to red. A Radio Beacon, only for use during fog was also established at that time. In 1964, Radio Beacon transmissions were altered to include clear weather, and in 1965 the character of the light was changed again; remaining Group flashing (2), but reduced to 30 seconds. The explosive fog signal was changed to a diaphone in 1969; later that year a Radar Responder Beacon (Racon), was established. In 1977, a foreign coaster mistook South Rock for Kilantringan, a Scottish Light near Portpatrick, on the Rhinns of Galloway. Both lights had identical characters. Consequently, in December of that year, the colour of the South Rock Light was changed from white to red.

As part of the general automation programme of Irish Lights an automated lightvessel was placed on South Rock on 14th July, 1981.

Angus Rock

Though an unlighted Beacon Tower had existed on Angus Rock for many years, it was not until the late 1960's that any serious consideration was given to lighting it. In 1969, the Commissioners of Irish Lights intimated that they were amenable to lighting Angus Rock, as part of a programme for improving the general lighting of Strangford Lough. Their lighting the Rock, however, was contingent on the East Down Industrial and Development Committee undertaking some work in the Lough. They would have to light the various leading marks up to the Narrows as, to light Angus Rock, without this being done, would be dangerous. It would be tantamount to enticing vessels up the Narrows to the vicinity of dangerous rocks.

Much discussion and exchange of letters followed and it was not until the early 1980's that the matter was resolved and Angus Rock light established. It was first exhibited at sunset on Thursday, 7th April, 1983, with a character of flashing red every 5 seconds, and a range of 6.5 miles. On that same date alterations were also made to the buoyage in the approaches, as part of a more efficient lighting system.

St. John's Point (Down)

Just South of Ardglass, on the coast of County Down, is St. John's Point. There has been a lighthouse here since the middle of the 19th century. The light was first established on 1st May, 1844, with an occulting character — 45 seconds. flash, 15 seconds. dark, 62 feet above high water. The tower was originally painted white. The light was changed from white to red in 1860, and in 1875 a gas works was built at the station when the light source changed from oil to coal gas.

During the 1880's there were many requests from mariners to improve the marking and lighting of the Co. Down coast. As part of a general effort to achieve this the height of the tower at St. John's Point was raised to almost double its original height; from 62 feet above high water to 120 feet above high water. A fog signal was established and an auxiliary light over Dundrum Bay was exhibited in one of the tower windows, on the third floor. In 1902 the colour of the tower was changed, from white to white with three black bands.

In 1909 the main light was improved, with the introduction of a biform lens and incandescent paraffin burners instead of gas jets. The colour was changed from red to white and the character to Group flashing (2) every 7.5 secs. There was a further colour change to the tower in 1954, to black with two yellow bands. On 18th February, 1981, the light was converted to electric, and an electric horn replaced the siren as fog signal. The station was demanned on 31st May, 1981.

Part Seven

Tenders, Buoys and Lightvessels -
Control and Administration -
Automation and the Lighthouse Keeper.

"The lighthouse was then a silvery, misty-looking tower, with a yellow eye, that opened suddenly and softly in the evening."

Virginia Woolf: "To The Lighthouse".

Captain Denis Gray (Retired Marine Superintendent) and
his son, Dermot Gray, Officer on the 'Gray Seal'

Tenders, Buoys and Lightvessels

Twenty-five years ago, the Commissioners of Irish Lights had a fleet of four tenders to service the lighthouses round our coast. To-day they have two; the flagship, *Granuaile*, and the *Gray Seal*. This is largely due to the advent of the helicopter and to the automation programme.

Since 1810, when the responsibility for the construction and maintenance of Irish lighthouses was vested in the Corporation for Preserving and Improving the Port of Dublin, vessels of many kinds have been deployed in the Service. Wooden hulled cutters and schooners, ex-RNLI life-boats, screw steamers, paddle steamers, steam tugs, motor vessels, diesel vessels, converted fishing craft, have all played an honourable part, over a period of 183 years, in servicing the lighthouses, buoys and lightvessels on the Irish coast. Some have been owned by, initially, the Ballast Board and then, since 1867, Irish Lights; others have been chartered for specific periods, or for specific work. At one time, in the mid-19th century, Trinity House loaned vessels for Inspection Tours. One of these the *Ierne*, loaned in 1855, was found unsuitable and the Tour was cancelled. The following year, the *Vestal* was taken on loan from Trinity House, and obviously proved satisfactory, for it was used, always on loan, for the following five years to take the Inspection Committee round the coast.

Over the years the various tenders have performed a wide range of tasks. In 1819, the *Alexander* anchored off Ringsend and was used as a hulk for men working on the construction of the South Wall and Poolbeg Lighthouse. In 1851, the steamer *John* was chartered for the construction of the new East lighthouse on Rathlin Island. The steamer *Ellen & Nancy* was chartered in 1854 for Insihtrahull reliefs. A screw steamer, the *Midge*, was chartered in 1858 for general buoy servicing. A steamer, the *Ierne*, was specially built, to service the building of the second Fastnet Lighthouse at the turn of the century.

Two of the tenders "died" during their working lives. The *Anne-Margaret*, a Light Vessel Tender, was wrecked off Wicklow in 1832. And, during the Second World War, the *ss Isolda* was sunk while carrying out a routine relief of the Coningbeg Lightvessel off the Wexford coast. On 19th December, 1940, a German bomber planted a stick of bombs into her, killing six members of the crew; W. Holland (Chief Steward), P. Dunne (Coxswain), W. Farrell (AB),

P. Short (Greaser), W. Rushby (Leading Fireman), and J. Hayden (Fireman). The sinking was particularly cynical, as the *Isolda* had 'LIGHTHOUSE SERVICE' painted in 5 feet high letters on her side, and was unarmed. Two survivors of that sinking, Jocelyn O'Hehir and Sam Williams are still living in Dunlaoghaire.

Ironically, it was the *ss Isolda*, which was involved, in 1936, in the saga of the last Daunt Lightvessel. The *Daunt*, off the Cork coast, had gone adrift in a fierce Sou'-Easterly gale, drifting helplessly for three days. During that time a rescue operation had been mounted. The Ballycotton lifeboat, the *ss Innisfallen* out of Cork, the Royal Naval destroyer HMS *Tenedos* and the *ss Isolda* all took part. The lifeboat's coxswain, Patrick Sliney, was an ins- piration to everyone and incredibly, there were no casualties. Unfortunately, the Daunt Rock, since 1974 marked by a new Focal Plane Buoy, was, to say the least, unkind to the lightships placed to mark it. The first, the *Gannet*, was placed on station in 1874, and nine years later was badly damaged when a barque, the *Largo Bay,* collided with her. Then, on 8th October, 1896, a violent storm caused the *Puffin* lightship, then on station, to sink with all hands. And there is a remarkable link between that tragedy and the present day; a link involving successive generations of a double-dynasty of lighthouse and lightship Keepers, the Higginbothams and the Scanlans. A link that goes back to 1750 and the oldest lighthouse in these islands. The Master of the *Puffin* was a Higginbotham, one of a long line that went back to Hook Head in 1750, when the first Higginbotham was a Keeper there. His son, John, was a Keeper at the Baily, and the next generation of the family gave 5 sons to the Lighthouse Service — 3 Lighthouse Keepers and 2 Masters of Lightships. One of these was the Master of the *Puffin*.

And that line continues to the present day, through the marriage of Isabella Higginbotham, a great-great-great grandaughter of that Hook Keeper of 1750, to Thomas Scanlan, of Scattery Island, in the Shannon Estuary. Thomas came of a long line of Shannon River Pilots, and was the first of his family to enter the Lighthouse Service. Both husband and wife were Lighthouse Keepers and lived on Mutton Island, in Galway Bay, from 1943 to 1951; he as Principal Keeper, she as Female Assistant Keeper. Their son Bill, was also a Principal Keeper with Irish Lights and is now retired and living in Galway. As many as 9 other members of the Scanlan clan have served with Irish Lights; one of them, Patrick Scanlan, Assistant Keeper on the Tuskar, was killed on 2nd December, 1941, when a drifting mine struck the rock and exploded. His grand-daughter, Patricia, is a best-selling author, now living in Dublin. And, the present Attendant Keeper at Youghal, in Co. Cork, is Donatius Scanlan.

The first lightships on our coast were, relatively speaking, quite primitive. Palmer's Lighhtship (1739) in the Liffey, and the first Kish Lightship (1811), were crudely converted craft, having been built for other work. The first of the old-type lightships to be 'custom' built was the Coningbeg (1824); she was built by Roberts & Co., Milford Haven.

But, even at their best, lightships were hell to live in; the cramped quarters, the constant rolling and pitching; the ever-present risk of breaking adrift without propulsive power; the hazard of collision in bad weather. The men who manned the lightvessels were, for the most part, seamen, well-used to the rolling and pitching and, in foul weather, sea water everywhere. By comparison the Lighthouse Keeper had a much better life, with, even at its worst, more freedom of movement and more comfortable and stable living quarters. Today, the lightship, or light-vessel, has been replaced by the L.A.N.B'Y (Large Navigational Buoy), at two stations on the East Coast — Codling and Arklow. The A.L.F. (Automatic Light-float) has replaced the Coninbeg L.V., and an A.L.F. now lights the South Rock, Co. Down, replacing the old Kilwarlin Lighthouse.

The officers and crews of the tenders have, over many years, displayed navigational skill and boatwork of the highest class. Theirs is an extremely demanding discipline; constantly working close inshore, negotiating dangerous shoals and sandbars; manoeuvering close to rocks in effecting reliefs and the landing of supplies and building materials; servicing buoyage systems in narrow estuaries. As with the Light Keepers, there is a tradition of family service here also. Captain Denis Gray, now retired, and for many years Inspector and Marine Superintendent, has been followed into the Irish Lights Service by his son, Dermot. Dermot is an officer on the *Gray Seal*, which ship takes its name from his father. Denis was responsible for purchasing the vessel for Irish Lights in 1988, and the Commissioners, appropriately, decided to name it after him.

Since the advent of the helicopter, and the automation of the lighthouses, the tenders have been largely deployed in the servicing of buoys and beacons. Some of these are the responsibility of the local Port Authority, but many of them are directly serviced by Irish Lights. Furthermore, the Commissioners have the statutory duty to inspect all of these marks periodically. Some of the buoys are lighted, but, fortunately only need refuelling every twelve months. The Service tenders, working on a planned rotation, place the buoys on station and in due course lift them again for servicing in one of the several Buoy Depots round the coast. The principal Depot for cleaning, repainting and refuelling is at Dun Laoghaire. Occasionally buoys break adrift and may be blown thousands of miles from their anchorage. Buoys from Florida and the East coast of America have been found drifting in Irish waters. The development of ever more sophisticated buoyage systems has brought us the "monster buoy", which is, in effect, an automated floating lighthouse.

Control and Administration

From Fair Head in Antrim to Hook Head in Wexford, our North-East, East and South-East coasts are contiguous to the British coast, from the Mull of Kintyre to the Bristol Channel. At some points the sea-journey is no greater than 20 or 30 miles; as in the North Channel between Donaghdee and Portpatrick, and between Rathlin Island and the Mull of Kintyre. It seems logical then that Irish Lights should, without having any formal obligation, liaise with Trinity House and the Northern Lighthouse Board on matters relating to navigational aids.

The three lighthouse authorities in these islands are; Trinity House, which controls the coasts and islands of England and Wales, with the exception of Jersey; the Northern Lighthouse Board which controls the coast and islands of Scotland, and the Isle of Man; the Commissioners of Irish Lights, who control all the coast and islands of Ireland, both North and South of the border. In an area of operation where, for instance, the duplication of the character of a light could prove disastrous, it make sense that all three authorities should work in close harmony to ensure safe passage for all vessels sailing in these waters.

When a ship docks at any port in any of these three "jurisdictions", she pays light dues, at a flat rate, based on her tonnage. The dues collected go into a General Lighthouse Fund, in London, and from that, allocation is made, according to their needs, to the three Authorities. This allocation, apart from certain financing from the Irish Government, is the only "income" available to Irish Lights, and out of this, the organisation is run. Head Office is at Lower Pembroke Street, Dublin, where the Commissioners hold a Board meeting once every week.

There are twenty-one Commissioners and one of these is always, *ex officio*, the Lord Mayor of Dublin; three are Aldermen or Councillors appointed by Dublin Corporation. The rest are a diverse lot, drawn from a variety of backgrounds; Business, Banking, the Law, Medicine; the pre-requisites being a genuine love of the sea and the welfare of those who sail on it, and sufficient time at their disposal to attend meetings on a regular basis. For instance, the current Chairman of the Board of the Commisioners of Irish Lights is John Gore-Grimes, a well-known Dublin Solicitor, who heads the family Law firm. He is also an internationally-known yachtsman, with a predilection, not for racing, but for cruising in Arctic and Antarctic waters, and such unspoilt and relatively undiscovered places. But, above all else, he is a man hypersensitive to the responsibility of the Irish Lights Service to actually serve those who go down to the sea in ships, of whatever size, and for whatever lawful reason.

The Commissioners of Irish Lights are elected for life, with the Chairmanship rotating. The appointment is an honorary one, with no emoluments. On formal occasions they wear naval uniform; as when on their Tour of Inspection. This Tour is very much a 'working' Tour; the *raison d'etre* being the need to fulfil their statutory obligation to inspect all lighthouses and other navigational aids on our coasts. Formerly carried out by ship, this Tour is now made by combination of ship and helicopter.

Granuaille awaiting Commissioners return - pre-helicopter

Automation and The Lighthouse Keeper

> "Having lived in a lighthouse
> On a bare rock
> Surrounded by sea
> For most of my life
> And now retired;
>
> The thing I remember
> Is dense fog clearing
> At the turn of high tide;
> And the stars coming out
> Like primroses in the sky."

D.J. O'Sullivan: "Memories".

In the years spent researching this book I visited most of the lighthouses round our coasts; took part in many helicopter reliefs; on occasion, took boat from mainland to offshore island; spent just hours on some, as the chopper schedule dictated; stayed a while on others, overnighting on many a wind-blown, wave-washed rock station; from Inishtrahull, saw the first, faint flush of dawn flood the cold, white sky behind the Mull of Kintyre; listened to the restive sea-birds settling for the night on the crags and in the crevices of Skellig Michael; saw dense fog clear at the turn of the tide on Slyne Head, and watched the stars, like clustered primroses, etched on the great vaulted ceiling of the indigo sky.

I have also taken part in some "evacuations", where, after the official automating of the light had taken place, the Keepers left the lighthouse for the last time. One such occasion is etched on my mind, as clearly as those primrose stars on the indigo sky above Slyne Head, and in it is resumed for me so much of the loss, the loneliness, the heartbreak and the awful finality of automation. We were leaving one of the remote rock stations, about to board the helicopter, when I remembered I had left a notebook in the Keepers' dwelling. I got the key from the Principal Keeper and went back to the house. Now, even though we had only vacated the place minutes before, it seemed to me that, as I went back into the recently deserted kitchen, I was stepping back into the past; a time where life had, in a sense, stopped, frozen forever.

Oh, yes, the Attendant would come here to make his regular visits; he might even stay overnight. And workmen and technicians would come to maintain the premises and the equipment. The occasional naturalist, ornithologist, or geologist would, with Irish Lights permission, come here for a short stay. But no one, no one would ever live here again, permanently, as Keepers latterly, and prior to that, whole families had lived. These rooms that had witnessed birth and death, happiness and unhappiness, would never be really lived in again. These rooms that had, through long days and nights under siege by the sea, been the forging-houses of so many talents, would never see such activitiy again. Here, poems and stories had been told and written down, pictures painted, songs sung, ships painstakingly, lovingly, constructed and placed in bottles. From stations such as this Keepers had, using the short wave radio, carried on marathon chess games with other Keepers, on other remote stations; had made their contributions to inter-lighthouse Christmas concerts, conducted 'over the air'.

One of the ramifications of automation that concerns many people, both inside and outside Irish Lights, is the fate of the various properties on which the lighthouses are located. Already it is planned to sell-off some of these, with just the lighthouse itself, and right-of-way for Irish Lights personnel, being retained. Many acres of some of the most valuable and picturesque land will pass into private ownership, and headlands and promontories once accessible to the public will now be closed. There will be no guarantee that very distinctive old lighthouse dwellings will be preserved; indeed, it most likely that they will be reconstructed with little sensitivity or care for their character. We raise a song-and-dance about the preservation of old, period buildings, some of them not always particularly beautiful, distinctive, or worth preserving. Should we not also be concerned for the very distinctive buildings and compounds that are now, since the Keepers and their families are gone, the only link with the great lost age of the manned lighthouse?

And now, despite all the careful maintenance, they would quickly acquire that unlived-in atmosphere; would lie dark and silent through the long nights, while the automated lantern in the lighthouse above cast its guiding beams across the trackless sea. And in that moment, it seemed to me, that every unwatched light, whether on remote wave-washed rock or lonely headland, was doomed to be a *Marie Celeste*, lit but abandoned, drifting in the dark.

Progress is the maddest, and most maddening, thing. It is inevitable and contradictory. Inevitable, in that, once started, it proceeds inexorably; contradictory, in that, as with the automation of Light-houses, excellent people with an accummulated and unique skill are made redundant. But, all genuine progress is simply evolu-tion; indeed, that is what makes it so inevitable and inexorable a process. I once asked an old Lighthouse Keeper what he cons-idered the most welcome 'innovation', 'progress', or whatever, in his time in the Service. I expected him to say "the helicopter", but he answered "the fridge and the deep-freeze". Well, whether it be fridge, freezer, helicopter, television, they were all milestones on the road of progress that inevitably led to automation. They were, with the added comforts and benefits they brought, the acceptable face of progress; automation, with the consequent hardships of redundancy and the need to make a new career, is the unaccept-able face. Flip sides of the same coin.

The automation process, for lighthouses, probably started the day someone discovered that, instead of manufacturing gas at some remote station, the light would function, equally effectively, on bottled gas. The next, logical step was to fit a timing device on the smaller harbour and pierhead lights, and make them unwatched. Then, in 1963, successful experiments were carried out on Haulbowline Lighthouse, in Carlingford Lough and it was made unwatched. This is a wave-washed tower, built on a rock so small it is exposed only at low-water. Accommodation was cramped for the Keepers living there, and automating it was seen primarily as a humane and kindly act; it also proved to be more economical. And so, once started, the process of automation rolled inexorably on.

A sad reminder of the effects of this automation, or progress, is the now largely unused building at the Baily Lighthouse, which was built in 1973 to accommodate Supernumerary Assistant Keepers. So modern, so well- equipped is this accommodation that it has been known as "The Baily Hilton". Now, because there has been no intake of people for so many years, it is, with the exception of the odd visiting tradesman, unoccupied.

Whether we romantics like it or not, Radar, Sonar and other shipboard navigational devices have greatly reduced the need for lighthouses and Lighthouse Keepers. Automation is reckoned to be more efficient, and cheaper than having human watchmen; just what shipping companies, who ultimately pay the dues, are looking for. And, in a Service whose primary duty is to serve the mariner at sea, it would be less than responsible to refuse to modernise and use all available navigational aids. So, the lighthouse Keeper must go. Those men, and women, who, for so many centuries have been symbols of heroism and philanthropy, will, by the end of this century have passed into history. First it was open fires; then candles; then coal; then oil; then gas; then electricity; now solar power. A far cry from the monks who tended fires on lonely headlands and rocky islets. A far cry from the heroism of Grace Darling and the spirit her very name evokes.

By 1997, all our Irish lighthouses will be unwatched automatic. And already ships are being fitted with electronic navigational devices which enable them to voyage with impunity in any waters without the aid of lighthouse beam or fog signal. Such technological advances will, ultimately, make the lighthouse as obsolete as the Lighthouse Keeper. Let us be grateful that, for the moment, though the Keepers are going, the Lights remain. For myself, I temper my acceptance of the inevitability of progress by remembering what my wise friend, that grand old man of the sea, Dr. John de Courcy Ireland said, in talking about the demanning of

the Kish Light. For many years he had been Secretary of Dun
Laoghaire Lifeboat, and in that time, to his certain knowledge,
the Keepers on Kish had, by their vigilance and quick, human
response in certain situations, saved at least twenty lives. A
thought to ruminate on as we progress into the unwatched, sonar
singing dark.

Building a lighthouse on a wave-washed rock. Callwell

Part Eight

Appendices

&

Index

COMMISSIONERS OF IRISH LIGHTS
CHAIRMEN

From 1867 until 1918 the third Commissioner to enter the Board Room took the Chair.

1918	Rt. Hon. Andrew Jameson, D.L., P.C.
1939	R.N. Guinness, B.A.
1957	J.H.J. Poole, M.A., M.A.I., Sc.D.,F.T.C.D., M.R.I.A.
1961	J. Purser, M.A., A.A.I., M.Sc., M.I.C.E.I.
1963	E.E. Benson, B.A.
1966	Captain J.C. Colvill, R.N.
1969	T.G. Wilson, M.B, Litt.D., F.R.C.S.I., M.R.I.A., Hon. R.H.A.
1970	Lt. Col. J.B. Hollwey, M.C.
1973	J. Harold Douglas, B.A., B.Comm.
1976	J.P. Jameson
1979	R.R. Stewart, M.A.
1981	Lieut. Commander Sir William Blunden, Bt., R.N.
1984	J.H. Guinness
1988	Capt. A.C. Tupper, D.S.C., R.N.
1990	V.A. Cooke, O.B.E, M.A., F.I.Mech.E., D.L.
1993	J. Gore-Grimes, B.A., LL.B.

COMMISSIONERS OF IRISH LIGHTS
VICE- CHAIRMEN

1918	Mr. E. White
1933	Mr. R.N. Guinness
1939	Captain J.H. Webb
1957	Professor J. Purser
1961	Mr. E.E. Benson
1963	Captain J.C. Colvill
1966	Dr. T.G. Wilson
1969	Lt. Col. J.B. Hollwey
1970	Mr. J.H. Douglas
1973	Mr. J.P. Jameson
1976	Mr. R.R. Stewart
1979	Lt. Commander Sir William Blunden
1981	Mr. J.H. Guinness
1984	Captain A.C. Tupper
1988	Mr. J. Gore-Grimes
1993	Mr. M.A. O'Neill

COMMISSIONERS OF IRISH LIGHTS
DEPUTY VICE-CHAIRMEN

1918	Mr. F. Brooke
1919	Sir D. Plunket Barton
1921	Mr. J.R. Blood
1922	Mr. R.N. Guinness
1933	Professor J.Joly
1934	Captain J.H. Webb
1939	Dr. E.J. Watson
1947	Professor H.H. Dixon
1954	Mr. Mr. J. Hubbard Clark
1957	Mr. E.E. Benson
1961	Captain J.C. Colvill
1963	Dr. T.G. Wilson
1966	Lt. Col. J.B. Hollwey
1969	Mr. J.H. Douglas
1970	Mr. J.P. Jameson
1973	Mr. R.R. Stewart
1976	Sir William Blunden
1979	Mr. J.H. Guinness
1981	Mr. P.H. Greer
1988	Mr. J. Gore-Grimes
1991	Mr. M.A. O'Neill
1993	Mr. M. W.S. Maclaran

COMMISSIONERS OF IRISH LIGHTS
CURRENT COMMISSION

Rt. Hon. the Earl of Meath

Mr. J.P. Jameson

Mr. L.D.G. Collen, B.A., M.A.I., F.I.E.I.

Mr. R.R. Stewart, M.A.

Mr. Richie Ryan

Captain A.C. Tupper, D.S.C., R.N.

Mr. M.A. O'Neill (Vice-Chairman)

Mr. H.P. Coneney, F.R.IC.S.

Mr. T. Sheppard

Mr. M. W.S. Maclaran, B.A. (Deputy Vivr-Chairman)

Mr. J. Gore-Grimes, B.A., LL.B. (Chairman)

Cammodore L.S. Moloney

Rt. Hon. The Lord Cooke of Islandreagh

The Hon. T.R.V. Dixon, C.B.E., D.L.

Mr. T.C. Johnson

Mr. L.D. McGonagle, B.A., LL.B.

(Vacancy)

REPRESENTATIVES OF
DUBLIN CORPORATON

Rt. Hon. The Lord Mayor, Councillor T. MacGiolla

Councillor J. Stafford

Councillor J. Connolly

Alderman S. 'Dublin Bay' Loftus

LIST OF OFFICIALS

Chief Executive   1985 -   T.M. Boyd

Secretary
1867-81	W. Lees
1881-05	O. Armstrong
1905-20	H.G. Cook
1920-33	J.B. Phelps
1934-46	E.A.M. Leggett
1946-54	D. Rowlands
1954-59	A.J. England
1959-61	H.V. Allman Smith
1961-81	P.G. Adams
1981-85	C.A. MacFarlan
	(Post Discontinued)

Secretary to the Board & Deputy Chief Exec.
1985-88	A. O'Hagan
1988-91	F.G. Kay
	(Post Discontinued)

Heads of Function

Engineering
1867-68	C.P. Cotton (Consultant)
1868-77	J.S. Sloane
1877-78	J.H. Morant
1878-00	W. Douglass
1900-30	C.W. Scott
1930-45	J.W. Tonkin
1945-56	J.H. Grose
1956-79	A.D.H. Martin
1979-81	N.D. Clotworthy
1981-85	T.M. Boyd
1985-87	0.M. Harvey
1987-	M.B. McStay

Marine
1867-69	Capt. E.F. Roberts
1869-74	Capt. E.H. Hawes, R.N.
1874-78	Capt. G.W. Morant
1878-81	Capt. Cole
1881-91	Capt. Boxer
1891-01	Capt. Galwey
1901-18	Capt. Deane
1918-39	Capt. W.H. Davis
1939-47	Capt. R.C. Hill
1947-59	Capt. W.J. Kelly
1960-62	Capt. E.C. Thornton
1962-69	Capt. W.H. Ball
1969-74	Capt. C.C. L'Estrange
1974-85	Capt. H.N. Greenlee
1985-91	Capt. D.A. Gray
1991-	Capt. G.C. Kinsella

Personnel
1985-88	F.G. Kay
1988-	R.T. Gully
	(with responsibility for Administration from 1991)

Finance
1920-34	E.A.M. Leggett
1934-36	H.W. Lea
1936-46	D. Rowlands
1946-54	A.J. England
1954-59	H.V. Allman Smith
1959-61	P.G. Adams
1961-82	S.G. Rogerson
1982-88	J.M. Wisdom
1988-	M.A. Dyas

LIGHTHOUSE KEEPERS ROLL CALL

No.	Surname	First
1	Redmond	Thomas
2	Tyrrell	Robert
3	Williams	James
4	Kennedy	Ambrose
5	Brownell	Jervis
6	Brownell	George
7	Kelly	John
8	Kelly	James
9	Donleavy	George
10	Dunne	William
11	Hawkins	Daniel
12	Tottenham	John
13	Brownell	George
14	Fortune	Thomas
15	Ryan	Francis
16	Sweeney	Thomas
17	St James	William
18	Hamilton	Rickard
19	Healy	Matthew
20	Boyle	Charles
21	O'Donnell	John
22	Redmond	John
23	Wilson	Alexander
24	Kerley	Thomas
25	Walsh	James
26	Barry	Michael
27	Keeney	Hugh
28	Armstrong	Robert
29	Meehan	Charles
30	Rohu	Edward
31	Lavelle	John
32	Kelly	Henry
33	Widdicambe	Richard
34	Mac Ginley	J. C.
35	Kennedy	John
36	Sole	Bradley
37	Hamilton	John
38	D'Arcy	Patrick
39	Grehan	Patrick
40	Maguire	Francis
41	McKenna	Edward
42	Kennedy	Edward, A.
43	Gillespie	George
44	Higginbotham	James
45	Hawkins	Charles
46	Kerr	Kenneth
47	Corish	Joseph
48	Kennedy	Hamilton
49	Griffen	Thomas
50	Carolin	Patrick
51	Staniforth	Samuel
52	Donovan	M. D.
53	Higginbotham	John
54	Duffy	Robert, J.
55	Duffy	Frederick, W.
56	Friel	James, F.
57	Corish	Patrick
58	Potter	John
59	Sampson	William
60	French	James
61	Wright	Richard, J.
62	O'Connell	Patrick
63	Glanville	William
64	Butler	William
65	Brownell	G. J.
66	Corish	William
67	Keeffe	John
68	Sheehy	Patrick
69	Cummain	Richard
70	Harrington	John
71	Jeffers	Benjamin, R.
72	Connell	John, J.
73	Twohig	James
74	Cotter	Thomas
75	Lyons	Richard
76	Twohig	Daniel
77	Watson	James
78	Colly	Michael
79	Morgan	William
80	Crowley	Henry
81	Glanville	John
82	Duffy	Thomas
83	Phelan	Robert, J.
84	Moore	John
85	Kennedy	David
86	Higginbotham	Patrick
87	Hammond	Henry
88	Glanville	Thomas
89	Lyons	William
90	Hawlin	James
91	Monks	John
92	Sullivan	Joseph
93	Roddy	Peter
94	Sloth	Alfred
95	Hamilton	David
96	Ryan	John
97	Murphy	Henry, T.
98	Trant	Jeremiah

No.	Surname	Name	No.	Surname	Name	No.	Surname	Name
99	Cunningham	John	133	Lavelle	Peter	167	Brannell	J. M.
100	Byrne	Murtha	134	Freeby	J. J.	168	Johnson	Michael
101	Murphy	John, Henry	135	Coughlan	John	169	Ward	Manus
102	Stocker	Leonard	136	Murray	Alexander	170	Connolly	John
103	Callaghan	W. J.	137	Murphy	Joseph, Denis	171	Smith	Samuel, J.
104	Grills	William	138	O'Reilly	John, J.	172	Jones	Thomas
105	Murphy	Thomas, J.	139	James	George, W.	173	McKeague	Robert
106	O'Donnell	Charles	140	Mc Minn	John	174	Crowley	John
107	Egan	William	141	Gillespie	Neal	175	Sweeney	Patrick
108	O'Brien	John	142	Sweeney	James, J.	176	Wall	John, Patrick
109	Higginbotham	Joseph	143	MacGinley	Patrick, J.	177	Devaney	James
110	King	Thomas	144	Boyle	Michael	178	O'Donnell	Richard, J.
111	Ryan	Thomas, F.	145	Murphy	John, Francis	179	Loughrey	Neil
112	Kelly	Richard, J.	146	McKeown	James	180	Kilgallon	Andrew
113	Birrells	Edward	147	Crowley	James	181	Sullivan	Eugene
114	Faulkner	Thomas	148	Moore	Michael, G.	182	Higginbotham	Leo
115	Hill	John	149	Healy	Matthew, J.	183	Healy	Joseph
116	Lavelle	J. H.	150	Bird	William	184	Rohu	Alfred
117	Lacy	William	151	Ahern	James	185	Kennedy	Martin
118	O'Donnell	T. J.	152	Woods	Michael	186	Morris	John, P.
119	James	R. H.	153	Duffy	Robert	187	Sloan	Philip
120	Cooper	John	154	Gillespie	J. J.	188	Maguire	Francis, M.
121	Hamilton	John	155	Duffy	F. J.	189	McQuaig	Alexander
122	O'Callaghan	M. J.	156	Brennan	Cornilius	190	McCloskey	A. J.
123	Keenan	Charles	157	Higginbotham	William	191	Reddin	Christopher
124	Wright	Jonathan	158	McGinley	Michael	192	McCann	Patrick
125	Coupe	Frederick	159	Sugrue	Thomas	193	O'Leary	Alphonses
126	Curling	Frederick	160	Williams	John	194	O'Connor	James, A.
127	Murran	D. J.	161	Healy	Patrick	195	Armstrong	Ambrose, Bloxham
128	Murphy	John	162	Ryan	Henry, R.	196	Godkin	Benjamin
129	Somers	R. S.	163	Johnson	John Martin	197	Hawkins	Francis
130	Wills	John	164	Duggan	John, J.	198	Finn	John
131	McKeague	Isaac	165	Smith	Edward, James	199	Loughrey	Charles
132	Neill	R. J.	166	Harrington	Timothy	200	Redmond	Thomas, Charles

No.	Surname	Forename		No.	Surname	Forename		No.	Surname	Forename
201	Martin	William, John		235	Friel	William		269	McShane	John
202	Hawkins	William		236	Connolly	Joseph, V.		270	McGowan	Joseph
203	Corish	Peter		237	Duff	Denis, J.		271	Staniforth	Henry
204	Boyle	Patrick, James		238	Carolan	F. J.		272	Trant	John, M.
205	Hill	Francis		239	McNelis	Charles		273	Whelan	Patrick
206	Bonfill	Martin		240	Donovan	Daniel		274	Duffy	Frederick, J.
207	McGinley	James		241	Ryan	F. J.		275	Higginbotham	John
208	Gillespie	Patrick		242	O'Donnell	Dominick		276	Haren	Hugh
209	Sullivan	Peter		243	Sutton	Patrick		277	Scanlan	Thomas
210	Donlon	John, Joseph		244	Kennedy	A. J.		278	Stocker	Leonard, V.
211	Snow	William		245	Roddy	James		279	Meehan	Edward, J.
212	McDevitt	John		246	Hegarty	James		280	Crowley	Daniel, C.
213	Scanlan	Patrick		247	Duffy	Michael		281	Dudley	Denis
214	O'Connor	James		248	Ernest	Clague, John		282	Meenan	Cornelius
215	Walsh	George		249	McMahon	George		283	Heneghan	Patrick
216	Hamilton	David, Joseph		250	Godkin	William, H.		284	Coughlan	John, W.
217	Brennan	Patrick		251	Sutton	Walter, F.		285	Staniforth	Samuel, J.
218	Blakely	Robert		252	Connolly	Denis, C.		286	O'Donnell	R. J.
219	Kennedy	Edward, H.		253	Gordon	Joseph		287	Doyle	James
220	Hawkins	Daniel, Thomas		254	Lance	James		288	Bird	Tom, J.
221	Fennell	John		255	Hawkins	Daniel		289	Scanlan	Patrick
222	Roche	Michael		256	Bonfill	John		290	King	James, M.
223	Fortune	Eugene		257	Blake	John		291	Scanlan	Thos (ii)
224	Coughlan	Andrew		258	Evans	William, E.		292	Roddy	Patrick, G.
225	Keaney-Mahony	Patrick Joseph		259	Keane	John		293	Scott	John, J.
226	Burke	Cornelius		260	Scanlan	Simon		294	Doyle	Michael
227	McMahon	Stephen		261	Boyle	John, J.		295	McGrath	Lawrence
228	Corish	Francis, J.		262	Bolger	Michael		296	King	John
229	Kearon	Richard		263	Meehan	Charles		297	Boyle	Patrick
230	O'Donnell	Daniel		264	McCann	Joseph		298	Conneely	John
231	Woods	William		265	Corish	John, Joseph		299	Stapleton	John
232	Power	Lawrence		266	McMahon	Michael		300	Kelly	John, J.
233	Barlow	John, J.		267	Hayes	Michael		301	Harding	John
234	Wall	William		268	Colfer	Thomas		302	Hammond	Thomas

303	Fitzgerald	Edmond
304	Sweeney	John, Francis
305	Monks	T. F.
306	Blakely	David
307	Glanville	Samuel, Michael
308	Murray	Gerald, Richard
309	Murphy	Daniel, David
310	Roddy	Peter
311	Hamilton	William, Alex
312	Deasy	John
313	Sullivan	Patrick, David
314	Boyle	Charles
315	Lavelle	John
316	Polly	James, R.
317	Staniforth	Patrick, Joseph
318	Glanville	John, K.
319	Lawlor	Thomas, J.
320	Stocker	Cecil
321	Ryan	Francis, James
322	O' Connor	Peter, Joseph
323	Murphy	Richard, Kevin
324	Sullivan	Daniel, James
325	Campbell	Neal
326	Glanville	Thomas
327	Boyle	Michael, Patrick
328	Crowley	John
329	James	George, Matthew
330	Roddy	Richard
331	Campbell	John, William
332	Duggan	Hugh
333	Huntingdon	Robert, Wilson
334	Hamilton	William, Joseph
335	Byrne	David
336	Coghlan	Richard, Francis

337	Geoghegan	James
338	Sullivan	David
339	Coupe	Walter
340	Howard	Robert
341	Crowley	Michael, J.
342	Jervis	James, William
343	Lavelle	James, Joseph
344	Cahill	William, John
345	Butler	Ambrose, Gerard
346	O'Connor	James, Joseph
347	Murphy	Thomas, Noel
348	Roche	John, Joseph
349	O'Donnell	David, M.
350	James	William, F.
351	Boyle	Martin, A.
352	Hegarty	James
353	Ryan	Francis, S.
354	Mc Cann	John, Joseph
355	Keenan	Edmond
356	Crowley	John
357	O'Donnell	John, Martin
358	Kennedy	Martin
359	Sullivan	Eugene
360	O'Donnell	Patrick, Joseph
361	Hegarty	James
362	Nelson	Robert
363	O'Connor	Michael, J.
364	Dillon	James, Joseph
365	Cleary	John
366	Butler	Richar, Ellis
367	Polly	William, John
368	Luccan	John
369	Ward	William, John
370	Sweeney	Michael, Francis

371	Hearne	Anthony, George
372	O'Donnell	Edward, Stanislaus
373	Connell	John, Frederick
374	Cahill	James, Joseph
375	Kennedy	John
376	Loughrey	Neil, Joseph
377	Walsh	James, Francis
378	Jones	Michael, Joseph
379	Byrne	Joseph
380	Hyde	Thomas
381	Cleary	James
382	Smith	Michael
383	McLaughlin	Edward
384	Roche	William, Patrick
385	Ryan	Francis, James
386	Scanlan	Michael, M.
387	Kilgallon	Hubert, A.
388	Hedderman	Kenneth, William
389	Lawler	Nicholas, Kevin
390	McMahon	Patrick
391	Butler	Lawrence, Joseph
392	Hickey	Edward, Francis
393	Ryan	Patrick
394	Stapleton	Joseph, T.
395	Doherty	Michael, J. C.
396	Whelan	Patrick, Vincent
397	Brennan	Patrick
398	Cullen	R.
399	Cahill	Denis
400	Duffy	Patrick
401	Gillespie	William, F.
402	Knox	William
403	Hayes	Richard, J.
404	O'Sullivan	Timothy

405	Leyden	James
406	Bell	Charles
407	Doyle	William
408	Lynch	Kevin
409	Scanlan	Thomas, M.
410	Cummins	Edward, J.
411	Roche	Patrick
412	Gillen	Michael, D.
413	McCarthy	Francis
414	O'Brien	Jeremiah, T.
415	Roche	Gerard
416	O'Connor	Joseph, M.
417	Bolger	Stephen, J.
418	Hawkins	Edward, J.
419	O'Donnell	Thomas
420	McMahon	Brendan
421	Ward	Richard, M.
422	Bolger	Patrick, M.
423	Connolly	John
424	Keane	Martin, J.
425	Campbell	James, J.
426	Hernan	Charles
427	O'Leary	Denis, V.
428	O'Donovan	William, G.
429	Linnane	Arthur, M.
430	Kilcoyne	John, G.
431	Spencer	John, J.
432	Scanlan	Senan, J.
433	Fox	J.
434	Devaney	Patrick, J.
435	Barr	Henry, Gerard
436	Murphy	J. J.
437	Coughlan	D.
438	Brennan	J.

439	Kelly	J. A.
440	Stapleton	J. J.
441	Duffy	F. G.
442	Power	J. V.
443	Gillen	E. P.
444	Walsh	T. A.
445	Sullivan	O.
446	Power	J. J.
447	Kennedy	A. J.
448	Scanlan	D. S.
449	O'Donnell	W. J.
450	Coughlan	A. F.
451	Spencer	R. A.
452	Keane	P. J.
453	O'Donnell	D. J.
454	Scanlan	J. P.
455	Connolly	C. P.
456	Stapleton	J. J.
457	Hamilton	A. R.
458	Scanlan	J. P.
459	Dumigan	William
460	Power	R.
461	Linnane	V.
462	Shanahan	W. C.
463	Rohu	S. A. M.
464	Meehan	C. A.
465	Barry	P.
466	Gaughan	D.
467	Murphy	M. J.
468	Barr	G. A.
469	Polly	M. J.
470	Spencer	C. J.
471	Stocker	L. C.
472	O'Driscoll	W. H.

473	Scanlan	P. W.
474	Roddy	T. J.
475	Coughlan	P. J.
476	Hamilton	W. R.
477	Grady	John, J.
478	Garvey	B. J.
479	Roddy	G.
480	McCroahn	P. J.
481	Harrington	C. J.
482	James	William, C.
483	Swan	J. R.
484	Coughlan	J.
485	Tweedy	James
486	Gallagher	John, Patrick
487	Fitzgerald	Richard
488	Keane	Patrick
489	McLaughlin	John, S.
490	Higginbotham	John, J.
491	Egan	Michael, Flannan
492	Farren	William
493	Notter	Robert, C.
494	O'Regan	Byran, P.
495	King	John, Richard
496	Sugrue	John, Reginald
497	Carmody	John
498	Stocker	Henry, Patrick
499	Murphy	Michael, J.
500	Coghlan	Matthew
501	Martin	Joseph, A.
502	Mc Laughlin	Hugh, A.
503	Hearty	Joseph, C.
504	O'Farrell	James, P.
505	Meehan	Gregory, M. P.
506	Roddy	John, J.

507	Polly	Robert, G.	541	Burke	Anthony	575	Jones	Patrick, Power
508	Kennedy	James, P.	542	White	James	576	Foran	Richard, Denis
509	Walsh	James	543	Polly	Adrian, Anthony	577	Weldon	John, E. D.
510	O'Boyle	Thomas, N.	544	Campbell	J. P.	578	Fitzgerald	Edward
511	Glanville	Thomas	545	Conway	Brendan, Patrick	579	Sullivan	Denis, Joseph
512	Cunningham	James, B.	546	Cavanagh	George, Francis	580	McCormack	Thomas, F.
513	Crowley	Oliver, F.	547	Ward	James	581	Whelan	James, Michael
514	Cashman	William	548	Wickham	Raymond	582	Kennedy	Martin
515	Kavanagh	John	549	O'Shea	Timothy, Michael	583	Busher	John, L.
516	O'Shea	Patrick, B.	550	O'Leary	Eugene, Francis	584	Neill	Robert
517	O'Farrell	Francis, J.	551	O'Brien	Christopher, Thomas	585	O'Sullivan	C. R. C.
518	Heneghan	William, F.	552	Murphy	Francis, Joseph	586	O'Driscoll	Anthony
519	Tweedy	Robert	553	McCouaig	Bernard, Phillip	587	Curtin	Patrick, J.
520	Duggan	Peter, Richard	554	O'Toole	John	588	Culligan	Michael, D.
521	Garvey	J. A.	555	Smyth	Robert, Augusta	589	O'Briain	Sean
522	Brennan	Kevin	556	Connor	Denis, Edward	590	Kennedy	Patrick, Edward
523	Sheridan	Michael, J.	557	O'Flaherty	James, Colman	591	Faherty	John, Joseph
524	Friel	Charles, Joseph	558	Gibson	Patrick, Joseph	592	Hennessy	Patrick, Joseph
525	Campbell	W. K. U.	559	Doherty	John, Joseph	593	Maloney	Michael
526	Boyers	Robert, Walpole	560	O'Sullivan	Daniel, Kevin	594	Keane	Patrick, Kevin
527	O'Connor	Padraig, Pearse	561	Enright	Patrick, J.	595	McNamara	William
528	Crowley	John, Noel	562	Crowley	B. A.	596	McGrath	John, David
529	O'Driscoll	Richard, Ignatius	563	Murphy	Thomas, P. J.	597	Murray	Phelim
530	Lyons	Joseph	564	McCurdy	Gerald	598	Hamilton	Alexander, M.
531	O'Sullivan	William	565	O'Leary	Denis, Anthony	599	Canning	James
532	Sullivan	Hugh, Joseph	566	Kennedy	Timothy, Paul	600	Ryan	Francis, James
533	Fitzgerald	Richard, John	567	O'Donnell	John, Martin	601	Sheehan	Thomas, Aquinas
534	Conneely	Robert	568	McLoughlin	John, Dominick	602	McCurdy	Noel, S.
535	Shannon	Michael, S.	569	O'Boyle	Peter, John	603	Kneafsey	Michael
536	O'Driscoll	Denis	570	O'Briain	Ciaran	604	Butler	Gerald, Patrick
537	O'Sullivan	Eugene, Paul	571	Tweedy	Nicholas	605	Butler	Edward, John
538	McCloskey	James, Hugh	572	Harrington	Brendan	606	Joyce	Thomas, Anthony
539	Tweedy	Thomas, Patrick	573	Dirrane	Patrick, Noel	607	Histon	John, Edward
540	O'Connor	John, Brendan	574	Jones	John, Leo	608	Polly	Brian, G.

609	Conneely	Michael, Anthony
610	Moran	Vincent, Mary
611	Cullen	James, Martin
612	Stocker	Stephen, Reginald
613	Holland	Daniel, Gerard,
614	Lane	Bryan
615	Aherne	David, Bennett,
616	Magner	John, Paul
617	Hedderman	Vincent
618	Tevlin	Michael, Francis
619	Tevlin	Gerard, Anthony
620	Cronin	Anthony, James
621	Deasy	Florence
622	Sweeney	Gerard
623	McCarthy	Eamonn
624	O'Connell	James, Vincent
625	Fitzpatrick	Michael, J.
626	Fitzgerald	John, G.
627	Doyle	Philip, James
628	Culligan	Senan
629	Flaherty	Patrick
630	Wickham	James, E.
631	Rohu	Gerard, Martin
632	Knox	Oliver
633	Copeland	Edward, Anthony
634	Cleary	Patrick, L.
635	Hassett	Martin, G.
636	Morrisey	William, Joseph
637	O'Brien	John, Patrick
638	Heneghan	Thomas
639	Butler	James, Maurice
640	Murphy	Martin, Joseph

641	Cliffe	John, Gerard
642	Stenning	Joseph
643	Magner	Kevin, Anthony
644	O'Byrne	Gerard, Mary
645	Collins	John, Senan
646	Clare	Colm, Denis
647	Hickey	Oliver
648	O'Driscoll	Ronald, Patrick
649	Polly	Nill, Columba
650	Barry	Michael, James
651	Sweeney	Vincent, Mary
652	Tubrid	Desmond, Mary
653	Millane	Patrick, Gerard
654	O'Donnell	Derek, Patrick
655	Larkin	John, Thomas
656	Murphy	John, Patrick
657	Walsh	William, Francis
658	O'Sullivan	Stephen, John
659	Condon	Oliver, Gerard
660	Kehoe	Robert, Anthony
661	Walsh	Aidan, John
662	OLeary	Francis, Joseph
663	McCarthy	Geoffrey, Francis
664	Kennedy	John, Patrick
665	Copeland	Brendan
666	Colfer	Thomas, Daniel
667	Kelly	John, Francis
668	Ryan	Brian, Marian
669	McCarthy	John, Dillon
670	Conneely	Enda, Kevin
671	Conneely	Martin, Joseph
672	Kelly	Richard, Thomas

673	McGrath	Gerard, Thomas
674	Hamilton	John, Alexander
675	Faherty	Thomas
676	Loughrey	Francis, James,
677	Coughlan	Patrick, Gerard
678	Cronin	Henry, Louis
679	Holmes	Noel, William
680	Power	P. B.
681	Cleary	M. J.
682	McMahon	C.
683	Kestell	P.
684	Verdon	Gerard, Joseph
685	Wickham	Anthony
686	Callaghan	Frank, Xavier
687	Thomson	George, Millar
688	Keane	Kevin, Joseph
689	Carty	Brendan
690	Cronin	Brendan, Joseph
691	Maloney	Eamon, Patrick
692	Brennan	Martin, Lawrence
693	Halpin	Nicholas, Martin
694	Boyers	Alan
695	Cummins	Richard
696	Griffin	Gerard
697	Butler	John, A.
698	Walshe	Gerard
699	O'Regan	M. G.
700	Gillen	E. A.
701	O'Farrell	P. F. J.

Glossary of Lighthouse Terms

Annular lens: A lens in the shape of a circular drum.

Apparatus: A term used to designate the complete optical system housed in the lantern.

Aragand lamp: An oil lamp with a circular wick, or several such wicks arranged concentrically.

Balcony: The projecting platform of the lighthouse, usually at the level of the lantern floor.

Beacon: 1. Open coal, or turf fire, lit in chauffer or atop cottage-type lighthouse.
2. Stone, pillar, or tower. Unlit. Used as sea-mark.
3. Radio direction finding aid. (see Radio-beacon).

Biform: Two optical systems, with separate light sources, mounted one above the other in the same lantern, to double the candlepower.

Caisson: A steel, or concrete container, inside which another structure is built.

Candela: The international unit of luminous intensity, for measuring candlepower.

Catadioptric: A combination of the catoptric and dioptric optical systems (q.v) in which a dioptric lens is augmented by glass reflecting prisms or metal reflectors.

Catoptric: A reflector system, using metal or glass prisms, for projecting light beams.

Character: The means by which a light is identified - e.g. the number of flashes per minute and duration of each.

Diaphone: A fog-signal consisting of a piston driven by compressed air, giving a very characteristic sound.

Dioptric: A lens system in which the rays of light are concentrated, by refraction on passing through glass prisms.

Explosive fog-signal: Explosive charges (4 oz.), detonated electrically by Keeper at regular intervals.

Fixed Light: A steady light of unvariable appearance.

Flashing Light:	A light in which short periods of light alternate with longer periods of darkness.
Focus:	The centre of an optical system.
Gallery:	The platform around the inside of a lantern from which the glass is cleaned.
Incandescent burner:	A burner in which paraffin oil is heated to form a gas and then burned in a mantle. Much used in Lighthouses prior to electrification.
Isophase light:	A light with equal periods of light and dark.
Lantern:	The house enclosing the optical system in a Lighthouse. Normally glazed to show the light in all directions, but sometimes glazed only over the required arc.
Leading lights:	Two lights, some distance apart, which, when kept in line, lead past a danger, or into a harbour.
Murette:	The portion of the lantern house between the balcony and the glass, usually of steel, or concrete.
Occulting light:	A light in which long periods of light alternate with short periods of darkness.
Perch:	An iron mast set into a rock, to mark the danger, and usually surmounted by characteristic top-mark.
Prism:	A piece of glass of triangular cross-section, having the property of either bending rays of light (refraction), or reflecting them, depending on the geometry of the prism.
Racon:	An electronic navigational aid which responds to an impulse from a ship's radar scanner, and makes an indentifiable mark at the position of the racon (e.g. the Lighthouse) on the ship's radar screen.
Radio-beacon:	A radio aid which transmits a coded signal automatically, wherby a mariner may obtain the bearing of the beacon (Lighthouse), using his direction-finding equipment.
Rotation machine:	A clockwork motor, driven by a falling weight, used to revolve many Lighthouse lenses.
Siren:	A fog signal in which compressed air is forced though slots in a rapidly revolving disc.

ACKNOWLEDGEMENTS

The researching of this book would not have been possible without the unstinted help of the Commissioners of Irish Lights, who gave me *carte blanche* to come and go as I pleased in all of their lighthouses. From the Chairman, John Gore-Grimes and Chief Executive, Mel Boyd, to the Receptionist at Head Office, I received nothing but courtesy and unfailing patience in my many, many visits there. I remember especially the helpfullness of Fred Kaye and Roy Watts in getting the project started four years ago. And, since then, at various stages of research and writing, the contributions of Richard Butler, Michael Taylor, Captain Owen Dignan, Richard Gulley, Alan McCann and Brian Maguire. A very special thanks to Michael Costeloe, who, magnanimously, made all his research available to me, and whose fine colour pictures help illustrate the book. The encyclopaedic knowledge of Dr. John de Courcy Ireland, called upon when I was straying off-course, is also greatly appreciated; as is the contribution made by Richie Hamilton in the many talks we had. Oscar Merne of the O.P.W. kindly supplied the data relating to bird life on the lighthouse islands. In the early stages of the project, the support of John Kane and the Lighthouse Club, was a great stimulus.

All round the coast I met with incredible courtesy and hospitality from the Keepers, the Attendants, and often their families; their contribution is not forgotten. The helpfulness of all those people was perfectly epitomised in the welcome afforded me by Principal Keeper Paud O'Connor, on my visits to Hook Head; the Sweeney family at Blacksod Bay; and by John Noel Crowley, Peter Duggan and their Assistant Keepers at the Baily, during my two year domicile there. Two retired Principal Keepers, Jack Roche of Skerries, and D. J. O'Sullivan of Donegal, were of inestimable help on many occasions, in matters relating to the lore of the stations at which they served. I thank D. J. for the excerpts from his poems used in the book. C. W. Scott's History of The Fastnet Rock Lighthouses (Hazell, Watson & Viney, 1906), T. G. Wilson's The Irish Lighthouse Service (Allen Figgis, 1968), Patrick Beaver's A History of Lighthouses (Peter Davies, 1971), J. S. Sloane's A Manual for Lightkeepers (Dublin, 1873), and Robert Callwell's 19th century manuscript A Short History of the Lighthouses of Ireland (unpublished, 1863), were required reading in the course of my research.

Bill Long, Dublin, September 1993.

Colour Photographs (between pages 96 - 97)

1: Mew Island, Belfast Lough. (RC)
2: Cromwell Point, Valentia Island. (MC)
3: Black Rock, Co Sligo. (MC)
4: Inishgort, with Croagh Patrick in background. (MC)
5: Metal Man, Rosses Point. (MC)
6: Rockabill. (RC)
7: A lighthouse lantern. (KH)
8: Spiral stairs, Ferris Point. (RC)
9: Ultra modern tower, Ferris Point. (RC)
10: Ballincourty Point, Dungarvan Bay. (MC)
11: Old Head of Kinsale. (MC)
12: Maiden's Rock. (RC)
13: Fastnet Rock. (RC)
14: Last Watch leaving Fastnet Rock on its automation. From left: Dick O'Driscoll (Principal Keeper), Mick Culligan, Kevin Magner (both Assistant Keepers), Captain Mick Hennessy (Pilot, Irish Helicopters). (A McC)
15: Bull Rock. (RC)
16: Peter Duggan (Principal Keeper, centre) with workmen. (KH)
17: Helicopter landing, Skellig Michael. (RC)
18: Skellig Michael. (MC)
19: Haulbowline, Carlingford Lough. (MC)
20: Eagle Island. (RC)
21: Ballycotton Island, Co Cork. (MC)
22: Tuskar Rock. (MC)
23: Roche's Point. (MC)
24: Tarbert. (MC)
25: Blacksod Bay. (RC)
26: Hook Head. (MC)
27: Pile light, Dundalk. (MC)
28: *Granuaille*, Irish Lights Flagship. (RC)
29: Kish Bank. (RC)
30: Inishtrahull. (RC)
31: Christmas, Baily, Co Dublin. (RC)
32: Tory Island, Co Donegal. (RC)

Photographers:
Richard Cummins (RC),
Michael Costeloe (MC),
Alan McCann (A McC),
K. Hobbs (K.H.)

218

Bright Light, White Water

Carey, Bryan (lighthouse builder), 156.

Casey, John (lighthouse attendant), 144.

Casey, Joseph (lighthouse attendant), 144.

Cashla Bay lighthouse, 146.

Castletownbere Depot & directional light, 102,111,124.

Chaine Tower lighthouse, 59,181, 182,184,186.

Chaine, James M.P., 181.

Chance Bros., 51,59,100,146.

Charles II, King, 65,85.

Charles Fort lighthouse, 66,84.

Christiani & Neilsen, 41.

Churchtown, 64.

City of Dublin Steam Packet Company, 33, 35,36.

Clare Island lighthouse, 31,147, 153,154.

Clear Island (Cape Clear), 48,91, 109,110.

Coal Harbour (Dun Laoghaire), 41.

Codling LV, 51, 52,195.

Collon Bros. (lighthouse builders), 175.

Colossus of Rhodes, 14.

Commerce, (sloop, wrecked Tramore Bay), 72.

Commissioners (Irish Lights), 17,35,38,41,47,83,87,88,93,94,99,101, 109,115,131,132,134, 135,167,176, 181,182,186,189,193,195,196,197.

Commissioners (Northern Lights), 180,196.

Comeragh Mountains, 73.

Coney Island lighthouse, 164.

Coningbeg lightvessel/rock, 60,61,62,195.

Continental Shelf, 155,158,174.

Convent of St. Anne, 75.

Cook, Hubert G., 132.

Copeland, Eddie (lighthouse keeper), 12.

Copeland Island, 66,184,185,186.

Copper Point lighthouse, 111.

'Cork Examiner', 90.

Cork Harbour, 71.

Corporation for Preserving & Improving the Port of Dublin, 49,54,60,65,66,72,75,180,185,193.

Corish, Josiah, 55.

Cork Steamship Co., 78.

Costeloe, Michael, 78.

Cotton, C.P. (engineer), 93.

Coveney, Hugh (Commissioner of Irish Lights), 106.

Cow Rock, 112,113.

Cranfield Point lighthouse, 21.

Croke, Samuel, 55.

Cromwell Point lighthouse, 127.

Crookhaven, 95,96,101,110.

Crookhaven lighthouse, 102.

Crowe, Daniel & Sons (lighthouse builders), 167.

Crowley, John Noel (lighthouse keeper), 12,52,102,106.

Crowley, Oliver (lighthouse keeper), 52.

Cumberland, The, 42.

Cunningham, Capt. (Irish Lights), 153.

Dark Ages, 11,15.

Dalkey, 35,44,47.

Darling, Grace, 123,201.

Daunt (lightvessel), 81,194.

David, St. (of Wales), 63,64.

Davis, Fr, 109.

Dean, Capt., 78,187.

de Courcy Ireland, John (lecturer & historian), 45,46,201.

Devereaux, William, 55.

Donaghadee lighthouse, 59,182,186.

Douglass, James (engineer), 93,116.

Douglass, William (engineer), 94,95,96.

Doyle, John (lighthouse keeper), 150.

Drogheda East lighthouse, 25.

Drogheda West lighthouse, 25.

Dubhán, Saint, 10,14,63.

"Dublin Evening Post", 60.

Dublin & Kingstown Railway Co., 36.

Dublin (lightvessel), 39.

LIMERICK COUNTY LIBRARY